6th Workshop on Structured Prediction for NLP (SPNLP 2022)

Dublin, Ireland
27 May 2022

ISBN: 978-1-7138-6753-1

Printed from e-media with permission by:

Curran Associates, Inc.
57 Morehouse Lane
Red Hook, NY 12571

Some format issues inherent in the e-media version may also appear in this print version.

Printed with permission by Curran Associates, Inc. (2023)

Association for Computational Linguistics
209 N. Eighth Street
Stroudsburg, Pennsylvania 18360

Phone: 1-570-476-8006
Fax: 1-570-476-0860

acl@aclweb.org

Additional copies of this publication are available from:

Curran Associates, Inc.
57 Morehouse Lane
Red Hook, NY 12571 USA
Phone: 845-758-0400
Fax: 845-758-2633
Email: curran@proceedings.com
Web: www.proceedings.com

SPNLP 2022

Sixth Workshop on Structured Prediction for NLP

Proceedings of the Workshop

May 27, 2022

Introduction

Welcome to the Sixth Workshop on Structured Prediction for NLP!

Structured prediction has a strong tradition within the natural language processing (NLP) community, owing to the discrete, compositional nature of words and sentences, which leads to natural combinatorial representations such as trees, sequences, segments, or alignments, among others. It is no surprise that structured output models have been successful and popular in NLP applications since their inception. Many other NLP tasks, including, but not limited to: semantic parsing, slot filling, machine translation, or information extraction, are commonly modeled as structured problems, and accounting for said structure has often lead to performance gain.

This year we received 19 submissions, 7 of which were reviewed by the ACL Rolling Review initiative and subsequently commited to our workshop and 12 of which were directly submitted to our workshop and double-blind peer reviewed by our program committee members. Of these 19, 13 were accepted (6 of which are non-archival papers) for presentation in this edition of the workshop, all exploring this interplay between structure and neural data representations, from different, important points of view. The program includes work on structure-informed representation learning, leveraging structure in problems like temporal knowledge graph completion, multilingual syntax-aware language modeling, mention detection models, etc. Our program also includes five invited presentations from influential researchers.

Our warmest thanks go to the program committee – for their time and effort providing valuable feedback, to all submitting authors – for their thought-provoking work, and to the invited speakers – for doing us the honor of joining our program.

Andreas Vlachos
Priyanka Agrawal
André Martins
Gerasimos Lampouras
Chunchuan Lyu

Organizing Committee

Organizers

Andreas Vlachos, University of Cambridge, UK
Priyanka Agrawal, Google Research, UK
André Martins, Unbabel and Instituto de Telecomunicações, Portugal
Gerasimos Lampouras, Huawei Noah's Ark Lab, UK
Chunchuan Lyu, University of Lisbon, Portugal

Program Committee

Program Committee

Manling Li, University of Illinois, Urbana-Champaign, USA
Sha Li, University of Illinois, Urbana-Champaign, USA
Julius Cheng, University of Cambridge, UK
Pietro Lesci, University of Cambridge, UK
Moy Yuan, University of Cambridge UK
Zhijiang Guo, University of Cambridge, UK
Ignacio Iacobacci, Huawei Noah's Ark Lab, UK
Philip John Gorinski, Huawei Noah's Ark Lab, UK
Parag Jain, University of Edinburgh, UK
Vivek Srikumar, University of Utah, USA
Michail Korakakis, University of Cambridge, UK
Parisa Kordjamshidi, Michigan State University, USA
Tatsuya Hiraoka, Tokyo Institute of Technology, Japan
Naoaki Okazaki, Tokyo Institute of Technology, Japan
Youmi Ma, Tokyo Institute of Technology, Japan
Pedro Henrique Martins, Instituto Superior Técnico, Portugal
Yangfeng Ji, University of Virginia, USA
Zhen Han, Institut für Informatik, Germany
Guirong Fu, Bytedance
Patrick Fernandes, Carnegie Mellon University, USA
Yusuke Miyao, University of Tokyo, Japan
Daniel Daza, Vrije Universiteit Amsterdam, Netherlands
Marcos Vinicius Treviso, Instituto Superior Técnico, Portugal

Table of Contents

Multilingual Syntax-aware Language Modeling through Dependency Tree Conversion
Shunsuke Kando, Hiroshi Noji and Yusuke Miyao 1

Joint Entity and Relation Extraction Based on Table Labeling Using Convolutional Neural Networks
Youmi Ma, Tatsuya Hiraoka and Naoaki Okazaki 11

TempCaps: A Capsule Network-based Embedding Model for Temporal Knowledge Graph Completion
Guirong Fu, Zhao Meng, Zhen Han, Zifeng Ding, Yunpu Ma, Matthias Schubert, Volker Tresp and Roger Wattenhofer 22

SlotGAN: Detecting Mentions in Text via Adversarial Distant Learning
Daniel Daza, Michael Cochez and Paul Groth 32

A Joint Learning Approach for Semi-supervised Neural Topic Modeling
Jeffrey Chiu, Rajat Mittal, Neehal Tumma, Abhishek Sharma and Finale Doshi-Velez 40

Neural String Edit Distance
Jindřich Libovický and Alexander Fraser 52

Predicting Attention Sparsity in Transformers
Marcos Vinicius Treviso, António Góis, Patrick Fernandes, Erick Rocha Fonseca and Andre Martins 67

Multilingual Syntax-aware Language Modeling through Dependency Tree Conversion

Shunsuke Kando[1,2] **Hiroshi Noji**[3,2] **Yusuke Miyao**[1,2]
[1] The University of Tokyo
[2] Artificial Intelligence Research Center, AIST
[3] LeapMind Inc.
kando-shunsuke@alumni.u-tokyo.ac.jp
noji@leapmind.io
yusuke@is.s.u-tokyo.ac.jp

Abstract

Incorporating stronger syntactic biases into neural language models (LMs) is a long-standing goal, but research in this area often focuses on modeling English text, where constituent treebanks are readily available. Extending constituent tree-based LMs to the multilingual setting, where dependency treebanks are more common, is possible via dependency-to-constituency conversion methods. However, this raises the question of which tree formats are best for learning the model, and for which languages. We investigate this question by training recurrent neural network grammars (RNNGs) using various conversion methods, and evaluating them empirically in a multilingual setting. We examine the effect on LM performance across nine conversion methods and five languages through seven types of syntactic tests. On average, the performance of our best model represents a 19 % increase in accuracy over the worst choice across all languages. Our best model shows the advantage over sequential/overparameterized LMs, suggesting the positive effect of syntax injection in a multilingual setting. Our experiments highlight the importance of choosing the right tree formalism, and provide insights into making an informed decision.

1 Introduction

The importance of language modeling in recent years has grown considerably, as methods based on large pre-trained neural language models (LMs) have become the state-of-the-art for many problems (Devlin et al., 2019; Radford et al., 2019). However, these neural LMs are based on general architectures and therefore do not explicitly model linguistic constraints, and have been shown to capture only a subset of the syntactic representations typically found in constituency treebanks (Warstadt et al., 2020). An alternative line of LM research aims to explicitly model the parse tree in order to make the LM syntax-aware. A representative example of this paradigm, reccurent neural network grammar (RNNG, Dyer et al., 2016), is reported to perform better than sequential LMs on tasks that require complex syntactic analysis (Kuncoro et al., 2019; Hu et al., 2020; Noji and Oseki, 2021).

The aim of this paper is to extend LMs that inject syntax to the multilingual setting. This attempt is important mainly in two ways. Firstly, English has been dominant in researches on syntax-aware LM. While multilingual LMs have received increasing attention in recent years, most of their approaches do not explicitly model syntax, such as multilingual BERT (mBERT, Devlin et al., 2019) or XLM-R (Conneau et al., 2020). Although these models have shown high performance on some cross-lingual tasks (Conneau et al., 2018), they perform poorly on a syntactic task (Mueller et al., 2020). Secondly, syntax-aware LMs have interesting features other than their high syntactic ability. One example is the validity of RNNG as a cognitive model under an English-based setting, as demonstrated in Hale et al. (2018). Since human cognitive functions are universal, while natural languages are diverse, it would be ideal to conduct this experiment based on multiple languages.

The main obstacle for multilingual syntax-aware modeling is that it is unclear how to inject syntactic information while training. A straightforward approach is to make use of a multilingual treebank, such as Universal Dependencies (UD, Nivre et al., 2016; Nivre et al., 2020), where trees are represented in a dependency tree (DTree) formalism. Matthews et al. (2019) evaluated parsing and language modeling performance on three typologically different languages, using a generative dependency model. Unfortunately, they revealed that dependency-based models are less suited to language modeling than comparable constituency-based models, highlighting the apparent difficulty of extending syntax-aware LMs to other languages using existing resources.

Proceedings of the Sixth Workshop on Structured Prediction for NLP, pages 1 - 10

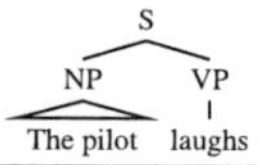	**Partial tree Stack-LSTM**	**Action**
0		NT(S)
1	(S [$\mathbf{e}_\mathrm{S}$]	NT(NP)
2	(S (NP [$\mathbf{e}_\mathrm{S}$ $\mathbf{e}_\mathrm{NP}$]	GEN(The)
3	(S (NP The [$\mathbf{e}_\mathrm{S}$ $\mathbf{e}_\mathrm{NP}$ $\mathbf{e}_\mathrm{The}$]	GEN(pilot)
4	(S (NP The pilot [$\mathbf{e}_\mathrm{S}$ $\underline{\mathbf{e}_\mathrm{NP}\ \mathbf{e}_\mathrm{The}\ \mathbf{e}_\mathrm{pilot}}$]	REDUCE
5	(S (NP The pilot) [$\mathbf{e}_\mathrm{S}$ $\underline{\mathbf{e}_\mathrm{NP'}}$]	NT(VP)
6	(S (NP The pilot) (VP [$\mathbf{e}_\mathrm{S}$ $\mathbf{e}_\mathrm{NP'}$ $\mathbf{e}_\mathrm{VP}$]	...

Figure 1: The illustration of stack-RNNG behavior. Stack-LSTM represents the current partial tree, in which adjacent vectors are connected in the network. At REDUCE action, the corresponding vector is updated with composition function (as underlined).

This paper revisits the issue of the difficulty of constructing multilingual syntax-aware LMs, by exploring the performance of multilingual language modeling using constituency-based models. Since our domain is a multilingual setting, our focus turns to how dependency-to-constituency conversion techniques result in different trees, and how these trees affect the model's performance. We obtain constituency treebanks from UD-formatted dependency treebanks of five languages using nine tree conversion methods. These treebanks are in turn used to train an RNNG, which we evaluate on perplexity and CLAMS (Mueller et al., 2020).

Our contributions are: (1) We propose a methodology for training multilingual syntax-aware LMs through the dependency tree conversion. (2) We found an optimal structure that brings out the potential of RNNG across five languages. (3) We demonstrated the advantage of our multilingual RNNG over sequential/overparameterized LMs.

2 Background

2.1 Recurrent Neural Network Grammars

RNNGs are generative models that estimate joint probability of a sentence $\boldsymbol{x}$ and a constituency tree (CTree) $\boldsymbol{y}$. The probability $p(\boldsymbol{x}, \boldsymbol{y})$ is estimated with top-down constituency parsing actions $\boldsymbol{a} = (a_1, a_2, \cdots, a_n)$ that produce $\boldsymbol{y}$:

$$p(\boldsymbol{x}, \boldsymbol{y}) = \prod_{t=1}^{n} p(a_t | a_1, \cdots, a_{t-1})$$

Kuncoro et al. (2017) proposed a stack-only RNNG that computes the next action probability based on the current partial tree. Figure 1 illustrates the behavior of it. The model represents the current partial tree with a stack-LSTM, which consists of three types of embeddings: nonterminal, word, and closed-nonterminal. The next action is estimated with the last hidden state of a stack-LSTM. There are three types of actions as follows:

- NT(X): Push nonterminal embedding of X ($\mathbf{e}_X$) onto the stack.
- GEN(w): Push word embedding of w ($\mathbf{e}_w$) onto the stack.
- REDUCE: Pop elements from the stack until a nonterminal embedding shows up. With all the embeddings which are popped, compute closed-nonterminal embedding $\mathbf{e}_{X'}$ using composition funcion COMP:

$$\mathbf{e}_{X'} = \textsc{Comp}(\mathbf{e}_X, \mathbf{e}_{w_1}, \cdots, \mathbf{e}_{w_m})$$

RNNG can be regarded as a language model that injects syntactic knowledge explicitly, and various appealing features have been reported (Kuncoro et al., 2017; Kuncoro et al., 2017; Hale et al., 2018). We focus on its high performance on *syntactic evaluation*, which is described below.

Difficulty in extending to other languages In principle, RNNG can be learned with any corpus as long as it contains CTree annotation. However, it is not evident which tree formats are best in a multilingual setting. Using the same technique as English can be inappropriate because each language has its own characteristic, which can be different from English. This question is the fundamental motivation of this research.

2.2 Cross-linguistic Syntactic Evaluation

To investigate the capability of LMs to capture syntax, previous work has attempted to create an evaluation set that requires analysis of the sentence structure (Linzen et al., 2016). One typical example is a subject-verb agreement, a rule that the form of a verb is determined by the grammatical category of the subject, such as person or number:

The pilot that the guards love laughs/*laugh. (1)

In (1), the form of *laugh* is determined by the subject *pilot*, not *guards*. This judgment requires

Algorithm 1: `lf` is short for left-first conversion. We omit right-first conversion because it can be defined just by swapping the codeblocks 6-9 and 10-13 of left-first conversion.

```
1  Function flat (w, ldeps, rdeps):
2      lNT ← [flat (lw, lw.ldeps, lw.rdeps) for lw in ldeps];
3      rNT ← [flat (rw, rw.ldeps, rw.rdeps) for rw in rdeps];
4      return [lNT [w] rNT].removeEmptyList;
5  Function lf (w, ldeps, rdeps):
6      if ldeps is not empty then
           /* Pop left-most dependent */
7          lw ← ldeps.pop();
8          lNT ← [lf (lw, lw.ldeps, lw.rdeps)];
9          rNT ← [lf (w, ldeps, rdeps)];
10     else if rdeps is not empty then
           /* Pop right-most dependent */
11         rw ← rdeps.pop();
12         lNT ← [lf (w, ldeps, rdeps)];
13         rNT ← [lf (rw, rw.ldeps, rw.rdeps)];
14     else return [w];
15     return [lNT rNT];
```

syntactic analysis; *guards* is not a subject of target verb *laugh* because it is in the relative clause of the real subject *pilot*.

Marvin and Linzen (2018) designed the English evaluation set using a grammatical framework. Mueller et al. (2020) extended this framework to other languages (French, German, Hebrew, and Russian) and created an evaluation set named CLAMS (Cross-Linguistic Assessment of Models on Syntax). CLAMS covers 7 categories of agreement tasks, including local agreement (e.g. The author laughs/*laugh) and non-local agreement that contains an intervening phrase between subject and verb as in (1). They evaluated LMs on CLAMS and demonstrated that sequential LMs often fail to assign a higher probability to the grammatical sentence in cases that involve non-local dependency.

Previous work has attempted to explore the syntactic capabilities of LMs with these evaluation sets. Kuncoro et al. (2019) compared the performance of LSTM LM and RNNG using the evaluation set proposed in Marvin and Linzen (2018), demonstrating the superiority of RNNG in predicting the agreement. Noji and Takamura (2020) suggested that LSTM LMs potentially have a limitation in handling object relative clauses. Since these analyses are performed on the basis of English text, it is unclear whether they hold or not in a multilingual setting. In this paper, we attempt to investigate this point by learning RNNGs in other languages and evaluating them on CLAMS.

3 Method: Dependency Tree Conversion

As a source of multilingual syntactic information, we use Universal Dependencies (UD), a collection of cross-linguistic dependency treebanks with a consistent annotation scheme. Since RNNG requires a CTree-formatted dataset for training, we perform DTree-to-CTree conversions, which are completely algorithmic to make it work regardless of language. Our method consists of two procedures: **structural conversion** and **nonterminal labeling**; obtaining a CTree skeleton with unlabeled nonterminal nodes, then assigning labels by leveraging syntactic information contained in the dependency annotations. While our structural conversion is identical to the baseline approach of Collins et al. (1999), we include a novel labeling method that relies on dependency relations, not POS tags.

Structural conversion We performed three types of structural conversion: *flat*, *left-first*, and *right-first*. Algorithm 1 shows the pseudo code and Figure 2 illustrates the actual conversions. These approaches construct CTree in a top-down manner following this procedure: 1) Introduce the root nonterminal of the head of a sentence ($\mathrm{NT}_{\mathrm{give}}$). 2) For each NT_w, introduce new nonterminals according to the dependent(s) of w. Repeat this procedure recursively until w has no dependents.

The difference between the three approaches is the ordering of introducing nonterminals. We describe their behaviors based on the example in Figure 2. (a) flat approach lets w and its dependents be children in CTree simultaneously. For example, $\mathrm{NT}_{\mathrm{give}}$ has four children: $\mathrm{NT}_{\mathrm{man}}$, $\mathrm{NT}_{\mathrm{give}}$, $\mathrm{NT}_{\mathrm{him}}$, $\mathrm{NT}_{\mathrm{box}}$, because they are dependents of the head word *give*. As the name suggests, this approach tends to produce a flat-structured CTree because each nonterminal can have multiple children. (b) left-first approach introduces the nonterminals from the left-most dependent. If there is no left dependent, the right-most dependent is introduced. In the example of Figure 2, the root $\mathrm{NT}_{\mathrm{give}}$ has a left child $\mathrm{NT}_{\mathrm{man}}$ because *man* is the left-most dependent of the head *give*. (c) right-first approach is the inversed version of left-first; handling the right-most dependent first. For methods (b) and (c), the resulting CTree is always a binary tree.

Nonterminal labeling We define three types of labeling methods for each NT_w; 1) X-label: Assign "X" to all the nonterminals. 2)POS-label: Assign POS tag of w. 3) DEP-label: Assign dependency

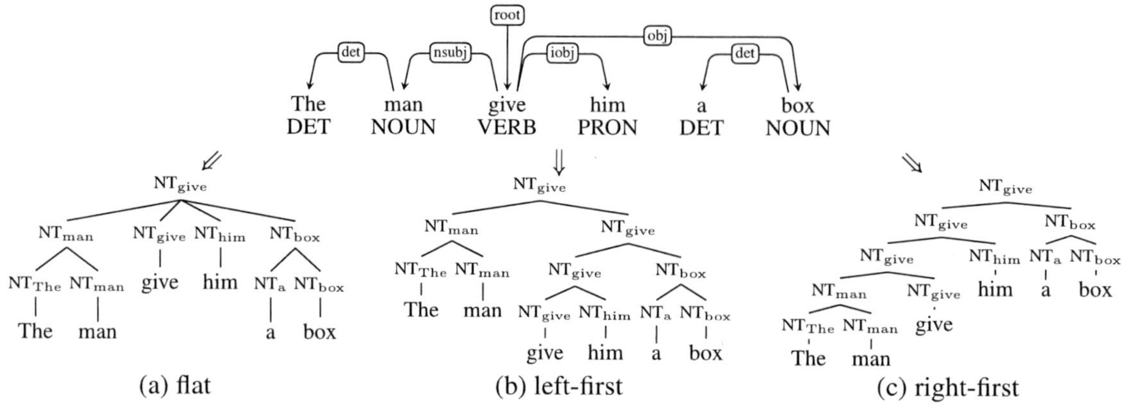

Figure 2: The illustration of structural conversion. NT_w is a temporal label of nonterminal which will be assigned at nonterminal labeling phase.

	X-label	POS-label	DEP-label
$\mathrm{NT}_{\mathrm{The}}$	X	DETP	det
$\mathrm{NT}_{\mathrm{man}}$	X	NOUNP	nsubj
$\mathrm{NT}_{\mathrm{give}}$	X	VERBP	root
$\mathrm{NT}_{\mathrm{him}}$	X	PRONP	iobj
NT_{a}	X	DETP	det
$\mathrm{NT}_{\mathrm{box}}$	X	NOUNP	obj

Table 1: Actual labels assigned to nonterminals.

relation between w and its head. Table 1 shows the actual labels that are assigned to CTrees in Figure 2.

Each method has its own intent. X-label drops the syntactic category of each phrase, which minimizes the structural information of the sentence. POS-label would produce the most common CTree structure because traditionally nonterminals are labeled based on POS tag of the head word. DEP-label is a more fine-grained method than POS-label because words in a sentence can have the same POS tag but different dependency relation, as in *man* and *box* in Figure 2.

Finally, we performed a total of nine types of conversions (three structures × three labelings). Although they have discrete features, they are common in that they embody reasonable phrase structures that are useful for capturing syntax. Figure 3 shows the converted structure of an actual instance from CLAMS. In all settings, the main subject phrase is correctly dominated by $\mathrm{NT}_{\mathrm{pilot}}$, which should contribute to solving the task.

4 What Is the Robust Conversion Which Works Well in Every Language?

In Section 3, we proposed language-independent multiple conversions from DTree to CTree. The intriguing question is; Is there a robust conversion that brings out the potential of RNNG in every language? To answer this question, we conducted a thorough experiment to compare the performances of RNNGs trained in each setting.

4.1 Experimental Setup

Treebank preparation Following Mueller et al. (2020), we extracted Wikipedia articles of target languages using WikiExtractor[1] to create corpora[2]. We fed it to UDify (Kondratyuk and Straka, 2019), a multilingual neural dependency parser trained on the entire UD treebanks, to generate a CoNLL-U formatted dependency treebank. Sentences are tokenized beforehand using Stanza (Qi et al., 2020) because UDify requires tokenized text for prediction. The resulting dependency treebank is converted into the constituency treebank using methods proposed in Section 3. Our treebank contains around 10% non-projective DTrees for all the language (between 9% in Russian and 14% in Hebrew), and we omit them in the conversion phase because we cannot obtain valid CTrees from them[3]. As a training set, we picked sentences with 10M tokens at random for each language. For a validation and a test set, we picked 5,000 sentences respectively.

Training details We used batched RNNG (Noji and Oseki, 2021) to speed up our training. Following Noji and Oseki (2021), we used subword units (Sennrich et al., 2016) with a vocabulary size of

[1] `https://github.com/attardi/wikiextractor`

[2] Although Mueller et al. (2020) publishes corpora they used, we extracted the dataset ourselves because they contain <unk> token which would affect parsing.

[3] Since other language can contain more non-projective DTrees, we have to consider how to handle it in the future.

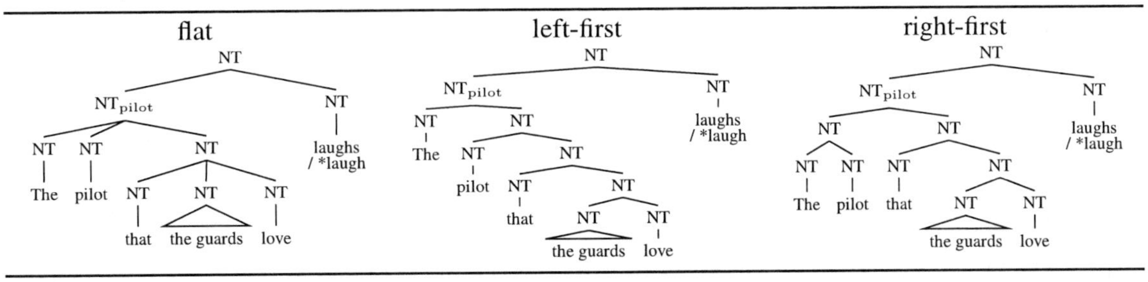

Figure 3: Examples of converted CTrees. A sentence is taken from CLAMS, which requires recognition of long distance dependency intervened by object relative clause (sentence (1)). For simplicity, we omit the corresponding word of each nonterminal except for *pilot*, the main subject of the sentence.

30K. We set the hyperparameters so as to make the model size 35M. We trained each model for 24 hours on a single GPU.

Evaluation metrics To compare the performance among conversions, we evaluated the model trained on each dataset in two aspects: **perplexity** and **syntactic ability** based on CLAMS.

Perplexity is a standard metric for assessing the quality of LM. Since we adopt subword units, we regard a word probability as a product of its subwords' probabilities. To compute it on RNNG, we performed word-synchronous beam search (Stern et al., 2017), a default approach implemented in batched RNNG. Following Noji and Oseki (2021), we set a beam size k as 100, a word beam size k_w as 10, and fast-track candidates k_s as 1. Syntactic ability is assessed by accuracy on CLAMS, which is calculated by comparing the probabilities assigned to a grammatical and an ungrammatical sentence. If the model assigns a higher probability to a grammatical sentence, then we regard it as correct. Chance accuracy is 0.5.

We run the experiment three times with different random seeds for initialization of the model, and report the average score with standard deviation.

4.2 Result

From now on, we refer to each conversion method according to a naming of the procedure, such as "left-first structure" or "flat-POS conversion".

Perplexity Table 2 shows the perplexities in each setting. As a whole, flat structures show the lowest perplexity, followed by left-first and right-first, which is consistent across languages. While flat structure produces stable and relatively low perplexity regardless of labeling methods and languages, left-first and right-first structures perform very poorly on X-label.

	flat	left	right	
X	259$_{\pm 1}$	707$_{\pm 19}$	1507$_{\pm 14}$	English
POS	278$_{\pm 3}$	417$_{\pm 2}$	512$_{\pm 3}$	
DEP	**241**$_{\pm 30}$	390$_{\pm 4}$	463$_{\pm 1}$	
X	133$_{\pm 0}$	405$_{\pm 10}$	691$_{\pm 10}$	French
POS	**129**$_{\pm 1}$	206$_{\pm 2}$	262$_{\pm 1}$	
DEP	137$_{\pm 22}$	190$_{\pm 5}$	223$_{\pm 2}$	
X	341$_{\pm 1}$	830$_{\pm 8}$	1124$_{\pm 18}$	German
POS	366$_{\pm 1}$	321$_{\pm 3}$	482$_{\pm 2}$	
DEP	330$_{\pm 43}$	**291**$_{\pm 3}$	398$_{\pm 4}$	
X	100$_{\pm 1}$	294$_{\pm 3}$	450$_{\pm 8}$	Hebrew
POS	97$_{\pm 0}$	153$_{\pm 1}$	183$_{\pm 1}$	
DEP	**93**$_{\pm 1}$	143$_{\pm 1}$	161$_{\pm 1}$	
X	508$_{\pm 5}$	1413$_{\pm 16}$	1910$_{\pm 59}$	Russian
POS	527$_{\pm 3}$	845$_{\pm 2}$	1067$_{\pm 16}$	
DEP	**473**$_{\pm 61}$	834$_{\pm 5}$	1030$_{\pm 27}$	

Table 2: Test set perplexity of each setting. Lower is better. "left" and "right" in the table are abbreviations of "left-first" and "right-first", respectively.

Syntactic ability Figure 4 shows the accuracies of CLAMS in each setting, and Table 3 shows the average scores. From Table 3, we observe clear distinctions across methods; the best model (shown in bold) is 19% more accurate in average than the worst one (shown in italic), across all languages, indicating the model's certain preference for the structure. Similar to perplexity, flat structure performs better and more stably than the others, regardless of labels and languages. While Mueller et al. (2020) reported a high variability in scores across languages when an LSTM LM is used, flat structure-based RNNGs do not show such a tendency; almost all the accuracies are above 90%.

Looking closely at the Figure 4, we can see that left-first and right-first structures exhibit unstable behavior depending on the labeling; the accuracy on X-label tends to be lower especially for the categories that require the resolution of a long-distance dependency, such as 'VP coord (long)', 'Across subj. rel.', 'Across obj. rel.', and 'Across prep'.

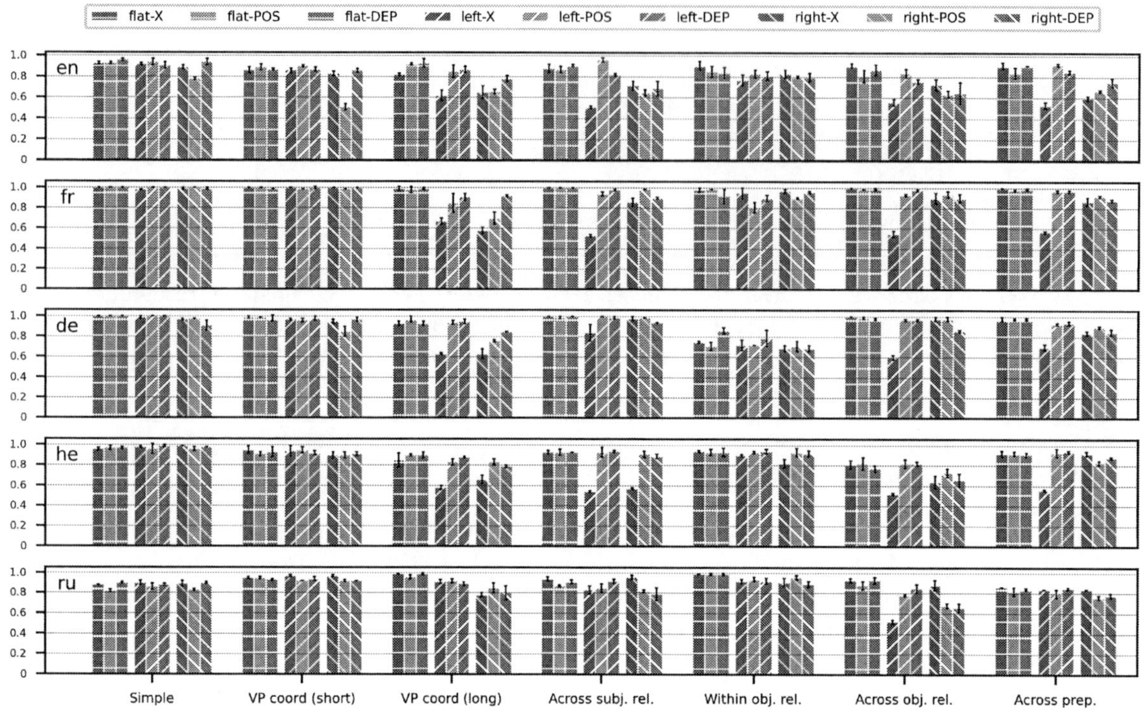

Figure 4: Accuracies of CLAMS for RNNGs trained on each setting.

	flat	left	right	
X	0.89$_{\pm.01}$	0.68$_{\pm.01}$	0.75$_{\pm.01}$	English
POS	0.87$_{\pm.02}$	0.89$_{\pm.01}$	*0.67*$_{\pm.01}$	
DEP	**0.90**$_{\pm.02}$	0.84$_{\pm.01}$	0.78$_{\pm.04}$	
X	**0.99**$_{\pm.00}$	*0.75*$_{\pm.00}$	0.88$_{\pm.02}$	French
POS	**0.99**$_{\pm.00}$	0.93$_{\pm.02}$	0.92$_{\pm.01}$	
DEP	0.98$_{\pm.01}$	0.96$_{\pm.01}$	0.94$_{\pm.01}$	
X	0.95$_{\pm.00}$	*0.78*$_{\pm.01}$	0.86$_{\pm.01}$	German
POS	0.95$_{\pm.01}$	0.93$_{\pm.01}$	0.88$_{\pm.01}$	
DEP	**0.96**$_{\pm.01}$	0.95$_{\pm.02}$	0.87$_{\pm.02}$	
X	0.91$_{\pm.01}$	*0.72*$_{\pm.01}$	0.78$_{\pm.01}$	Hebrew
POS	0.91$_{\pm.01}$	0.91$_{\pm.03}$	0.87$_{\pm.01}$	
DEP	0.90$_{\pm.01}$	**0.92**$_{\pm.00}$	0.86$_{\pm.01}$	
X	**0.93**$_{\pm.00}$	0.84$_{\pm.01}$	0.89$_{\pm.02}$	Russian
POS	0.90$_{\pm.01}$	0.87$_{\pm.01}$	0.83$_{\pm.01}$	
DEP	**0.93**$_{\pm.01}$	0.89$_{\pm.00}$	*0.82*$_{\pm.01}$	

Table 3: CLAMS scores averaged by task category.

Discussion Basically, we observed a similar tendency in perplexity and CLAMS score; (1) flat structures show the highest scores. (2) left-first and right-first structures perform poorly on X-label. We conjecture that these tendencies are due to the resulting structure of each conversion; while flat structure is non-binary, the rest two are binary. Since nonterminals in a non-binary tree can have multiple words as children, parsing actions obtained from it contain more continuous GEN actions than a binary tree. This nature helps the model to predict the next word by considering lexical relations, which would contribute to its lower perplexity. Although binary trees get better with the hint of informative labels (POS/DEP), it is difficult to reach the performance of flat structures due to their confused actions; GEN actions tend to be interrupted by other actions. Besides, there are too many NT actions in a binary tree, which can hurt the prediction because the information of an important nonterminal (e.g. $\mathrm{NT}_{\mathrm{pilot}}$ in Figure 3) can be diluted through the actions. The situation becomes worse on X-label; the model cannot distinguish the nonterminal of the main subject and that of the other, resulting in missing what the subject is.

It is worth noting that perplexity does not always reflect the CLAMS accuracy. For example, while right-X conversion produces the worst perplexity for all the languages, it achieves better CLAMS accuracy than left-X conversion for almost all the cases. This observation is in line with Hu et al. (2020), who report a dissociation between perplexity and syntactic performance for English.

4.3 Why Does Flat Structure Perform Well?

As one possible reason why flat structure is optimal among the three structures presented, we conjecture that the parseability of the structure is involved. To test this hypothesis, we calculated the F1 score

	flat	left	right	
X	$0.80_{\pm.00}$	$0.34_{\pm.00}$	$0.48_{\pm.00}$	English
POS	$0.79_{\pm.00}$	$0.57_{\pm.00}$	$0.70_{\pm.00}$	
DEP	$\mathbf{0.82}_{\pm.01}$	$0.59_{\pm.01}$	$0.70_{\pm.00}$	
X	$0.79_{\pm.00}$	$0.37_{\pm.00}$	$0.58_{\pm.00}$	French
POS	$\mathbf{0.86}_{\pm.00}$	$0.63_{\pm.00}$	$0.74_{\pm.00}$	
DEP	$\mathbf{0.86}_{\pm.01}$	$0.65_{\pm.01}$	$0.75_{\pm.00}$	
X	$0.90_{\pm.00}$	$0.44_{\pm.00}$	$0.59_{\pm.00}$	German
POS	$0.85_{\pm.00}$	$0.74_{\pm.00}$	$0.76_{\pm.00}$	
DEP	$\mathbf{0.91}_{\pm.08}$	$0.76_{\pm.00}$	$0.77_{\pm.00}$	
X	$0.81_{\pm.01}$	$0.41_{\pm.00}$	$0.58_{\pm.00}$	Hebrew
POS	$\mathbf{0.83}_{\pm.00}$	$0.65_{\pm.00}$	$0.73_{\pm.00}$	
DEP	$\mathbf{0.83}_{\pm.00}$	$0.65_{\pm.00}$	$0.72_{\pm.00}$	
X	$0.80_{\pm.00}$	$0.41_{\pm.00}$	$0.59_{\pm.00}$	Russian
POS	$\mathbf{0.83}_{\pm.00}$	$0.62_{\pm.00}$	$0.73_{\pm.00}$	
DEP	$0.82_{\pm.01}$	$0.58_{\pm.00}$	$0.68_{\pm.00}$	

Table 4: F1 score of predicted CTree. We regard a resulting CTree of each conversion as a gold tree.

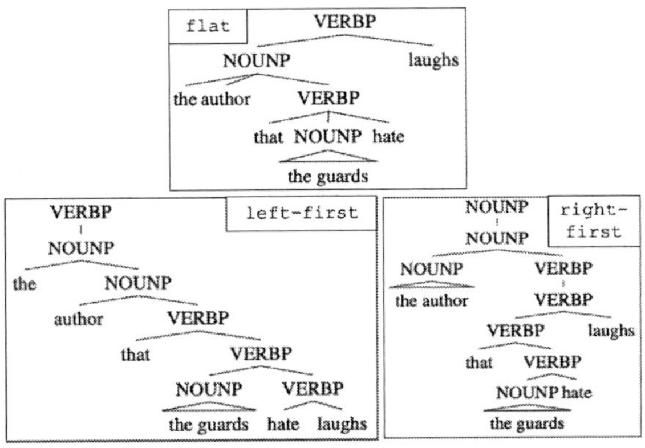

Figure 5: Structures of a CLAMS example predicted by {flat, left-first, right-first}-POS RNNG. This example is solvable only by flat-POS RNNG across all seeds.

between the gold CTrees of the test set and the structures predicted by RNNG for each setting. Table 4 shows the result. The tendencies of F1 scores are consistent across languages: 1) Flat structures show highest F1 score. 2) While scores of flat structures are stable regardless of their labelings, the rest two structures exhibit lower score on X-label. As a whole, the result reflects the tendency discussed in Section 4.2, which supports our hypothesis.

To further investigate the link between parseability and the capability of solving the task, we obtained parse trees of CLAMS examples that are solvable only by flat RNNG across all seeds. We found that only flat RNNG produces a correct constituency tree, and structures obtained from left-first and right-first RNNGs are incorrect on a critical point. For example, in Figure 5, while the relation between the subject "author" and the target verb "laughs" is analyzed clearly in the flat structure, it is ambiguous in the rest, possibly causing the misinterpretation that the subject is "guards".

These findings indicate the importance of choosing the correct tree structure for syntax-aware language modeling; it should be not only hierarchical, but also as parseable as possible.

Through analysis of the conversions, we found that (1) flat structure performs stably well in every setting. (2) while CLAMS accuracy of flat structure does not differ significantly depending on its labeling, for perplexity, flat-DEP performs the best for more than half of the languages and no inferiority can be observed for the other languages. Therefore, we conclude that *flat-DEP* conversion is the most robust conversion among languages.

5 Advantage of Syntax Injection to LMs in a Multilingual Setting

In this section, we demonstrate the benefits of injecting syntactic biases into the model in a multilingual setting. We obtained the CLAMS score of RNNG trained on the flat-DEP treebank (*flat-DEP RNNG* for short) and compared it against baselines.

Experimental setup The experiment was conducted in as close setting to the previous work as possible. Following Mueller et al. (2020), we extracted Wikipedia articles of 80M tokens as training set. The hyperparameters of LSTM LM are set following Noji and Takamura (2020) because it performs the best for the dataset of Marvin and Linzen (2018)[4]. We used subword units with a vocabulary size of 30K, and the sizes of RNNG and LSTM LM are set to be the same (35M).

Result Table 5 shows the result. In addition to scores from the models we trained (flat-DEP RNNG, LSTM (N20)), we display scores of LSTM LM and mBERT reported in the original paper (LSTM (M20) and mBERT (M20), Mueller et al., 2020). Overall, we can see the superiority of RNNG across languages, especially for the tasks that require analysis on long distance dependency; 'VP coord (long)', 'Across subj. rel.', 'Across obj. rel.', and 'Across prep'. While previous work suggested that LSTM LMs potentially have a limitation in handling object relative clauses (Noji and Takamura, 2020), our result suggests that RNNG does not have such a limitation thanks to explicitly injected syntactic biases.

[4]Since English set of CLAMS is a subset of Marvin and Linzen (2018), it is reasonable to choose this model to validate the multilingual extendability.

	Simple	VP coord (short)	VP coord (long)	Across subj. rel.	Within obj rel.	Across obj rel.	Across prep.	Average	
flat-DEP RNNG	$0.99_{\pm.01}$	$0.87_{\pm.02}$	$0.91_{\pm.04}$	$0.95_{\pm.02}$	$0.92_{\pm.05}$	$0.92_{\pm.06}$	$0.93_{\pm.04}$	$\mathbf{0.93}_{\pm.02}$	English
LSTM (N20)	$0.93_{\pm.03}$	$0.85_{\pm.01}$	$0.83_{\pm.04}$	$0.85_{\pm.04}$	$0.83_{\pm.05}$	$0.77_{\pm.04}$	$0.87_{\pm.02}$	$0.85_{\pm.02}$	
LSTM (M20)	$1.00_{\pm.00}$	$0.94_{\pm.01}$	$0.76_{\pm.06}$	$0.60_{\pm.06}$	$0.89_{\pm.01}$	$0.55_{\pm.05}$	$0.63_{\pm.02}$	$0.77_{\pm.03}$	
mBERT (M20)	1.00	1.00	0.92	0.88	0.83	0.87	0.92	0.92	
flat-DEP RNNG	$1.00_{\pm.00}$	$1.00_{\pm.00}$	$1.00_{\pm.00}$	$1.00_{\pm.00}$	$1.00_{\pm.00}$	$1.00_{\pm.00}$	$1.00_{\pm.00}$	$\mathbf{1.00}_{\pm.00}$	French
LSTM (N20)	$1.00_{\pm.00}$	$1.00_{\pm.00}$	$0.97_{\pm.03}$	$0.92_{\pm.06}$	$0.85_{\pm.03}$	$0.75_{\pm.01}$	$1.00_{\pm.00}$	$0.93_{\pm.01}$	
LSTM (M20)	$1.00_{\pm.00}$	$0.97_{\pm.01}$	$0.85_{\pm.05}$	$0.71_{\pm.05}$	$0.99_{\pm.01}$	$0.52_{\pm.01}$	$0.74_{\pm.02}$	$0.83_{\pm.02}$	
mBERT (M20)	1.00	1.00	0.98	0.57	—	0.86	0.57	0.83	
flat-DEP RNNG	$1.00_{\pm.00}$	$0.99_{\pm.01}$	$0.98_{\pm.01}$	$1.00_{\pm.00}$	$0.88_{\pm.04}$	$0.99_{\pm.01}$	$0.97_{\pm.02}$	$\mathbf{0.97}_{\pm.01}$	German
LSTM (N20)	$0.99_{\pm.01}$	$0.97_{\pm.03}$	$0.92_{\pm.05}$	$0.99_{\pm.01}$	$0.72_{\pm.01}$	$0.97_{\pm.02}$	$0.94_{\pm.01}$	$0.93_{\pm.01}$	
LSTM (M20)	$1.00_{\pm.00}$	$0.99_{\pm.02}$	$0.96_{\pm.04}$	$0.94_{\pm.04}$	$0.74_{\pm.03}$	$0.81_{\pm.09}$	$0.89_{\pm.06}$	$0.90_{\pm.04}$	
mBERT (M20)	0.95	0.97	1.00	0.73	—	0.93	0.95	0.92	
flat-DEP RNNG	$0.97_{\pm.01}$	$0.99_{\pm.00}$	$0.92_{\pm.03}$	$0.95_{\pm.02}$	$1.00_{\pm.00}$	$0.84_{\pm.05}$	$0.95_{\pm.01}$	$\mathbf{0.95}_{\pm.01}$	Hebrew
LSTM (N20)	$0.97_{\pm.00}$	$0.95_{\pm.04}$	$0.85_{\pm.02}$	$0.89_{\pm.02}$	$0.94_{\pm.01}$	$0.63_{\pm.04}$	$0.93_{\pm.01}$	$0.88_{\pm.00}$	
LSTM (M20)	$0.95_{\pm.01}$	$1.00_{\pm.01}$	$0.84_{\pm.06}$	$0.91_{\pm.03}$	$1.00_{\pm.01}$	$0.56_{\pm.01}$	$0.88_{\pm.03}$	$0.88_{\pm.02}$	
mBERT (M20)	0.70	0.91	0.73	0.61	—	0.55	0.62	0.69	
flat-DEP RNNG	$0.89_{\pm.02}$	$0.94_{\pm.02}$	$1.00_{\pm.00}$	$0.93_{\pm.00}$	$0.99_{\pm.01}$	$0.92_{\pm.02}$	$0.85_{\pm.03}$	$\mathbf{0.93}_{\pm.01}$	Russian
LSTM (N20)	$0.91_{\pm.01}$	$0.97_{\pm.00}$	$0.97_{\pm.02}$	$0.98_{\pm.00}$	$0.90_{\pm.04}$	$0.85_{\pm.07}$	$0.86_{\pm.02}$	$0.92_{\pm.01}$	
LSTM (M20)	$0.91_{\pm.01}$	$0.98_{\pm.02}$	$0.86_{\pm.04}$	$0.88_{\pm.03}$	$0.95_{\pm.04}$	$0.60_{\pm.03}$	$0.76_{\pm.02}$	$0.85_{\pm.03}$	
mBERT (M20)	0.65	0.80	—	0.70	—	0.67	0.56	0.68	

Table 5: CLAMS scores for flat-DEP RNNG and baselines. LSTM (N20) is a model of which hyperparameters are set as with Noji and Takamura (2020). LSTM (M20) and mBERT (M20) scores are quoted from Table 1, 2 and 5 in Mueller et al. (2020). Hyphen means that all focus verb for the corresponding setting were out-of-vocabulary.

6 Discussion

We discussed the CTree structure that works robustly regardless of the language and the superiority of injecting syntactic bias to the model. Our claim is that we can construct language-independent syntax-aware LMs by seeking the best structure for learning RNNGs, which is backed up by our experiments based on five languages. To make this claim firm, more investigations are needed from two aspects: **fine-grained syntactic evaluation** and **experiment on typologically diverse languages**.

Fine-grained syntactic evaluation The linguistic phenomenon covered in CLAMS is only an agreement. However, previous works have invented evaluation sets that examine more diverse syntactic phenomena for English (Hu et al., 2020, Warstadt et al., 2020). We need such a fine-grained evaluation even in a multilingual setting, as superiority in agreement does not imply superiority in every syntactic knowledge; Kuncoro et al. (2019) suggested that RNNG performs poorer than LSTM LM in capturing sentential complement or simple negative polarity items. It is challenging to design a multiliugnal syntactic test set because even an agreement based on grammatical categories is not a universal phenomenon. It is required to seek reasonable metrics that cover broad syntactic phenomena and are applicable to many languages.

Experiment on typologically diverse languages Languages included in CLAMS (English, French, German, Hebrew and Russian) are actually not typologically diverse. Apart from language-specific features, all of them take the same ordering of (1) subject, verb, and object (SVO) (2) relative clause and noun (Noun-Relative clause) (3) adposition and noun phrase (preposition), and so on[5]. If we run the same experiment for a typologically different language, the result could be somewhat different. Although some previous work focused on syntactic assessment of other languages (Ravfogel et al., 2018; Gulordava et al., 2018), such attempts are scarce. As future work, it is needed to design an evaluation set based on other languages and explore the extendability to more diverse languages.

7 Conclusion

In this paper, we propose a methodology to learn multilingual RNNG through dependency tree conversion. We performed multiple conversions to seek the robust structure which works well multilingually, discussing the effect of multiple structures. We demonstrated the superiority of our model over baselines in capturing syntax in a multilingual setting. Since our research is the first step for multilingual syntax-aware LMs, it is necessary to conduct experiments on more diverse languages to seek a better structure. We believe that this research would contribute to the field of theoretical/cognitive linguistics as well because an ultimate goal of linguistics is finding the universal rule of natural language. Finding a reasonable structure in engineering would yield useful knowledge for that purpose.

[5]Typological information is obtained from WALS: `https://wals.info/`

Acknowledgements

This paper is based on results obtained from a project JPNP20006, commissioned by the New Energy and Industrial Technology Development Organization (NEDO). For experiments, computational resource of AI Bridging Cloud Infrastructure (ABCI) provided by National Institute of Advanced Industrial Science and Technology (AIST) was used.

References

Michael Collins, Jan Hajic, Lance Ramshaw, and Christoph Tillmann. 1999. A statistical parser for Czech. In *Proceedings of the 37th Annual Meeting of the Association for Computational Linguistics*, pages 505–512, College Park, Maryland, USA. Association for Computational Linguistics.

Alexis Conneau, Kartikay Khandelwal, Naman Goyal, Vishrav Chaudhary, Guillaume Wenzek, Francisco Guzmán, Edouard Grave, Myle Ott, Luke Zettlemoyer, and Veselin Stoyanov. 2020. Unsupervised cross-lingual representation learning at scale. In *Proceedings of the 58th Annual Meeting of the Association for Computational Linguistics*, pages 8440–8451, Online. Association for Computational Linguistics.

Alexis Conneau, Ruty Rinott, Guillaume Lample, Adina Williams, Samuel Bowman, Holger Schwenk, and Veselin Stoyanov. 2018. XNLI: Evaluating cross-lingual sentence representations. In *Proceedings of the 2018 Conference on Empirical Methods in Natural Language Processing*, pages 2475–2485, Brussels, Belgium. Association for Computational Linguistics.

Jacob Devlin, Ming-Wei Chang, Kenton Lee, and Kristina Toutanova. 2019. BERT: Pre-training of deep bidirectional transformers for language understanding. In *Proceedings of the 2019 Conference of the North American Chapter of the Association for Computational Linguistics: Human Language Technologies, Volume 1 (Long and Short Papers)*, pages 4171–4186, Minneapolis, Minnesota. Association for Computational Linguistics.

Chris Dyer, Adhiguna Kuncoro, Miguel Ballesteros, and Noah A. Smith. 2016. Recurrent neural network grammars. In *Proceedings of the 2016 Conference of the North American Chapter of the Association for Computational Linguistics: Human Language Technologies*, pages 199–209, San Diego, California. Association for Computational Linguistics.

Kristina Gulordava, Tal Linzen, and Marco Baroni. 2018. Colorless green recurrent networks dream hierarchically. In *Proceedings of the 2018 Conference of the North American Chapter of the Association for Computational Linguistics: Human Language Technologies, Volume 1 (Long Papers)*, pages 1195–1205, New Orleans, Louisiana. Association for Computational Linguistics.

John Hale, Chris Dyer, Adhiguna Kuncoro, and Jonathan Brennan. 2018. Finding syntax in human encephalography with beam search. In *Proceedings of the 56th Annual Meeting of the Association for Computational Linguistics (Volume 1: Long Papers)*, pages 2727–2736, Melbourne, Australia. Association for Computational Linguistics.

Jennifer Hu, Jon Gauthier, Peng Qian, Ethan Wilcox, and Roger Levy. 2020. A systematic assessment of syntactic generalization in neural language models. In *Proceedings of the 58th Annual Meeting of the Association for Computational Linguistics*, pages 1725–1744, Online. Association for Computational Linguistics.

Dan Kondratyuk and Milan Straka. 2019. 75 languages, 1 model: Parsing Universal Dependencies universally. In *Proceedings of the 2019 Conference on Empirical Methods in Natural Language Processing and the 9th International Joint Conference on Natural Language Processing (EMNLP-IJCNLP)*, pages 2779–2795, Hong Kong, China. Association for Computational Linguistics.

Adhiguna Kuncoro, Miguel Ballesteros, Lingpeng Kong, Chris Dyer, Graham Neubig, and Noah A. Smith. 2017. What do recurrent neural network grammars learn about syntax? In *Proceedings of the 15th Conference of the European Chapter of the Association for Computational Linguistics: Volume 1, Long Papers*, pages 1249–1258, Valencia, Spain. Association for Computational Linguistics.

Adhiguna Kuncoro, Chris Dyer, Laura Rimell, Stephen Clark, and Phil Blunsom. 2019. Scalable syntax-aware language models using knowledge distillation. In *Proceedings of the 57th Annual Meeting of the Association for Computational Linguistics*, pages 3472–3484, Florence, Italy. Association for Computational Linguistics.

Tal Linzen, Emmanuel Dupoux, and Yoav Goldberg. 2016. Assessing the ability of LSTMs to learn syntax-sensitive dependencies. *Transactions of the Association for Computational Linguistics*, 4:521–535.

Rebecca Marvin and Tal Linzen. 2018. Targeted syntactic evaluation of language models. In *Proceedings of the 2018 Conference on Empirical Methods in Natural Language Processing*, pages 1192–1202, Brussels, Belgium. Association for Computational Linguistics.

Austin Matthews, Graham Neubig, and Chris Dyer. 2019. Comparing top-down and bottom-up neural generative dependency models. In *Proceedings of the 23rd Conference on Computational Natural Language Learning (CoNLL)*, pages 227–237, Hong Kong, China. Association for Computational Linguistics.

Aaron Mueller, Garrett Nicolai, Panayiota Petrou-Zeniou, Natalia Talmina, and Tal Linzen. 2020. Cross-linguistic syntactic evaluation of word prediction models. In *Proceedings of the 58th Annual Meeting of the Association for Computational Linguistics*, pages 5523–5539, Online. Association for Computational Linguistics.

Joakim Nivre, Marie-Catherine de Marneffe, Filip Ginter, Yoav Goldberg, Jan Hajič, Christopher D. Manning, Ryan McDonald, Slav Petrov, Sampo Pyysalo, Natalia Silveira, Reut Tsarfaty, and Daniel Zeman. 2016. Universal Dependencies v1: A multilingual treebank collection. In *Proceedings of the Tenth International Conference on Language Resources and Evaluation (LREC'16)*, pages 1659–1666, Portorož, Slovenia. European Language Resources Association (ELRA).

Joakim Nivre, Marie-Catherine de Marneffe, Filip Ginter, Jan Hajič, Christopher D. Manning, Sampo Pyysalo, Sebastian Schuster, Francis Tyers, and Daniel Zeman. 2020. Universal Dependencies v2: An evergrowing multilingual treebank collection. In *Proceedings of the 12th Language Resources and Evaluation Conference*, pages 4034–4043, Marseille, France. European Language Resources Association.

Hiroshi Noji and Yohei Oseki. 2021. Effective batching for recurrent neural network grammars. In *Findings of the Association for Computational Linguistics: ACL-IJCNLP 2021*, pages 4340–4352, Online. Association for Computational Linguistics.

Hiroshi Noji and Hiroya Takamura. 2020. An analysis of the utility of explicit negative examples to improve the syntactic abilities of neural language models. In *Proceedings of the 58th Annual Meeting of the Association for Computational Linguistics*, pages 3375–3385, Online. Association for Computational Linguistics.

Peng Qi, Yuhao Zhang, Yuhui Zhang, Jason Bolton, and Christopher D. Manning. 2020. Stanza: A python natural language processing toolkit for many human languages. In *Proceedings of the 58th Annual Meeting of the Association for Computational Linguistics: System Demonstrations*, pages 101–108, Online. Association for Computational Linguistics.

Alec Radford, Jeffrey Wu, Rewon Child, David Luan, Dario Amodei, and Ilya Sutskever. 2019. Language models are unsupervised multitask learners.

Shauli Ravfogel, Yoav Goldberg, and Francis Tyers. 2018. Can LSTM learn to capture agreement? The case of Basque. In *Proceedings of the 2018 EMNLP Workshop BlackboxNLP: Analyzing and Interpreting Neural Networks for NLP*, pages 98–107, Brussels, Belgium. Association for Computational Linguistics.

Rico Sennrich, Barry Haddow, and Alexandra Birch. 2016. Neural machine translation of rare words with subword units. In *Proceedings of the 54th Annual Meeting of the Association for Computational Linguistics (Volume 1: Long Papers)*, pages 1715–1725, Berlin, Germany. Association for Computational Linguistics.

Mitchell Stern, Daniel Fried, and Dan Klein. 2017. Effective inference for generative neural parsing. In *Proceedings of the 2017 Conference on Empirical Methods in Natural Language Processing*, pages 1695–1700, Copenhagen, Denmark. Association for Computational Linguistics.

Alex Warstadt, Alicia Parrish, Haokun Liu, Anhad Mohananey, Wei Peng, Sheng-Fu Wang, and Samuel R. Bowman. 2020. BLiMP: A benchmark of linguistic minimal pairs for English. In *Proceedings of the Society for Computation in Linguistics 2020*, pages 409–410, New York, New York. Association for Computational Linguistics.

Joint Entity and Relation Extraction Based on Table Labeling Using Convolutional Neural Networks

Youmi Ma **Tatsuya Hiraoka** **Naoaki Okazaki**
Tokyo Institute of Technology
{youmi.ma, tatsuya.hiraoka}@nlp.c.titech.ac.jp
okazaki@c.titech.ac.jp

Abstract

This study introduces a novel approach to the joint extraction of entities and relations by stacking convolutional neural networks (CNNs) on pretrained language models. We adopt table representations to model the entities and relations, casting the entity and relation extraction as a table-labeling problem. Regarding each table as an image and each cell in a table as an image pixel, we apply two-dimensional CNNs to the tables to capture local dependencies and predict the cell labels. The experimental results showed that the performance of the proposed method is comparable to those of current state-of-art systems on the CoNLL04, ACE05, and ADE datasets. Even when freezing pretrained language model parameters, the proposed method showed a stable performance, whereas the compared methods suffered from significant decreases in performance. This observation indicates that the parameters of the pretrained encoder may incorporate dependencies among the entity and relation labels during fine-tuning.

1 Introduction

The purpose of a joint entity and relation extraction is to recognize entities and relations in a text. A task can be decomposed into two subtasks: named entity recognition (NER) and relation extraction (RE). In recent years, several researchers have built high-performance NER and RE systems based on contextualized representations (Yan et al., 2021; Zhong and Chen, 2021; Wang and Lu, 2020; Eberts and Ulges, 2020; Lin et al., 2020). These contextualized representations obtained from pretrained language models, such as bidirectional encoder representations from transformers (BERT) Devlin et al., 2019, have significantly improved the performance for various NLP tasks. As a result, studies on NER and RE have focused on the design of task-specific layers stacked on top of pretrained language models.

A common idea is to formulate NER and RE as table-filling problems (Miwa and Sasaki, 2014). The core concept is to extract entities and relations by filling a table with entity labels in the diagonal cells and relation labels in the off-diagonal cells. Based on this concept, Ma et al. (2022) proposed TablERT, which is a combined system of NER and RE based on a pretrained BERT. TablERT predicts the diagonal cells sequentially and off-diagonal cells simultaneously. Although the system is simple and effective, it ignores the dependencies among predicted relation labels. As noted in Ma et al. (2022), this does not improve the performance with label dependencies incorporated through refined decoding orders.

We propose TablERT-CNN, a novel NER and RE system that encodes the dependencies among the cells within the table. Our method employs two-dimensional convolutional neural networks (2D-CNNs), which are widely used neural architectures for object detection (Krizhevsky et al., 2012). We considered each table as a 2D image and each cell as a pixel, transforming the task into a table-labeling problem at the cell level. By applying 2D-CNNs to the output of BERT, the system is expected to implicitly perceive local information and label dependencies from neighboring cells. Notably, the range of cells to be processed is expandable by stacking multiple CNN layers, we model the dependencies among distant cells.

We evaluated TablERT-CNN based on multiple benchmarks: CoNLL04 (Roth and Yih, 2004), ACE05 (Walker et al., 2006), and ADE (Gurulingappa et al., 2012). The experimental results showed that the performance of the proposed method is on par with those of current state-of-art systems. We hypothesized that parameter updates during fine-tuning helped the BERT encoder capture the necessary dependencies for label predictions; thus, incorporating dependencies using the CNN became less helpful. To verify this hy-

Proceedings of the Sixth Workshop on Structured Prediction for NLP, pages 11 - 21

pothesis, we compared the performance of several NER and RE systems while keeping the BERT parameters frozen and updating them during fine tuning. In addition, we used different layers from which the prediction model extracts token embeddings to analyze how parameter updates within each layer contribute to the performance. As a result, TablERT-CNN still performed well while keeping the BERT parameters unchanged, whereas the performance of the other systems significantly decreased. This observation indicates the ability of the BERT architecture to consider token- and label-wise dependencies during task-specific fine tuning. The source code for the proposed system is publicly available at `https://github.com/YoumiMa/TablERT-CNN`.

2 Related Work

2.1 NER and RE Using Contextualized Representations

BERT and its variants have recently achieved significant performance improvements on various NLP tasks (Devlin et al., 2019; Lan et al., 2020). These transformer-based (Vaswani et al., 2017) encoders learn syntactic and semantic languages, generating a contextualized representation of each input token (Jawahar et al., 2019; Rogers et al., 2020). Owing to the superiority of BERT encoders, recent studies on NER and RE have tended to focus on the design of a good prediction model that fully utilizes BERT embeddings to further improve the performance.

Promising and straightforward prediction models for NER and RE have been developed. Eberts and Ulges (2020) proposed SpERT, which employs span-level representations obtained from BERT encoders for linear classification based on a negative sampling strategy during training. In addition, Zhong and Chen (2021) introduced a pipelined system, which performs span-based NER similarly to that of SpERT but re-encodes the input sentence using BERT to perform RE. In the RE model, the context and predicted entity labels are jointly encoded, enabling the computation of token-label attention. These approaches rely mainly on parameter updates in the BERT encoder during fine-tuning, where the encoder learns to capture task-specific dependencies. This study compares our system with SpERT to distinguish the dependencies captured by the encoder from those captured by the prediction model.

Some studies have used NER and RE for generative NLP tasks. Li et al. (2019) cast NER and RE as a multiturn question-answering problem. They designed natural language question templates whose answers specify the entities and relations within each sentence. In addition, Paolini et al. (2021) tackled structured language prediction tasks as sequence-to-sequence translations between augmented languages. Structural information can be extracted by postprocessing the target augmented language. Huguet Cabot and Navigli (2021) followed their idea and built a translation system that auto-regressively generates linearized relation triplets, considering an input text. These approaches utilize the attention mechanism within the transformer to capture long-range dependencies; however, they tend to be computationally burdensome. Inspired by their study, we have explored ways to incorporate token and label dependencies into the prediction model. However, our goal is to develop a mechanism that is more explainable and computationally efficient.

Another common approach is building a directed graph, modelling entity with spans as nodes and relations as arcs. Luan et al. (2019) and Wadden et al. (2019) focused on information propagation among span pairs to obtain effective span representations for a prediction. Based on their study, Lin et al. (2020) explicitly modeled cross-task and cross-instance dependencies by introducing a predefined set of global features. Instead of manually defining the global features, Ren et al. (2021) introduced a text-to-graph extraction model that automatically captures global features based on the auto-regressive generation process of a graph. These approaches are delicately designed to involve graph propagation and beam search strategies, resulting in a relatively high complexity.

Formulating the task as a table-filling problem is also a common idea (Miwa and Sasaki, 2014; Gupta et al., 2016; Zhang et al., 2017). Efforts have recently been made to incorporate BERT into this framework. Wang and Lu (2020) designed separate encoders for entities and relations. To use word-word interactions captured within the BERT model, the authors leveraged the attention weights computed from BERT into a relation encoder. Yan et al. (2021) applied a partition filter to divide neurons into multiple partitions and generated task-specific features based on a linear combination of these partitions. Moreover,Ma et al. (2022) built

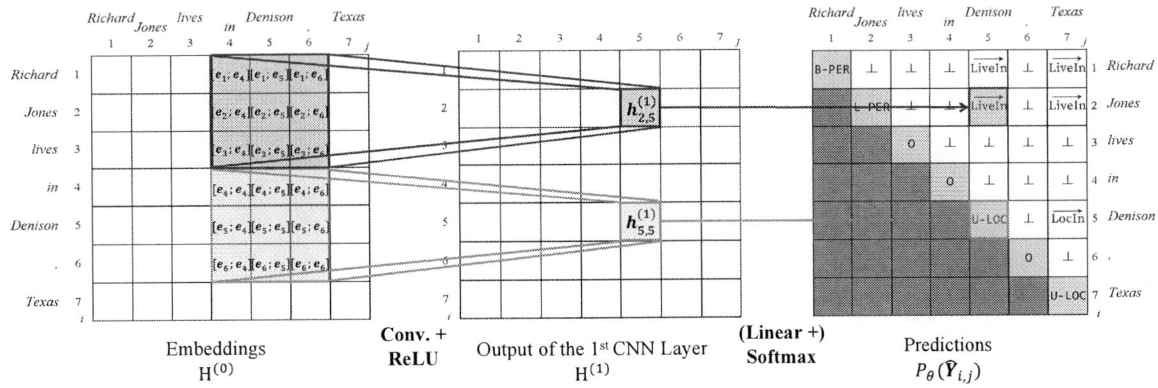

Figure 1: Overview of the proposed TablERT-CNN method when setting the number of CNN layers to 1. An example of a table-filling representation is shown on the right side. We employ the entire table to represent the features and the upper triangular part to represent the labels.

the straightforward TablERT system by predicting entities sequentially and relations simultaneously. Although the model exhibited state-of-art performance when published, it was unable to leverage the interactions among the table cells, especially for RE. This study applies their system as a strong baseline and explores the effect of incorporating local dependencies at the top of BERT. Because the proposed system is an extension of TablERT, we recap this approach (Ma et al., 2022) in the following subsection.

2.2 TablERT

TablERT (Ma et al., 2022) is a simple and effective method for a combined system applying both NER and RE. As shown on the right side of Figure 1, the method uses the upper triangular part of a table to represent the label spaces of NER and RE. The diagonal entries of the table are filled by entity labels, adopting the BILOU scheme to identify the **b**eginning, **i**nside, **l**ast words of multi-word and **u**nit-length spans (Ratinov and Roth, 2009). The off-diagonal entries in the table are filled with relation labels, with directions hard-coded onto each label. For each entity, the corresponding relation is annotated for all component words. For the sentence shown in Figure 1, the relation "LiveIn" pointing from "Richard Jones" to "Denison" is labeled as $\overrightarrow{\text{LIVEIN}}$ for the entries $(i = 1, j = 5)$ and $(i = 2, j = 5)$, corresponding to (*Richard*, *Denison*) and (*Jones*, *Denison*), respectively.

Ma et al. (2022) designed two separate prediction models for NER and RE. For NER, they sequentially assign a label to each word using features at the current and previous timesteps. For RE, they concatenate word embeddings with their corresponding entity label embeddings as relation embeddings. The relation scores of each word pair are computed based on a matrix multiplication of the linearly transformed relation embeddings.

Despite its simplicity, TablERT has shown promising performance. However, the system predicts the relation labels simultaneously, discarding label dependencies between the table cells. It has been reported that the performance of TablERT has shown little improvement, even when the off-diagonal cells are decoded individually following a predefined order Ma et al. (2022). In this study, we are interested in the effect of incorporating label dependencies at the top of contextualized representations. In contrast to Ma et al. (2022), we address this problem using 2D-CNNs.

3 Proposed Method

3.1 Problem Formulation

The goal of NER and RE systems is to extract entities and relations between pairs of entities, based on word sequences. Specifically, we consider a sentence $w_1, \cdots, w_N$. NER aims to identify every word span $s_i = w_b, \cdots, w_e$ that forms an entity with entity type $t_i \in \mathcal{E}$. By contrast, RE aims to extract every relation triple $(s_0\langle t_0\rangle, r, s_1\langle t_1\rangle)$, where $r \in \mathcal{R}$ represents the relation type between s_0 and s_1. Here, $\mathcal{E}$ and $\mathcal{R}$ represent the label sets of entities and relations, respectively.

3.2 TablERT-CNN

We propose TablERT-CNN as an extension of TablERT (Ma et al., 2022), considering the dependencies among labels by applying 2D-CNNs. Figure 1 shows an overview of TablERT-CNN under a setting in which the prediction model contains only one CNN layer. Based on existing studies (Miwa and Sasaki, 2014; Gupta et al., 2016; Zhang et al., 2017; Ma et al., 2022), we use the upper triangular part of a table to represent the entity and relation labels. The table representation is formally defined as follows:

Table Representation We define a matrix $\boldsymbol{Y} \in \mathbb{R}^{N \times N}$ and use the upper triangular part to represent the label space of NER and RE. A diagonal entry $\boldsymbol{Y}_{i,i}$ represents the entity label of word w_i, and an off-diagonal entry $\boldsymbol{Y}_{i,j} (j > i)$ represents the relation label of the word pair (w_i, w_j). We adopt the labeling rules of NER and RE, as in Ma et al. (2022); i.e., we annotate an entity using the BILOU notation and annotate a relation to every composing word of an entity span, with the direction hard-encoded into the label.

Word Embeddings We obtain word embeddings from contextualized representations generated from the pretrained BERT model (Devlin et al., 2019). Based on the existing study, we compute the embedding of each word by max-pooling its composing sub-words (Liu et al., 2019; Eberts and Ulges, 2020; Ma et al., 2022). Specifically, for word w_i composed of subwords $\text{start}(i), \cdots, \text{end}(i)$, the embedding of $\boldsymbol{e}_i$ is computed as follows:

$$\boldsymbol{e}_i := \max(\boldsymbol{x}^{(l)}_{\text{start}(i)}, \cdots, \boldsymbol{x}^{(l)}_{\text{end}(i)}). \tag{1}$$

Here, $\boldsymbol{x}^{(l)} \in \mathbb{R}^{d_{\text{emb}}}$ is the output of the pretrained BERT model, where l is the layer index[1], d_{emb} is the dimension size, and $\max(\cdot)$ is the max-pooling function. Therefore, we obtain $\boldsymbol{e}_i \in \mathbb{R}^{d_{\text{emb}}}$.

Prediction Model We adopt a 2D-CNN to capture the local dependencies among neighboring cells. 2D-CNNs are widely used for extracting image-classification and object-detection features (Krizhevsky et al., 2012). To apply a 2D-CNN to jointly extract entities and their relations, we treat the 2D table as an image and each cell within the table as a pixel. We then employ the 2D-CNN to encode the representation of each cell, as shown in Figure 1. The convolution network enables the model to capture local dependencies, and for each cell, a 2D-CNN layer yields a weighted linear combination among all surrounding cells within the convolutional window. The dependency range can be extended by stacking multiple 2D-CNN layers.

Specifically, for each word pair (w_i, w_j), we concatenate the word embeddings $\boldsymbol{e}_i, \boldsymbol{e}_j$, and construct the bottom layer $\mathsf{H}^{(0)} \in \mathbb{R}^{N \times N \times 2d_{\text{emb}}}$ (i.e., layer 0) of the 2D-CNN.

$$\mathsf{H}^{(0)}_{i,j,:} = \boldsymbol{h}^{(0)}_{i,j} := [\boldsymbol{e}_i;\ \boldsymbol{e}_j]. \tag{2}$$

Here, $[\cdot;\cdot]$ represents the concatenation of two vectors. Hence, the representation of each cell is a vector of dimension $2 \times d_{\text{emb}}$, which is denoted as d_0. Similarly, we denote the dimension number of the vector representation for each cell in layer l as d_l.

We then compute the output of the first 2D-CNN layer $\mathsf{H}^{(1)}$ based on the output of the bottom layer $\mathsf{H}^{(0)}$. Analogously, the output of any layer l can be computed by applying convolutions to the output of the previous layer, $l-1$. For any word pair (w_i, w_j), we obtain its corresponding output at the lth layer $\mathsf{H}^{(l)}_{i,j,:} = \boldsymbol{h}^{(l)}_{i,j} \in \mathbb{R}^{d_l}$ as follows:

$$\mathsf{H}^{(l)}_{i,j,:} = \boldsymbol{h}^{(l)}_{i,j} := \boldsymbol{b}^{(l)} + \sum_{c=0}^{d_{l-1}} (\mathsf{K}^{(l)}_{c,:,:} * \mathsf{H}^{(l-1)}_{:,:,c})_{i,j}, \tag{3}$$

where $\mathsf{H}^{(l-1)} \in \mathbb{R}^{N \times N \times d_{l-1}}$ is the output of layer $l-1$, $\mathsf{K}^{(l)} \in \mathbb{R}^{d_l \times d_h \times d_w}$ is a convolution kernel with window size $d_h \times d_w$, and $\boldsymbol{b}^{(l)} \in \mathbb{R}^{(l)}$ is the bias. Thus, for any dimension (i.e., channel) c, we have $\mathsf{K}^{(l)}_{c,:,:} \in \mathbb{R}^{d_h \times d_w}$ and $\mathsf{H}^{(l-1)}_{:,:,c} \in \mathbb{R}^{N \times N}$. $\boldsymbol{A} * \boldsymbol{B}$ represents the operation of computing 2D correlations. Given that $\boldsymbol{A} \in \mathbb{R}^{(2\alpha+1) \times (2\beta+1)}$, the computation is defined as follows:

$$(\boldsymbol{A} * \boldsymbol{B})_{m,n} := \sum_{h=-\alpha}^{\alpha} \sum_{w=-\beta}^{\beta} A_{\alpha+h,\beta+w} B_{m+h,n+w}. \tag{4}$$

The last layer of the 2D-CNN is a convolutional classifier for RE. That is, for the last layer L, we set its output dimension number to be the same as the number of relation labels; i.e., $d_L := |\mathcal{R}|$. Thus, for each word pair (w_i, w_j) where $i \neq j$, we obtain the relation label distribution $P_\theta(\hat{\boldsymbol{Y}}_{i,j})$ by applying a softmax function to $\mathsf{H}^{(L)}_{i,j,:}$:

$$P_\theta(\hat{\boldsymbol{Y}}_{i,j}) := \text{softmax}(\mathsf{H}^{(L)}_{i,j,:}), \tag{5}$$

[1]Previous studies have adopted the top layer (Li et al., 2019; Wadden et al., 2019; Eberts and Ulges, 2020) or the average of the top three layers (Wang and Lu, 2020) to generate word representations.

where P is the estimated probability function, and θ represents the model parameters.

For NER, we linearly transform the representations of the diagonal cells at layer L to compute the entity label distribution of each word w_i.

$$P_\theta(\hat{\boldsymbol{Y}}_{i,i}) := \text{softmax}(\boldsymbol{W} \cdot \mathsf{H}^{(L)}_{i,i,:} + \boldsymbol{b}), \quad (6)$$

where $\boldsymbol{W} \in \mathbb{R}^{|\mathcal{E}|\times|\mathcal{R}|}$ and $\boldsymbol{b} \in \mathbb{R}^{|\mathcal{E}|}$ are the trainable weight matrix and the bias vector, respectively.

Training and Prediction During training, we use the sum of cross-entropy losses of NER and RE as the objective function. Given the ground-truth label matrix of table $\boldsymbol{Y} \in \mathbb{R}^{N\times N}$, we compute the cross-entropy loss for NER ($\mathcal{L}^{\text{NER}}$) and RE ($\mathcal{L}^{\text{RE}}$).

$$\mathcal{L}^{\text{NER}} = -\sum_{1\le i\le N} \log P_\theta(\hat{\boldsymbol{Y}}_{i,i} = Y_{i,i}), \quad (7)$$

$$\mathcal{L}^{\text{RE}} = -\sum_{\substack{1\le i\le N\\ i<j\le N}} \log P_\theta(\hat{\boldsymbol{Y}}_{i,j} = Y_{i,j}). \quad (8)$$

We minimize $\mathcal{L}^{\text{NER}} + \mathcal{L}^{\text{RE}}$ to update the model parameters θ.

To predict the entity label of each word w_i, we select the label yielding the highest probability from $P_\theta(\hat{\boldsymbol{Y}}_{i,i})$ as the predicted result. When a conflict occurs with regard to the entity type within an entity span, we select the entity type labeled to the last word as the final prediction. To predict the relation label for each entity pair (s_i, s_j), we select the last words of both entity spans to represent the corresponding span s_i, s_j. For example, supposing the last word of entity span s_i, s_j is indexed as $\text{end}(i), \text{end}(j)$, the predicted relation label for entity pair (s_i, s_j) is determined as the label yielding the highest probability from $P_\theta(\hat{\boldsymbol{Y}}_{\text{end}(i),\text{end}(j)})$.

4 Experiments

4.1 Datasets

We evaluated the performance of our proposed system on CoNLL04 (Roth and Yih, 2004), ACE05 (Walker et al., 2006), and ADE (Gurulingappa et al., 2012), the statistics of which are listed in Table 1. Based on the conventional evaluation scheme for CoNLL04 and ACE05, we measured the micro F1-scores, and for ADE, we measured the macro F1-scores.

Dataset	# Sentences train	dev	test	$\lvert\mathcal{E}\rvert$	$\lvert\mathcal{R}\rvert$
CoNLL04	922	231	288	4	5
ACE05	10,051	2,424	2,050	7	6
ADE	4,272 (10-fold)			2	1

Table 1: Statistics of each dataset used in this study.

CoNLL04 is an annotated corpus collected from newswires. We processed the data released by Eberts and Ulges (2020)[2] to obtain the BILOU notations of the entities. Thus, our data split is the same as that in Eberts and Ulges (2020).

ACE05 is an annotated corpus collected from various sources, including newswires and online forums. We used the data preprocessing scripts provided by Wadden et al. (2019)[3] and Luan et al. (2019), which inherits that of Miwa and Bansal (2016)[4]. After preprocessing, an entity is regarded as correct if its label and head region are identical to the ground truth.

Adverse **D**rug **E**ffect (**ADE**, Gurulingappa et al., 2012) is a corpus constructed based on the medical reports of drug usages and their adverse effects. Based on existing studies (Eberts and Ulges, 2020; Wang and Lu, 2020), we removed overlapping entities from the dataset, which comprises only 2.8% of the total number of entities.

4.2 Experimental Settings

We implemented the proposed system using PyTorch (Li et al., 2020) and applied the pretrained BERT model provided by the Huggingface libraries (Wolf et al., 2020). Except for those within the pretrained BERT model, the parameters were randomly initialized. During training, we adopted the AdamW algorithm (Loshchilov and Hutter, 2019) for parameter updates. The details of hyperparameters are listed in Appendix A.

All experiments were conducted on a single GPU of an NVIDIA Tesla V100 (16 GiB). Throughout this study, we report the average values of 5 runs with different random seeds for all evaluation metrics.

4.3 Main Results

The main results of the proposed method are presented in Table 2. We adopted TablERT (Ma et al., 2022) for the primary comparison and trained the system from scratch with different pretrained en-

[2]`https://github.com/lavis-nlp/spert`
[3]`https://github.com/dwadden/dygiepp`
[4]`https://github.com/tticoin/LSTM-ER`

Dataset	Method	Encoder	NER	RE	RE+
CoNLL04△	SpERT (Eberts and Ulges, 2020)	$BERT_{BASE}$	88.9	-	71.5
	Table-Sequence (Wang and Lu, 2020)	$ALBERT_{XXLARGE}$	90.1	**73.8**	73.6
	TablERT (Ma et al., 2022)	$BERT_{BASE}$	90.2	72.8	72.6
	TablERT (Ma et al., 2022)	$BERT_{LARGE}$	**90.5**	**73.8**	**73.8**
	TablERT-CNN (Ours)	$BERT_{BASE}$	**90.5**	73.2	73.2
ADE▲	SpERT (Eberts and Ulges, 2020)	$BERT_{BASE}$	89.3	-	79.2
	Table-Sequence (Wang and Lu, 2020)	$ALBERT_{XXLARGE}$	89.7	80.1	80.1
	PFN (Yan et al., 2021)	$BERT_{BASE}$	89.6	-	80.0
	PFN (Yan et al., 2021)	$BERT_{LARGE}$	**91.3**	–	**83.2**
	TablERT(Ma et al., 2022)	$BERT_{BASE}$	89.9	**80.6**	80.6
	TablERT-CNN (Ours)	$BERT_{BASE}$	89.7	80.5	80.5
ACE05△	DyGIE++ (Wadden et al., 2019)	$BERT_{BASE}$	88.6	63.4	-
	Table-Sequence (Wang and Lu, 2020)	$BERT_{LARGE}$	88.2	67.4	-
	Table-Sequence (Wang and Lu, 2020)	$ALBERT_{XXLARGE}$	89.5	67.6	64.3
	PURE (Zhong and Chen, 2021)	$BERT_{BASE}$	88.7	66.7	63.9
	PURE (Zhong and Chen, 2021)	$BERT_{XXLARGE}$	89.7	**69.0**	65.6
	PFN (Yan et al., 2021)	$ALBERT_{XXLARGE}$	89.0	-	**66.8**
	TablERT (Ma et al., 2022)	$BERT_{BASE}$	87.6	66.2	62.6
	TablERT (Ma et al., 2022)	$BERT_{LARGE}$	88.4	67.5	64.6
	TablERT (Ma et al., 2022)	$ALBERT_{XXLARGE}$	**89.8**	67.7	65.2
	TablERT-CNN (Ours)	$BERT_{BASE}$	87.8	65.0	61.8

Table 2: Comparison between the existing and the proposed method (TablERT-CNN). Here, △ and ▲ denote the use of micro-and macro-average F1 scores for evaluation, respectively. The results of TablERT are our replications, and the results of the others are reported values from the original papers. To ensure a fair comparison, the reported values of PURE follow the single-sentence setting.

coders[5].

We evaluated the RE performance based on two criteria: RE and RE+. Specifically, REregards each predicted relation triple as correct if the relation label and spans of both entities are identical to the ground truth, whereas RE+ requires the labels of both entities to be correct. Because comparing systems using different encoders is unfair, we discuss the condition in which the encoders are aligned.

With regard to the CoNLL04 and ADE datasets, we observed that TablERT-CNN achieved high and stable performance on all datasets, on par with that of TablERT. In particular, for CoNLL04, the performance of the proposed method surpassed TablERT for both NER and RE. One possible explanation for this performance gain is that CoNLL04 is a relatively small dataset, as listed in Table 1. Such a low-resource setting possibly brought out the advantage of TablERT-CNN, as the CNN layers helped to utilize rich information about dependencies among entities and relations.

However, regarding the ACE05 dataset, we did not observe any performance gain by stacking the CNN layers. As listed in Table 2, TablERT-CNN lagged its competitor TablERT for around 1.0 point on the F1 score of RE. The reason for this can be multifactorial, and the nature of the ACE05 dataset might provide an answer. The dataset contains entities that do not contribute to any relation triple, which significantly confuses the model during the RE.

[5]The code is available at https://github.com/YoumiMa/TablERT.

5 Analysis

Although our system exhibited a good performance based on multiple datasets, no significant improvement was observed against TablERT (Ma et al., 2022). We hypothesize that the reason for this is the parameter updates within the BERT encoder during fine-tuning, which overshadowed the ability of the CNNs in the prediction model. Self-attention modules within BERT potentially learn to encode the dependencies between word pairs during fine-tuning, overlapping with those captured by the CNNs.

Experiments were conducted to verify this hypothesis. Specifically, we trained multiple BERT-based NER and RE systems (i.e., systems using a pretrained BERT as the encoder) while freezing the BERT parameters (§ 5.1). In this manner, we prevented the encoder from obtaining task-specific features during fine-tuning. The performance of these encoder-frozen systems was compared with that of their counterparts, whose encoder parameters were updated during fine-tuning. Based on this comparison, we investigated the extent to which the parameter updates within BERT contribute to

Method	Parameter Updates	Encoder Layer 0	1	2	4	6	8	10	12
SpERT (Eberts and Ulges, 2020)	No	27.4	30.9	32.1	36.5	41.0	40.6	37.2	8.0
	Yes	51.0	70.7	79.9	85.4	85.9	86.9	86.5	87.7
TablERT (Ma et al., 2022)	No	62.4	68.0	74.8	78.6	81.4	82.0	81.5	80.2
	Yes	66.9	78.2	84.1	87.4	88.7	88.2	88.5	88.5
TablERT-CNN (Ours)	No	80.3	81.1	83.1	85.1	86.6	86.2	86.0	85.9
	Yes	80.5	83.7	85.6	87.0	88.4	88.4	88.3	88.0

Table 3: Micro-average NER F1 scores on the CoNLL04 development set with/without parameter updates within the encoder ($\text{BERT}_{\text{BASE}}$) during fine-tuning. We fed the hidden states at different encoder layers into the prediction model for task-specific predictions.

Method	Parameter Updates	Encoder Layer 0	1	2	4	6	8	10	12
SpERT (Eberts and Ulges, 2020)	No	3.0	3.3	3.7	4.6	7.8	6.0	5.8	0.0
	Yes	16.4	35.4	49.6	64.7	67.2	69.3	70.2	69.1
TablERT (Ma et al., 2022)	No	28.8	37.4	39.3	47.1	53.0	54.0	55.9	51.7
	Yes	36.0	47.9	60.9	66.5	71.3	70.5	71.0	70.7
TablERT-CNN (Ours)	No	53.5	54.8	57.6	64.4	66.2	67.1	64.4	61.5
	Yes	54.0	59.9	62.3	67.8	70.6	70.3	70.1	70.6

Table 4: Micro-average F1 scores of the RE on the CoNLL04 development set with/without parameter updates within the encoder ($\text{BERT}_{\text{BASE}}$) during fine-tuning. We fed the hidden states at different encoder layers into the prediction model for task-specific predictions.

the performance of NER and RE.

In addition, we are interested in how each BERT layer encodes dependencies that are helpful for NER and RE. Previous studies have utilized the outputs of the top BERT layers to produce word representations (Wadden et al., 2019; Eberts and Ulges, 2020; Ma et al., 2022; Wang and Lu, 2020). However, we are curious whether the bottom or middle BERT layers also store useful information for solving the NER and RE. Therefore, we fed hidden states at the $\{0, 1, 2, 4, 6, 8, 10, 12\}$th BERT layer into the prediction model and examined the difference in performance (§ 5.2). Here, the 0th layer denotes the embedding layer of the BERT encoder.

Our analysis includes SpERT (Eberts and Ulges, 2020), TablERT (Ma et al., 2022) and the proposed method. We included TablERT for comparison because it is a counterpart of our system, incorporating no dependencies while performing RE. We included SpERT for comparison because it is a strong baseline utilizing a pretrained BERT encoder. Systems were trained on the CoNLL04 (Roth and Yih, 2004) training set and evaluated on the development set, using $\text{BERT}_{\text{BASE}}$ (Devlin et al., 2019) as the encoder. The experimental results are listed in Tables 3 and 4. The plots corresponding to these results are presented in Appendix B. Finally, we analyze the effect of 2D-CNNs (§ 5.3).

5.1 Effect of Parameter Updates within BERT

As listed in Tables 3 and 4, while freezing the parameters within BERT, we observed a decrease in the performance of both NER and RE for all target systems. SpERT exhibits a drastic decrease in performance while disabling the parameter updates within the encoder. This observation suggests that the system relies heavily on parameter updates of the encoder during task-specific fine-tuning to solve specific tasks.

By contrast, TablERT-CNN exhibited the best performance among the target systems, even with BERT parameters frozen. This result indicates that in a situation in which the parameter updates within the encoder are infeasible (e.g., computational resources are limited), TablERT-CNN can be more promising than TablERT or SpERT in terms of achieving high performance.

Furthermore, while freezing the BERT parameters, utilizing the hidden states of the top layers (i.e., layer 10 and higher) hindered the performance of all target systems. This phenomenon corresponds to the study by Rogers et al. (2020), which concluded that the final layers of BERT are usually the most task-specific. For a pretrained BERT encoder without any parameter updates, the top layers of the model are specified to the pretraining task, i.e., the masked-language modeling (MLM) task. It can therefore be assumed that while using the hidden

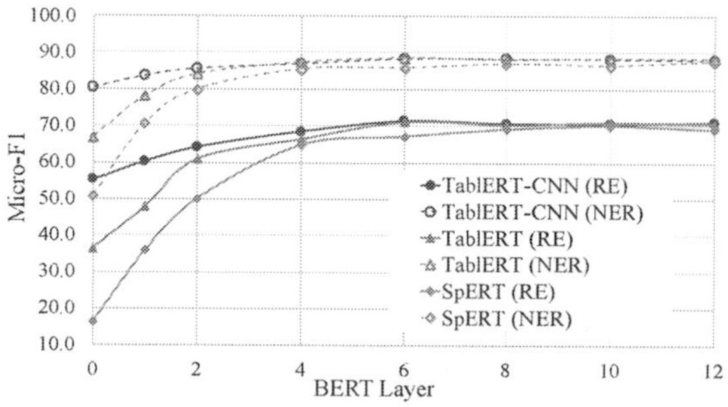

Figure 2: Micro-F1 scores of all target systems while varying the encoder layer whose outputs were fed into the prediction model (CoNLL04 development set).

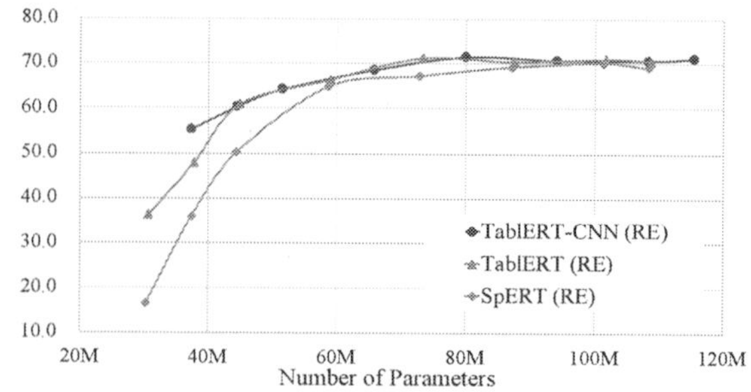

Figure 3: Performance of all target systems while varying the number of trainable parameters, as measured using the RE micro-F1 score (CoNLL04 development set).

states of the top layers of BERT without any task-specific parameter updates, the specificity toward the MLM task adversely affects the performance of the prediction model for both NER and RE.

5.2 Effect of BERT Layer

To visualize the performance change caused by the choice of BERT layer, the hidden states of which were utilized as word embeddings, we plotted the micro-F1 scores of all target systems, as shown in Figure 2.

Incorporating outputs from deeper BERT layers generally improves the prediction of all target systems. The improvement was significant at the bottom layers, but subtle at the top. Specifically, as shown in Figure 2, from layers 0 to 6, we observed a significant boost in the performance of NER and RE for all target systems. The change in performance was more evident with RE than with NER. By contrast, the performance of all target systems remained flat, starting from layer 8. This tendency suggests that, while building a BERT-based NER and RE system, it may be sufficient to employ up to 8 layers for text encoding.

Our findings match those reported by Jawahar et al. (2019), suggesting that BERT encodes a hierarchy of linguistics from bottom to top. Jawahar et al. (2019) found that BERT learns to encode long-distance dependencies, e.g., subject-verb agreements at deeper layers, which possibly explains the significant improvement in the RE performance while using outputs of the deeper BERT layers.

5.3 Effect of 2D-CNNs

As shown in Figure 2, while employing the outputs from the bottom BERT layers (i.e., from layers 0 to 4), TablERT-CNN outperformed the other systems by a relatively large margin. We owe the performance gap to the ability of TablERT-CNN to capture local dependencies. As noted in an existing study, the bottom BERT layers encode the surface information, for example, the phrasal syntax and word order (Jawahar et al., 2019; Rogers et al., 2020). As a result, the outputs at the bottom BERT layers lack contextualized information incorporating long-range dependencies, which are crucial for extracting relations. Therefore, whereas SpERT and TablERT suffer from the absence of word-word interactions, TablERT-CNN overcomes this issue by encoding them in the prediction model. By observing the table representation as a 2D image and each cell as a pixel, our method captures the local dependencies within each convolution kernel using 2D-CNNs. This advantage is apparent when word embeddings are not properly contextualized.

However, the superiority of TablERT-CNN becomes inconspicuous when the depth of the BERT layers increases. This phenomenon indicates that, when the contextualization ability of the encoder improves, the strength of a 2D-CNN to incorporate dependencies diminishes because the encoder has already captured the necessary information.

Notably, although we have shown the superiority of TablERT-CNN when utilizing the bottom BERT layers, it is natural to suspect that the performance gain resulted from the additional parameters introduced by the convolutional layers. Compared with SpERT and TablERT, TalERT-CNN introduces more trainable parameters, thereby increasing the ability of the system to fit the training data. To determine whether the performance gain resulted from the ability of the CNN to capture local dependencies or merely from an increased number of parameters, we replotted Figure 2, as shown in

Figure 3, the result of which shows the relationship between the RE micro-F1 scores and the number of trainable parameters of each target system. From Figure 3, we observed that TablERT-CNN lies on the left-most side among all of the target systems. To paraphrase, when keeping the number of trainable parameters the same, TablERT-CNN performs better than its competitors. This tendency is apparent when the number of trainable parameters is small, which indicates that TablERT-CNN can be a prospective option when the computational resources are limited.

To conclude, TablERT-CNN can be a promising architecture when parameter updates within the encoder are infeasible or when the encoder is not well-contextualized. Under these situations, a 2D-CNN plays an important role in encoding the local dependencies, thus improving the NER and RE predictions.

6 Conclusion

We presented TablERT-CNN, a novel method for jointly extracting entities and relations with 2D-CNNs. The method casts NER and RE as table-labeling problems, representing each table cell as a pixel and each table as a 2D image. By applying 2D-CNNs, the method predicts the label of each table cell to extract entities and relations. Experiments conducted on CoNLL04, ACE05, and ADE demonstrated that TablERT-CNN performed on par with current state-of-art systems when the pretrained encoders were aligned.

To explore why TablERT-CNN did not outperform existing systems by a significant margin, we conducted experiments to compare their performance with and without parameter updates of the BERT encoder during the fine-tuning. We observed that TablERT-CNN performed reasonably well even without updating the encoder parameters, whereas its competitors suffered a decrease in performance. These results indicate that the BERT encoder can capture task-specific dependencies among tokens and labels within its architecture, based on parameter updates during fine-tuning.

In the future, we plan to model the dependencies among table cells using other neural architectures. Prospective directions include 2D-transformers that compute the attention across element pairs in a 2D array, or Routing Transformers that utilize local attentions.

Acknowledgements

This paper is based on results obtained from a project, JPNP18002, commissioned by the New Energy and Industrial Technology Development Organization (NEDO). We appreciate the insightful comments and suggestions of the anonymous reviewers.

References

Jacob Devlin, Ming-Wei Chang, Kenton Lee, and Kristina Toutanova. 2019. BERT: Pre-training of deep bidirectional transformers for language understanding. In *Proceedings of the 2019 Conference of the North American Chapter of the Association for Computational Linguistics: Human Language Technologies, Volume 1 (Long and Short Papers)*, pages 4171–4186, Minneapolis, Minnesota. Association for Computational Linguistics.

Markus Eberts and Adrian Ulges. 2020. Span-based joint entity and relation extraction with transformer pre-training. In *24th European Conference on Artificial Intelligence (ECAI)*.

Pankaj Gupta, Hinrich Schütze, and Bernt Andrassy. 2016. Table filling multi-task recurrent neural network for joint entity and relation extraction. In *Proceedings of COLING 2016, the 26th International Conference on Computational Linguistics: Technical Papers*, pages 2537–2547, Osaka, Japan. The COLING 2016 Organizing Committee.

Harsha Gurulingappa, Abdul Mateen Rajput, Angus Roberts, Juliane Fluck, Martin Hofmann-Apitius, and Luca Toldo. 2012. Development of a benchmark corpus to support the automatic extraction of drug-related adverse effects from medical case reports. *Journal of Biomedical Informatics*, 45(5):885–892. Text Mining and Natural Language Processing in Pharmacogenomics.

Pere-Lluís Huguet Cabot and Roberto Navigli. 2021. REBEL: Relation extraction by end-to-end language generation. In *Findings of the Association for Computational Linguistics: EMNLP 2021*, pages 2370–2381, Punta Cana, Dominican Republic. Association for Computational Linguistics.

Ganesh Jawahar, Benoît Sagot, and Djamé Seddah. 2019. What does BERT learn about the structure of language? In *Proceedings of the 57th Annual Meeting of the Association for Computational Linguistics*, pages 3651–3657, Florence, Italy. Association for Computational Linguistics.

Alex Krizhevsky, Ilya Sutskever, and Geoffrey E Hinton. 2012. Imagenet classification with deep convolutional neural networks. In *Advances in Neural Information Processing Systems*, volume 25. Curran Associates, Inc.

Zhenzhong Lan, Mingda Chen, Sebastian Goodman, Kevin Gimpel, Piyush Sharma, and Radu Soricut. 2020. Albert: A lite bert for self-supervised learning of language representations. In *International Conference on Learning Representations (ICLR)*.

Shen Li, Yanli Zhao, Rohan Varma, Omkar Salpekar, Pieter Noordhuis, Teng Li, Adam Paszke, Jeff Smith, Brian Vaughan, Pritam Damania, and Soumith Chintala. 2020. Pytorch distributed: Experiences on accelerating data parallel training. *Proc. VLDB Endow.*, 13(12):3005–3018.

Xiaoya Li, Fan Yin, Zijun Sun, Xiayu Li, Arianna Yuan, Duo Chai, Mingxin Zhou, and Jiwei Li. 2019. Entity-relation extraction as multi-turn question answering. In *Proceedings of the 57th Annual Meeting of the Association for Computational Linguistics*, pages 1340–1350, Florence, Italy. Association for Computational Linguistics.

Ying Lin, Heng Ji, Fei Huang, and Lingfei Wu. 2020. A joint neural model for information extraction with global features. In *Proceedings of the 58th Annual Meeting of the Association for Computational Linguistics*, pages 7999–8009, Online. Association for Computational Linguistics.

Yijin Liu, Fandong Meng, Jinchao Zhang, Jinan Xu, Yufeng Chen, and Jie Zhou. 2019. GCDT: A global context enhanced deep transition architecture for sequence labeling. In *Proceedings of the 57th Annual Meeting of the Association for Computational Linguistics*, pages 2431–2441, Florence, Italy. Association for Computational Linguistics.

Ilya Loshchilov and Frank Hutter. 2019. Decoupled weight decay regularization. In *International Conference on Learning Representations (ICLR)*.

Yi Luan, Dave Wadden, Luheng He, Amy Shah, Mari Ostendorf, and Hannaneh Hajishirzi. 2019. A general framework for information extraction using dynamic span graphs. In *Proceedings of the 2019 Conference of the North American Chapter of the Association for Computational Linguistics: Human Language Technologies, Volume 1 (Long and Short Papers)*, pages 3036–3046, Minneapolis, Minnesota. Association for Computational Linguistics.

Youmi Ma, Tatsuya Hiraoka, and Naoaki Okazaki. 2022. Named entity recognition and relation extraction using enhanced table filling by contextualized representations. *Journal of Natural Language Processing*, 29(1):187–223.

Makoto Miwa and Mohit Bansal. 2016. End-to-end relation extraction using LSTMs on sequences and tree structures. In *Proceedings of the 54th Annual Meeting of the Association for Computational Linguistics (Volume 1: Long Papers)*, pages 1105–1116, Berlin, Germany. Association for Computational Linguistics.

Makoto Miwa and Yutaka Sasaki. 2014. Modeling joint entity and relation extraction with table representation. In *Proceedings of the 2014 Conference on Empirical Methods in Natural Language Processing (EMNLP)*, pages 1858–1869, Doha, Qatar. Association for Computational Linguistics.

Giovanni Paolini, Ben Athiwaratkun, Jason Krone, Jie Ma, Alessandro Achille, RISHITA ANUBHAI, Cicero Nogueira dos Santos, Bing Xiang, and Stefano Soatto. 2021. Structured prediction as translation between augmented natural languages. In *International Conference on Learning Representations (ICLR)*.

Lev Ratinov and Dan Roth. 2009. Design challenges and misconceptions in named entity recognition. In *Proceedings of the Thirteenth Conference on Computational Natural Language Learning (CoNLL-2009)*, pages 147–155, Boulder, Colorado. Association for Computational Linguistics.

Liliang Ren, Chenkai Sun, Heng Ji, and Julia Hockenmaier. 2021. HySPA: Hybrid span generation for scalable text-to-graph extraction. In *Findings of the Association for Computational Linguistics: ACL-IJCNLP 2021*, pages 4066–4078, Online. Association for Computational Linguistics.

Anna Rogers, Olga Kovaleva, and Anna Rumshisky. 2020. A primer in BERTology: What we know about how BERT works. *Transactions of the Association for Computational Linguistics*, 8:842–866.

Dan Roth and Wen-tau Yih. 2004. A linear programming formulation for global inference in natural language tasks. In *Proceedings of the Eighth Conference on Computational Natural Language Learning (CoNLL-2004) at HLT-NAACL 2004*, pages 1–8, Boston, Massachusetts, USA. Association for Computational Linguistics.

Ashish Vaswani, Noam Shazeer, Niki Parmar, Jakob Uszkoreit, Llion Jones, Aidan N Gomez, Łukasz Kaiser, and Illia Polosukhin. 2017. Attention is all you need. In *Advances in neural information processing systems (NeurIPS)*, pages 5998–6008.

David Wadden, Ulme Wennberg, Yi Luan, and Hannaneh Hajishirzi. 2019. Entity, relation, and event extraction with contextualized span representations. In *Proceedings of the 2019 Conference on Empirical Methods in Natural Language Processing and the 9th International Joint Conference on Natural Language Processing (EMNLP-IJCNLP)*, pages 5784–5789, Hong Kong, China. Association for Computational Linguistics.

Christopher Walker, Stephanie Strassel, Julie Medero, and Kazuaki Maeda. 2006. Ace 2005 multilingual training corpus. *Philadelphia: Linguistic Data Consortium*.

Jue Wang and Wei Lu. 2020. Two are better than one: Joint entity and relation extraction with table-sequence encoders. In *Proceedings of the 2020 Conference on Empirical Methods in Natural Language Processing (EMNLP)*, pages 1706–1721, Online. Association for Computational Linguistics.

Thomas Wolf, Lysandre Debut, Victor Sanh, Julien Chaumond, Clement Delangue, Anthony Moi, Pierric Cistac, Tim Rault, Remi Louf, Morgan Funtowicz, Joe Davison, Sam Shleifer, Patrick von Platen, Clara Ma, Yacine Jernite, Julien Plu, Canwen Xu, Teven Le Scao, Sylvain Gugger, Mariama Drame, Quentin Lhoest, and Alexander Rush. 2020. Transformers: State-of-the-art natural language processing. In *Proceedings of the 2020 Conference on Empirical Methods in Natural Language Processing: System Demonstrations*, pages 38–45, Online. Association for Computational Linguistics.

Zhiheng Yan, Chong Zhang, Jinlan Fu, Qi Zhang, and Zhongyu Wei. 2021. A partition filter network for joint entity and relation extraction. In *Proceedings of the 2021 Conference on Empirical Methods in Natural Language Processing*, pages 185–197, Online and Punta Cana, Dominican Republic. Association for Computational Linguistics.

Meishan Zhang, Yue Zhang, and Guohong Fu. 2017. End-to-end neural relation extraction with global optimization. In *Proceedings of the 2017 Conference on Empirical Methods in Natural Language Processing*, pages 1730–1740, Copenhagen, Denmark. Association for Computational Linguistics.

Zexuan Zhong and Danqi Chen. 2021. A frustratingly easy approach for entity and relation extraction. In *Proceedings of the 2021 Conference of the North American Chapter of the Association for Computational Linguistics: Human Language Technologies*, pages 50–61, Online. Association for Computational Linguistics.

A Hyper-parameters

The values of the hyperparameters used during the experiments are listed in Table 5. CNN configurations were determined by conducting grid searches on the development split of each dataset, whereas the training configurations were adopted directly from Ma et al. (2022). We applied a scheduler that linearly increases the learning rate from 0 to the maximum value during the warm-up period and gradually decreases it afterward.

B Effect of Parameter Updates with BERT (cont.)

Figures 4(a) and 4(b) correspond to Tables 3 and 4, respectively. As we can see, TablERT-CNN exhibited a relatively high performance, even when the BERT parameters were frozen. In addition, when the BERT parameters were frozen, the performance of all target systems decreased while incorporating the hidden states of the top (10–12) encoder layers.

	CoNLL04	ACE05	ADE
CNN Config.			
kernel size $F_h \times F_w$	3×3	5×5	3×3
# layers L	2	2	3
hidden dim $d^{(l)}$	512	512	512|256
Training Config.			
batch size	8	8	16
Learning rate (BERT)	5e-5	5e-5	5e-5
Learning rate (others)	1e-3	1e-3	1e-3
dropout	0.3	0.3	0.3
warm-up period	0.2	0.2	0.2
# epochs	30	30	30

Table 5: Hyperparameters of our proposed method (TablERT-CNN).

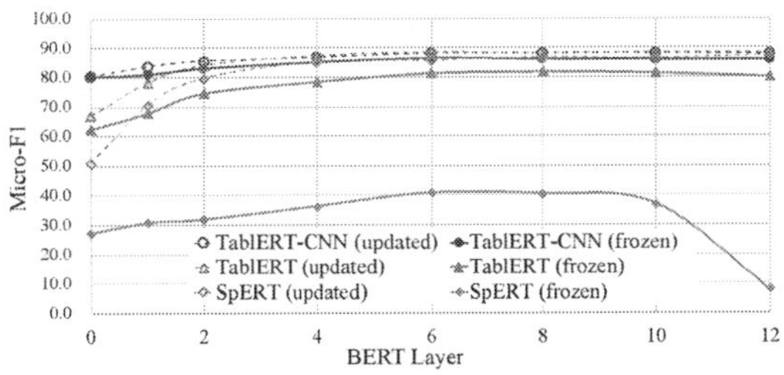

(a) NER micro-F1 scores.

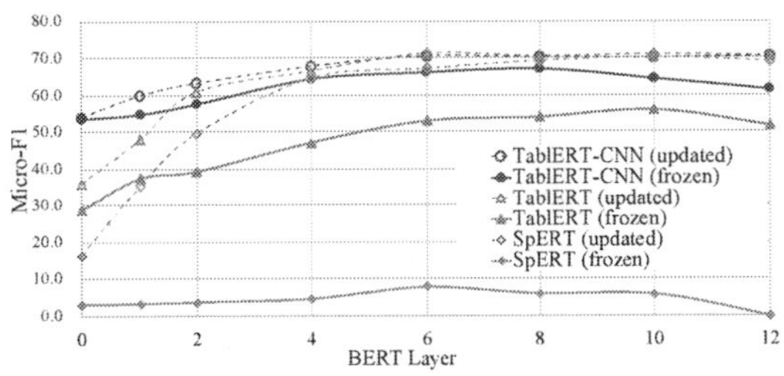

(b) RE micro-F1 scores.

Figure 4: Micro-F1 scores of all target systems while varying the encoder layer whose outputs were fed into the prediction model (CoNLL04 development set). Here, "updated" and "frozen" indicate the status of each parameter within BERT during the fine-tuning process.

TempCaps: A Capsule Network-based Embedding Model for Temporal Knowledge Graph Completion

Guirong Fu*[1], Zhao Meng*[1], Zhen Han*[2,3], Zifeng Ding[2,3],
Yunpu Ma[2], Matthias Schubert[2] Volker Tresp[2,3] Roger Wattenhofer[1]
[1]ETH Zürich [2]LMU Munich [3]Siemens AG
{fug, zhmeng, wattenhofer}@ethz.ch, zhen.han@campus.lmu.de
{zifeng.ding,volker.tresp}@siemens.com,
cognitive.yunpu@gmail.com, schubert@dbs.ifi.lmu.de

Abstract

Temporal knowledge graphs store the dynamics of entities and relations during a time period. However, typical temporal knowledge graphs often suffer from incomplete dynamics with missing facts in real-world scenarios. Hence, modeling temporal knowledge graphs to complete the missing facts is important. In this paper, we tackle the temporal knowledge graph completion task by proposing **TempCaps**, which is a **Caps**ule network-based embedding model for **Temp**oral knowledge graph completion. TempCaps models temporal knowledge graphs by introducing a novel dynamic routing aggregator inspired by Capsule Networks. Specifically, TempCaps builds entity embeddings by dynamically routing retrieved temporal relation and neighbor information. Experimental results demonstrate that TempCaps reaches state-of-the-art performance for temporal knowledge graph completion. Additional analysis also shows that TempCaps is efficient[1].

1 Introduction

Knowledge graphs (KGs) organize and integrate information in a structured manner, which is human-readable and suitable for computer processing. This advantage of knowledge graphs is helping to bridge the gap between humans and computers. Numerous real-world applications have benefited from KGs. In particular, recent advances in artificial intelligence have motivated researchers to use knowledge graphs to boost performance in downstream applications, including natural language processing (IV et al., 2019; Bosselut et al., 2019) and computer vision (Yu et al., 2021; Marino et al., 2017).

Despite the usefulness of knowledge graphs, existing knowledge graphs are often incomplete, which means important facts might be missing. To tackle this problem, researchers have developed various methods for the task of knowledge graph completion (Nickel et al., 2011; Bordes et al., 2013), aiming to recover missing facts for existing knowledge graphs. In particular, Nguyen et al. (2019) explored the Capsule Network (CapsNet) (Sabour et al., 2017) for modeling knowledge graphs. CapsE(Nguyen et al., 2019) demonstrate that each dimension of the entity, as well as relation, embeddings also have diverse variations in different contexts. Thus, they used capsules to encode many characteristics in the embedding triple and represent the entries at the corresponding dimension, showing superior performance to other KG models.

Existing studies, including CapsE, focus on completing static knowledge graphs. In reality, however, multi-relational data is often time-dependent. Moreover, static knowledge graphs fail to adequately describe the changing essence of the world, indicating that knowledge or facts being true in the past might not always stay true. For instance, social networks constantly change. Static knowledge graphs fail to model these changes. To this end, temporal knowledge graphs (tKGs) are introduced to grasp these dynamic changes. Specifically, temporal facts are represented as a quadruple by extending the static triplet with a timestamp describing when these facts occurred, i.e. (Barack Obama, inaugurated, president of the US, 2009). Similar to static KG, tKGs also suffer from the problem of incompleteness, making the task of temporal knowledge graph completion eminent (Bordes et al., 2013; Lin et al., 2015).

In this paper, we take advantage of the Capsule Network paradigm and generalize it for modeling tKGs. We introduce TempCaps, which is a **Caps**ule network-based embedding model for **Temp**oral knowledge graph completion. As shown in Figure 1, TempCaps consists of a neighbor selector, an

*The first three authors contributed equally to this work.
[1]Our code is available at `https://github.com/fuguigui/tempcaps`

Proceedings of the Sixth Workshop on Structured Prediction for NLP, pages 22 - 31
May 27, 2022 ©2022 Association for Computational Linguistics

entity embedding layer, a dynamic routing aggregator and a multi-layer perceptron (MLP) decoder. Unlike CapsE, we incorporate the temporal information of tKGs into our model: First, we pose temporal constraints on neighbor selection by introducing a time window. At a given time step, we only take the neighbors that interact with the source entity within the time window into account for capturing the entity features. Second, we propose a time-dependent dynamic routing mechanism that incorporates time information into routing weight matrix. Third, we exploit the temporal weighting vectors generated during the dynamic routing to calculate the output probability, which reflects how tightly lower capsules connect with higher capsules.

Our contributions are in the following: **(i)** We propose TempCaps, which leverages Capsule Networks by dynamically routing retrieved temporal relations and neighboring entities. An advantage of our model is that different capsules can capture different aspects of the same entity. Such advantage is important for modeling temporal knowledge graphs, which are dynamic, and often involve one entity in multiple timestamps. **(ii)** Our TempCaps improves the performance of temporal knowledge graph completion. Experimental results show that our model achieves state-of-the-art performance on the GDELT and ICEWS datasets. Furthermore, our model is light-weighted and efficient compared to previous methods for modeling tKGs. **(iii)** As far as we know, we are the first to use Capsule Networks for tKGs. Our experiments show that by leveraging dynamic routing, TempCaps is suitable for both discrete and continuous timestamps and can be easily generalized to unseen timestamps. **(iv)** We conduct additional ablation studies to understand how each part of TempCaps contributes to the model performance. We also show that TempCaps is efficient by analyzing time and space complexity.

2 Related Work

2.1 Knowledge Graph Embedding

Knowledge Graph Embedding (KGE) maps entities and relations into low-dimensional continuous vectors. Two types of KGEs, including static KGE and temporal KGE, have attracted attention from the community. In the rest of this subsection, we give an overview of static and temporal KGE.

Static Knowledge Graph Embedding. Embedding approaches for static KGs can generally be categorized into bilinear models and transition-based models. TransE (Bordes et al., 2013) leverages the transition-based approach, which measures the plausibility of a triple as the distance between the object entity's embedding and the embedding of the subject after the relational transition. Similarly, by using additional projection vectors, Wang et al. (2014) extend TransE to translate entity embeddings into the vector space of relations. Other works including RESCAL (Nickel et al., 2011), DisMult (Yang et al., 2015), and SimplE (Kazemi and Poole, 2018) use a bilinear score function, which represents predicates as linear transformations of entity embeddings. However, these KGE methods are not suitable for tKGs as they cannot capture the temporal dynamics of tKGs.

Temporal Knowledge Graph Embedding. Temporal KGE approaches aim to capture both temporal and relational information to improve the performance of the completion task. Han et al. (2021b) assessed well-known temporal embeddings of tKGE models via an extensive experimental study and released the first open unified open-source framework for temporal KG completion models with full composability. HyTE (Dasgupta et al., 2018) embeds time information in the entity-relation space by arranging a temporal hyperplane to each timestamp and uses TransE as interaction model to compute the plausibility score of facts. DE-SimplE (Goel et al., 2020) extends SimplE by exploring the diachronic function to model entity embeddings at different timestamps. TA-DistMult (García-Durán et al., 2018) utilizes recurrent neural networks to learn time-aware representations of relations and adopt DistMult as the score function. Moreover, Han et al. (2020a) introduced a non-Euclidean embedding approach that learns evolving entity representations in a product of Riemannian manifolds. Besides, Han et al. (2022) enhanced temporal knowledge embedding using contextualized language representations and achived state-of-the-art results. Besides the completion task, researchers have also paid attention to use temporal KGE for forecasting on tKGs (Trivedi et al., 2017; Jin et al., 2020; Han et al., 2020b,c, 2021a; Sun et al., 2021). Forecasting tasks predict future links based on past observations, while the completion tasks interpolate missing links at observed timestamps. In this work, we focus on the tKG completion task.

2.2 Capsule Network

Sabour et al. (2017) propose Capsule Networks to capture different entities in images by leveraging dynamic routing between different layers of Capsule Networks. As a result, capsule Networks reach comparable or even better performance when compared to convolutional neural networks, while at the same time being more efficient and more robust to affine transformation. Following Sabour et al. (2017), researchers have proposed various methods to improve the performance of Capsule Networks. Hahn et al. (2019) boost the performance of Capsule Networks by using a novel self-routing mechanism. Tsai et al. (2020) propose to use inverted dot-product attention routing to improve Capsule Networks. We give more details on the basics of Capsule Networks in Section 3.2.2.

Apart from the vision domain, previous work has shown that Capsule Networks are also useful for modeling static knowledge graphs. (Nguyen et al., 2019) propose CapsE, which represents each triplet fact *(subject, relation, object)* in a knowledge graph as a 3-column matrix, each of which corresponds to an entity in a fact. CapsE reaches state-of-the-art performance on static knowledge graph completion tasks.

This paper proposes TempCaps, which uses Capsule Networks to model tKGs. Despite all previous works on Capsule Networks, we are the first to model tKGs with Capsule Networks to the best of our knowledge. Experimental results show that TempCaps achieves competitive performance on the temporal knowledge graph completion task. We present the details of TempCaps in Section 3.2.

3 Methodology

3.1 Task Formulation

A temporal knowledge graph (tKG) is a collection of valid facts with temporal information. A fact in tKG is a quadruple of (s, r, o, t), which consists of subject s, relation r, object o, and timestamp t. We use E, R, and T to denote the sets of entities, relations, and timestamps involved in at least one fact in a given tKG. $|E|$, $|R|$ and $|T|$ are the number of elements in each set, respectively. A tKG can be viewed as the union of KG snapshots at each timestamp. Formally, we have:

$$G = G(t_1) \cup G(t_2) \cup \cdots G(t_i) \cdots \cup G(t_{max}),$$

where $G(t_i) = \{(s, r, o, t_i) | t_i \in T\}$ is a snapshot of G at timestamp t_i, and $t_{max} = \max(t_i | t_i \in T)$.

Temporal Knowledge Graph Completion (TKGC) aims to predict unobserved missing facts from incomplete tKGs. In TKGC, both unobserved and observed facts share the same period of time. Let O be the observed true facts from a complete tKG G (G contains both observed true facts and to-be-predicted facts), we denote the set of missing facts as $\bar{O} = G \setminus O$ which should be predicted in the context of TKGC. In our work, we only consider predicting the missing subject or the missing object of the missing facts. For every missing fact $(s, r, o, t) \in \bar{O}$, two prediction queries $(s, r, ?, t)$ and $(?, r, o, t)$ are generated, and our model aims to rank the ground-truth subject entity s from $(?, r, o, t)$, as well as the ground-truth object entity o from $(s, r, ?, t)$, as high as possible among all candidate entities. For simplicity, we present the equations and illustrate our method with only object prediction. During training and evaluation of our experiments, we include both subject prediction and object prediction.

3.2 Model Architecture

3.2.1 Overview

We propose TempCaps, a **Caps**ule network-based embedding model for **Temp**oral knowledge graph completion. TempCaps first selects two types of neighboring entities, i.e., local entities and global relational entities, for each entity of the tKG. Then it learns the embeddings of entities based on the retrieved neighbors using a dynamic routing module (see Section 3.2.5). Finally, TempCaps ranks the entities from the candidate set by feeding the embeddings of the entities to a scoring module. Figure 1 gives an illustration of TempCaps.

3.2.2 Capsule Network

Capsule networks are built with two critical components: capsules and the dynamic routing mechanism.

A capsule is a set of neurons processing different information about an entity, and the activities of the neurons within an active capsule represent the various properties of a particular entity (Sabour et al., 2017). We use a squash function proposed by Sabour et al. to guarantee that the length of the

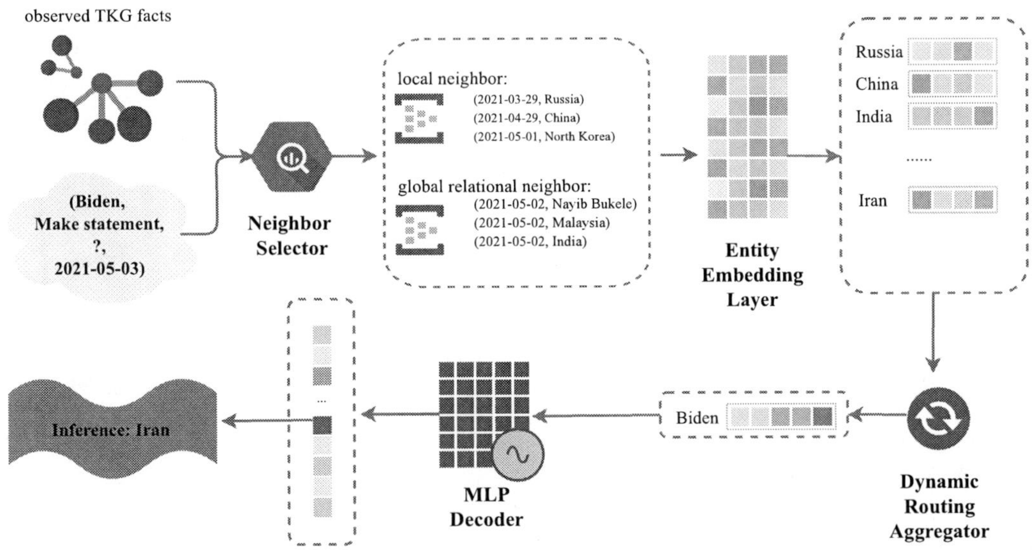

Figure 1: Overview of TempCaps. Assume we want to predict the ground truth object of a prediction query (Biden, Make statement, ?, 2021-05-03), given all the observed facts. TempCaps first selects different types of neighboring entities of the query subject Biden, and embeds these neighbors with capsules. Then it utilizes the dynamic routing aggregator to learn Biden's contextualized embedding. A multi-layer perceptron (MLP) decoder takes the learned embedding and performs a multi-class classification over all candidates, producing scores for every entity in the candidate set. The entity with the highest score (Iran in this example) is the predicted object.

vector stays between 0 and 1:

$$\mathbf{v}_j = \frac{||\mathbf{s}_j||^2}{1+||\mathbf{s}_j||^2}\frac{\mathbf{s}_j}{||\mathbf{s}_j||}, \tag{1}$$

where $\mathbf{s}_j$ is the input of a capsule and $\mathbf{v}_j$ is its squashed output.

Routing by agreements regulates how capsules communicate between layers. The dynamic routing mechanism (Sabour et al., 2017) works as follows. All output vectors $\mathbf{u}_i$ of capsules in the lower layer are first multiplied by a weight matrix $\mathbf{W}_{ij}$. Then, the weighted sum of newly obtained vectors are input into a capsule $\mathbf{s}_j$ in the next layer:

$$\hat{\mathbf{u}}_{j|i} = \mathbf{W}_{ij}\mathbf{u}_i, \quad \mathbf{s}_j = \sum_i c_{ij}\hat{\mathbf{u}}_{j|i}, \tag{2}$$

where c_{ij} is the coupling coefficient between capsule i and capsule j. In our work, we initialize each entity's embedding with a capsule in the first capsule layer. By performing routing by agreements, we achieve information aggregation between an entity and its selected neighbors.

3.2.3 Neighbor Selector

Similar to static KGs, in tKGs, we can still treat entities as nodes (relations as edges). Inspired by previous works in graph neural network (Kipf and Welling, 2017; Velickovic et al., 2018; Xu et al., 2019), where the embeddings of nodes are derived by the n-hop neighbors of the nodes, TempCaps computes the embedding of each node, i.e., entity in the context of tKGs, by leveraging information from the temporal neighbors of that node in the tKG. Given a prediction query $(s, r, ?, t)$, TempCaps selects two types of neighbors, namely, local entities and global relational entities, for the query subject s.

A **local entity** is an object entity o' which originates from an observed fact (s, r, o', t'), where t' can be any timestamp within a fixed range around the query timestamp. We denote the set of all local entities at all timestamps as $E^l(s, r)$:

$$E^l(s,r) = \{o'|(s,r,o',t'), \\ \mathtt{max}(t-\Delta t_e, t_1) \leq t' \leq \mathtt{min}(t+\Delta t_e, t_{max})\}\}.$$

To avoid including excessive entities into E^l, TempCaps samples local entities from all observed facts within a pre-defined time window Δt_e.

A **global relational entity** is an object entity o' which originates from an observed fact (s', r, o', t'), where s' can be any entity and t' can be any timestamp within a fixed range around the query timestamp. We denote the set of all local entities at all timestamps as E^g:

$$E^g(r) = \{o'|(s', r, o', t'), \\ \mathtt{max}(t - \Delta t_r, t_1) \leq t' \leq \mathtt{min}(t + \Delta t_r, t_{max})\}.$$

Similarly, global relational entities are selected within a time window Δt_r.

We further define the set of all selected neighbors as $E^n = \{E^l, E^g\}$. By restricting neighbors within time windows around the query timestamp, TempCaps selects entities that have greater influence on the query subject s. We employ different time windows to select local entities, and global relational entities as different types of neighbors have different influence on the query subject s. We treat the time windows, i.e., Δt_e and Δt_r, as hyperparameters during finetuning.

3.2.4 Temporal Weighting Function

In CapsNet (Sabour et al., 2017), the log prior probability b_{ij} between two capsules i and j are learned depending on the locations and the types of both capsules. It is used to compute the coupling coefficient stated in Equation 2: $c_{ij} = \frac{\exp(b_{ij})}{\sum_k \exp(b_{ik})}$. Inspired by CapsNet, we initialize the log prior probability between the query subject s and its selected neighbor o' with a temporal weighting function, as we consider the time difference between these two entities as the difference of capsule locations. The intuition is that, for a prediction query $(s, r, ?, t)$, a neighbor that connects with s near to t should have more influence on s than a temporally-farther neighbor. Hence, we assign a higher probability to nearer neighbors than farther neighbors. Formally, given a prediction query $(s, r, ?, t)$ and a selected neighbor o' (derived from an observed fact at t'), $b_{o'}$ is initialized as:

$$b_{o'} = \frac{\gamma + 1}{\gamma + |t' - t| + 1}, \tag{3}$$

where γ is a hyperparameter. Figure 2 illustrates the temporal weighting function with different γ. The temporal weighting function with a lower γ leads to higher differences in the values of coupling coefficients regarding various neighboring entities.

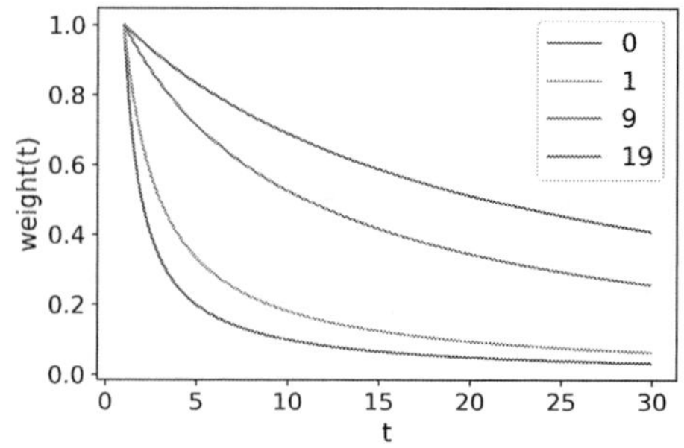

Figure 2: Temporal weighting function with different γ. The horizontal axis is t and the vertical axis is the value of $\mathtt{weight}(t)$.

3.2.5 Dynamic Routing Aggregator

Based on the selected neighboring entities from the neighbor selector, TempCaps then learns the representation of an entity by leveraging a dynamic routing aggregator. Inspired by CapsE (Nguyen et al., 2019) that uses Capsule Networks to model static KGs, we design two layers of capsules for TempCaps, and then apply a modified dynamic routing algorithm. The first capsule layer consists of N capsules, where N is the number of the selected neighboring entities from the neighbor selector. Assume we have a prediction query $(s, r, ?, t)$, and for the query subject s, we have the selected neighbors E^n. For every neighboring entity $e \in E^n$, a capsule maps its embedding $\mathbf{u}^{(0)}$ with a multi-layer perceptron to obtain $\mathbf{u}^{(1)}$. Then in the second capsule layer, we use the dynamic routing algorithm to compute the contextualized representation $\mathbf{e}_s$ of the query subject s. Let $\sigma(\cdot)$ be an activation function, we use the following functions to compute contextualized representations:

$$\mathbf{u}_i^{(1)} = \sigma(\mathbf{W}\mathbf{u}_i^{(0)} + \epsilon), \tag{4}$$

$$\mathbf{e} = \mathtt{DynamicRouting}(\mathbf{u}_1^{(1)}, \cdots, \mathbf{u}_N^{(1)}), \tag{5}$$

where W is the weighting matrix, ϵ is a bias, and N is the number of selected neighbors. Algorithm 1 shows the details of the dynamic routing module.

3.2.6 MLP Decoder

The multi-layer perceptron (MLP) decoder takes the representation $\mathbf{e}$ from the dynamic routing module as the input and estimates the probabilities of all candidates being the predicted answer by leveraging a softmax function:

$$P_{\text{MLP}}(o|s, r, t) = \frac{\exp(\sigma(\mathbf{W}_{\text{MLP}}\mathbf{e}_o + \epsilon_{\text{MLP}}))}{\sum_{o' \in E} \exp(\sigma(\mathbf{W}_{\text{MLP}}\mathbf{e}_{o'} + \epsilon_{\text{MLP}}))}, \tag{6}$$

where $\mathbf{W}_{\text{MLP}}$ is a weight matrix, $\epsilon_{\text{MLP}} \in \mathbb{R}^{|E|}$ is a bias vector, and $\sigma(\cdot)$ is the activation function.

Algorithm 1: Modified dynamic routing algorithm

```
input  : {u_i^(0)}, number of iteration m
output : e, c
for all capsule i ∈ first capsule layer do
  | b_i ← weight(t_i)
end
for m iterations do
  for all capsule i ∈ first capsule layer do
    | c_i ← exp(b_i) / Σ_k exp(b_k);
  end
  for all capsule i ∈ second capsule layer do
    | s ← Σ_i c_i u_i^(0);
  end
  for all capsule i ∈ second capsule layer do
    | e ← squash(s);
  end
  for all capsule i ∈ first capsule layer do
    | b_i ← b_i + u_i^(0)T · e
  end
end
```

3.2.7 Parameter Estimation and Inference

Following previous works about tKG reasoning (Jin et al., 2020; Zhu et al., 2021), we treat temporal knowledge graph completion as a multi-class classification task, where each class corresponds to a candidate entity. The learning objective is to minimize the negative log-likelihood L on all observed facts with the object (or subject) masked during training:

$$L = -\sum_{(s,r,o,t)\in G} \log[P(o|s,r,t)], \qquad (7)$$

where $P(o|s,r,t) = (1-\alpha)\cdot P_{\mathtt{MLP}}(o|s,r,t) + \alpha \cdot P_{\mathtt{DyR}}(o|s,r,t)$ is the probability of the entity o being the ground truth missing object given $(s,r,?,t)$. This probability consists of two parts: $P_{\mathtt{MLP}}(o|s,r,t)$ and $P_{\mathtt{DyR}}(o|s,r,t)$, where $P_{\mathtt{MLP}}(o|s,r,t)$ is defined by Equation 6 and $P_{\mathtt{DyR}}(o|s,r,t)$ is the softmax output c from the last iteration of Algorithm 1. For the entities not selected into the set of neighbors, we force the value of their $P_{\mathtt{DyR}}$ to 0. $\alpha \in [0,1]$ is the balancing parameter that controls the importance of each probability term.

During inference time, for a prediction query $(s,r,?,t)$, we follow the training process and retrieve the combined probabilities of all entities. The candidate entity with the highest combined probability is selected as the model prediction:

$$o_{\mathtt{pred}} = \arg\max_{o'\in E} P(o|s,r,t). \qquad (8)$$

The learning objective for subject prediction is similar. We omit it in the paper for simplicity.

4 Experimental Results

4.1 Experimental Setup

Datasets We use three datasets for evaluation in our experiments: Global Database of Events, Language, and Tone (GDELT) (Leetaru and Schrodt, 2013), two subsets of Integrated Crisis Early Warning System (ICEWS) (Boschee et al., 2015), i.e, ICEWS05-15 and ICEWS14. GDELT collects human societal-scale behaviors and events occurring from April 1, 2015, to March 31, 2016 in news media. The ICEWS dataset records political events with timestamps. ICEWS14 and ICEWS05-15 are two subsets from ICEWS, which contains events in 2014, and from 2005 to 2015, respectively. For all our experiments, we split the dataset by 80%/10%/10% for train/validation/test. Table 2 gives the statistics of the datasets.

Metrics For each fact (s,r,o,t) in the dataset, we create two sub-tasks: (1) predicting the object $(s,r,?,t)$ and (2) predicting the subject $(?,r,o,t)$. We report four metrics for the two tasks separately and take the average between the two sub-tasks. The metrics we used are MRR and Hits@1/3/10. Let |Q| denote the number of queries. MRR, defined as $\frac{1}{|Q|}\sum_i \frac{1}{\text{rank}_i}$, is the average of reciprocal ranks. Hits@K $= \frac{1}{|Q|}\sum_i \mathbb{1}[\text{rank}_i \le K]$ shows the ratio of the cases where the ground-truth entities are ranked within the top K. We filter the candidate object set during evaluation in the same manner as (Goel et al., 2020) do. During the evaluation, in one timestamp, a subject may be connected with multiple objects under the same relation. Hence, objects except the groundtruth o are not necessarily wrong. We therefore filter the candidate set E during evaluation. In other words, instead of considering all the entities E, the model gives the rank of the actual missing object among entities in $o\cup\bar{E}_t$, where $\bar{E}_t$ are entities not connected to s under r at time t. To be specific, $\bar{E}_t = \{o'|(s,r,o',t) \notin G_t\}$.

Baselines We compare the performance of our model with both static and temporal state-of-the-art

Model	GDELT				ICEWS05-15				ICEWS14			
	MRR	Hits@1	Hits@3	Hits@10	MRR	Hits@1	Hits@3	Hits@10	MRR	Hits@1	Hits@3	Hits@10
TransE	11.3	0.0	-	15.8	29.4	9.0	-	66.3	28.0	9.4	-	63.7
DistMult	19.6	11.7	20.8	34.8	45.6	33.7	-	69.1	43.9	32.3	-	67.2
SimplE	20.6	12.4	22.0	36.6	47.8	35.9	53.9	70.8	45.8	34.1	51.6	68.7
HyTE	11.8	0.0	16.5	32.6	31.6	11.6	44.5	68.1	29.7	10.8	41.6	65.5
TA-DistMult	20.6	12.4	21.9	36.5	47.4	34.6	-	72.8	47.7	36.3	-	68.6
DE-SimplE	23.0	14.1	24.8	40.3	51.3	39.2	**57.8**	**74.8**	**52.6**	**41.8**	**59.2**	**72.5**
TempCaps	**25.8**	**18.0**	**27.7**	**40.4**	**52.1**	**42.3**	57.6	70.5	48.9	38.8	54.4	67.9

Table 1: Model performance on GDELT, ICEWS05-15 and ICEWS14. We use MRR and Hits@1/3/10 as our evaluation metric. Results of the baseline models are directly adapted from the original papers. "-" indicates the number is not available.

Dataset	#Ent	# Rel	#Train	#Valid	#Test	Gap	#Gaps
ICEWS14	7,128	230	72,826	8,941	8,963	24H	365
ICEWS05-15	10,488	251	368,962	46,275	46,092	24H	4,017
GDELT	500	20	2,735,685	341,961	341,961	24H	366

Table 2: Statistics on datasets. The columns are the name of the dataset, the number of all entities, the number of all relation types, the number of facts in the train/validation/test sets, the time gap, and total time gaps. In the column **Gap**, "H" indicates hours. For example, "24H" means that the difference between two consecutive timestamps is 24 hours.

KG embedding models. The static models include TransE (Bordes et al., 2013), DistMult (Yang et al., 2015) and SimplE (Kazemi and Poole, 2018) while temporal models are HyTE (Dasgupta et al., 2018), TA-DistMult (García-Durán et al., 2018), and DE-SimplE (Goel et al., 2020).

Implementations Details All our experiments are conducted on a single Titan Xp GPU. We use the ADAM optimizer with a weight decay rate of 1e-5. In addition, we set the learning rate to 1e-3, batch size to 300, the initial entity embedding size to 100, the size of the linear transformation in dynamic routing aggregator to 200 $\times$ 100, the routing iteration times as 1, the temporal weighting decay γ to 4, the loss balancing factor α to 0.1 and dropout rate to 0.3. The neighborhood candidate numbers are 80 for local entities and 40 for global relational entities.

4.2 Results

Table 1 gives the results of our model performance. We can observe that our model reaches state-of-the-art performance on the GDELT and ICEWS05-15 datasets. On GDELT, our model outperforms the baseline models on all four metrics. For MRR, our model outperforms the second-best model by 2.8%, and leads Hits@1 by 3.9%. On ICEWS05-15, our model is state-of-the-art on two of the most important metrics, MRR and Hits@1. Additionally, our model leads the second-best model by 3.1% for Hits@1, indicating that our model can retrieve the ground-truth entity with high accuracy.

On ICEWS14, our model is not the best but is still comparable to the state-of-the-art model. For example, our model reaches an MRR of 48.9% on ICEWS14, while the best-performed model DE-SimplE reaches an MRR of 52.6%.

4.3 Ablation Studies

We study the following hyperparameters or design choices on ICEWS14: (1) the number of candidate entities (local/global relational);(2) the length of visible time window (t_r, t_e, t_a); (3) the number of routing iterations; (4) the temporal weighting decay rate γ; (5) whether or not we use an MLP decoder in the final layer of the model; (6) the loss balancing factor α. Table 3 details the results of the ablation studies.

From model variants on the number of candidate numbers, we can see that mixing different types of neighbors is helping. The local entities are particularly helpful, and adding global relational entities further improves the performance.

For the length of visible time window, the optimal number is 6 days ($t_r = t_a = 3\ days$) according to the results in Figure 3(a). We argue that a too-short window results in insufficient information, while a too-long window would contain too much noise, which might harm the model performance.

From Figure 4, we can see how the number of routing iterations affects model performance and that the dynamic routing aggregator outperforms the mean aggregator on MRR. Finally, figure 3(b) illustrates the model performance when using different weight decay rates γ, where we can observe that the optimal value of γ is 4. Additionally, we

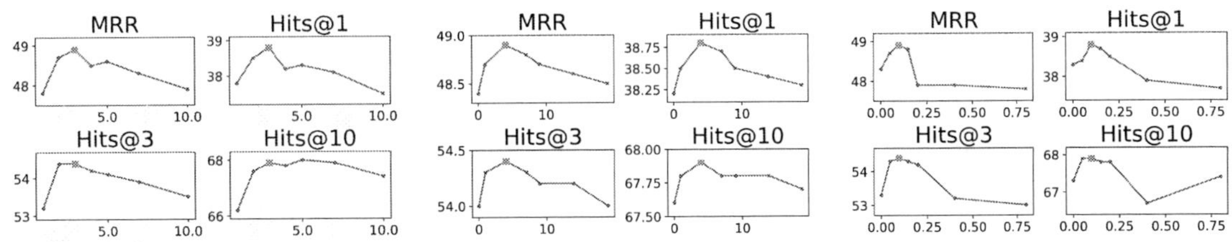

(a) Time window size (days). (b) Temporal weighting decay γ. (c) Balancing factor α.

Figure 3: Ablation studies. The configuration in our final model is marked in orange.

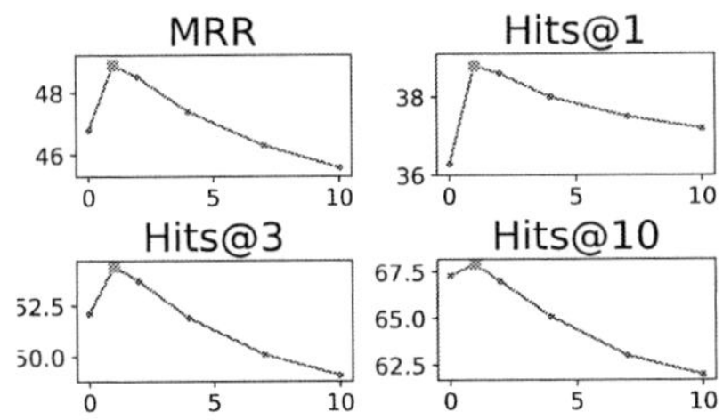

Figure 4: Ablation studies. Effects of the number of iterations. 0 indicates the model uses a mean aggregator, otherwise the model uses the dynamic routing aggregator.

Variants		MRR	Hits@1	Hits@3	Hits@10
Candidates	(120,0)	47.7	37.4	53.2	67.0
	(0,120)	16.7	8.3	18.0	34.8
	(60,60)	48.3	38.1	54.0	67.4
	(80,40)*	**48.9**	**38.8**	**54.4**	**67.9**
	(90,30)	48.6	38.4	54.1	67.7
	(100,20)	48.2	38.0	53.6	67.4
Neighbor length	1	47.8	37.8	53.2	66.2
	2	48.7	38.5	54.4	67.6
	3*	**48.9**	**38.8**	**54.4**	67.9
	4	48.5	38.2	54.2	67.8
	5	48.6	38.3	54.1	**68.0**
	7	48.3	38.1	53.9	67.9
	10	47.9	37.5	53.5	67.4
Iterations	0 (mean)	46.8	36.3	52.1	67.3
	1*	**48.9**	**38.8**	**54.4**	**67.9**
	2	48.5	38.6	53.7	67.0
	4	47.4	38.0	51.9	65.1
	7	46.3	37.5	50.1	63.0
	10	45.6	37.2	49.1	62.0
Weight decay γ	0	48.4	38.2	54.0	67.6
	1	48.7	38.5	54.3	67.8
	4*	**48.9**	**38.8**	**54.4**	**67.9**
	7	48.8	38.7	54.3	67.8
	9	48.7	38.5	54.2	67.8
	14	48.6	38.4	54.2	67.8
	19	48.5	38.3	54.0	67.7
Final MLP decoder	No	48.6	38.6	53.8	67.1
	Yes*	**48.9**	**38.8**	**54.4**	**67.9**
Loss weight α	0	48.3	38.3	53.3	67.3
	0.05	48.7	38.4	54.3	**67.9**
	0.1*	**48.9**	**38.8**	**54.4**	**67.9**
	0.15	48.8	38.7	54.3	67.8
	0.2	48.7	38.5	54.2	67.8
	0.4	47.9	37.9	53.2	66.7
	0.8	47.8	37.7	53.0	67.4
	1.0	0.017	0.017	0.017	0.017

Table 3: The complete results of our ablation studies. * indicates configurations used in our final model.

notice that dropping the final MLP decoder results decreases model performance (see Table 3). In Figure 3(c), we show that a loss balance factor $\alpha = 0.1$ leads to better performance than when setting $\alpha = 0$. This indicates that our model benefits from both $P_{\texttt{MLP}}$ and $P_{\texttt{DyR}}$.

4.4 Analysis

We analyze the space and time complexity of our model from the empirical and theoretical points of view. As is shown in Figure 1, the trainable parameters of our model consists of three parts: (1) $\mathbf{E}_1 \in \mathbb{R}^{|E|\times D_1}$ in the entity embedding layer, (2) $\mathbf{W}_1 \in \mathbb{R}^{D_2\times D_1}$ and $\mathbf{e}_1 \in \mathbb{R}^{D_2}$ in the dynamic routing aggregator and (3) $\mathbf{W}_2 \in \mathbb{R}^{|E|\times D_2}$ and $\mathbf{e}_2 \in \mathbb{R}^{|E|\times D_2}$ in the final MLP decoder. In summary, our model has $O(|E|)$ parameters, which is optimal for representing a knowledge graph with $|E|$ entities. In our experiments, taking the ICEWS14 dataset as an example, each training epoch costs only 54 seconds on average, and the total evaluation process for the testing dataset costs 21 seconds. This indicates our model is efficient both in training and inference and saves considerable time and memory compared to previous works for temporal knowledge graph completion.

The space complexity of the embedding computation before aggregation is $O(|B|D_1D_2)$ where $|B|$ is the batch size and D_i is the embedding size defined in the model. Then, the space complexity of going through the dynamic routing aggregator (Algorithm 1) is $O(r|B||C|D_2^2)$, where $|C|$ is the candidate number. At last, the MLP decoder takes another $O(|B||E|D_2)$, where $|E|$ is the total number of entities. Thus, for each epoch of training or testing, the space complexity is $O(|Q|(D_1D_2+|C|D_2^2+|E|D_2))$, which can be simplified as $O(c \cdot |Q||E|)$. Here c is a constant related to pre-defined parameters, and $|Q|$ is the training/testing dataset size.

5 Conclusion

In this paper, we propose TempCaps, which is a light-weighted Capsule Network-based embedding model for temporal knowledge graph completion. TempCaps consists of a neighbor selector, a dynamic routing aggregator, and an MLP decoder. Experimental results show that TempCaps reaches state-of-the-art performance on the GDELT and ICEWS05-15 dataset. We conduct additional ablation studies to understand how each part of TempCaps and hyperparameter choices contribute to the model performance. Our analysis also shows that TempCaps is efficient both in time and space. In the future, we plan to extend TempCaps to forecasting in temporal knowledge graphs.

Acknowledgements

This work has been funded by the German Federal Ministry of Education and Research (BMBF) under Grant No. 01IS18036A. The authors of this work take full responsibilities for its content.

References

Antoine Bordes, Nicolas Usunier, Alberto García-Durán, Jason Weston, and Oksana Yakhnenko. 2013. Translating embeddings for modeling multi-relational data. In *NeurIPS*.

Elizabeth Boschee, Jennifer Lautenschlager, Sean O'Brien, Steve Shellman, James Starz, and Michael Ward. 2015. ICEWS Coded Event Data.

Antoine Bosselut, Hannah Rashkin, Maarten Sap, Chaitanya Malaviya, Asli Celikyilmaz, and Yejin Choi. 2019. COMET: commonsense transformers for automatic knowledge graph construction. In *ACL*.

Shib Sankar Dasgupta, Swayambhu Nath Ray, and Partha P. Talukdar. 2018. Hyte: Hyperplane-based temporally aware knowledge graph embedding. In *EMNLP*.

Alberto García-Durán, Sebastijan Dumancic, and Mathias Niepert. 2018. Learning sequence encoders for temporal knowledge graph completion. In *EMNLP*.

Rishab Goel, Seyed Mehran Kazemi, Marcus Brubaker, and Pascal Poupart. 2020. Diachronic embedding for temporal knowledge graph completion. In *AAAI*.

Taeyoung Hahn, Myeongjang Pyeon, and Gunhee Kim. 2019. Self-routing capsule networks. In *NeurIPS*.

Zhen Han, Peng Chen, Yunpu Ma, and Volker Tresp. 2020a. Dyernie: Dynamic evolution of riemannian manifold embeddings for temporal knowledge graph completion. In *EMNLP*.

Zhen Han, Peng Chen, Yunpu Ma, and Volker Tresp. 2020b. Explainable subgraph reasoning for forecasting on temporal knowledge graphs. In *ICLR*.

Zhen Han, Zifeng Ding, Yunpu Ma, Yujia Gu, and Volker Tresp. 2021a. Temporal knowledge graph forecasting with neural ode. *arXiv preprint arXiv:2101.05151*.

Zhen Han, Ruotong Liao, Beiyan Liu, Yao Zhang, Zifeng Ding, Heinz Köppl, Hinrich Schütze, and Volker Tresp. 2022. Enhanced temporal knowledge embeddings with contextualized language representations. *arXiv preprint arXiv:2203.09590*.

Zhen Han, Yunpu Ma, Yuyi Wang, Stephan Günnemann, and Volker Tresp. 2020c. Graph hawkes neural network for forecasting on temporal knowledge graphs. In *AKBC*.

Zhen Han, Gengyuan Zhang, Yunpu Ma, and Volker Tresp. 2021b. Time-dependent entity embedding is not all you need: A re-evaluation of temporal knowledge graph completion models under a unified framework. In *EMNLP*.

Robert L. Logan IV, Nelson F. Liu, Matthew E. Peters, Matt Gardner, and Sameer Singh. 2019. Barack's wife hillary: Using knowledge graphs for fact-aware language modeling. In *ACL*.

Woojeong Jin, Meng Qu, Xisen Jin, and Xiang Ren. 2020. Recurrent event network: Autoregressive structure inferenceover temporal knowledge graphs. In *EMNLP*.

Seyed Mehran Kazemi and David Poole. 2018. Simple embedding for link prediction in knowledge graphs. In *NeurIPS*.

Thomas N. Kipf and Max Welling. 2017. Semi-supervised classification with graph convolutional networks. In *ICLR*.

Kalev Leetaru and Philip A. Schrodt. 2013. Gdelt: Global data on events, location, and tone. *ISA Annual Convention*.

Yankai Lin, Zhiyuan Liu, Maosong Sun, Yang Liu, and Xuan Zhu. 2015. Learning entity and relation embeddings for knowledge graph completion. In *AAAI*.

Kenneth Marino, Ruslan Salakhutdinov, and Abhinav Gupta. 2017. The more you know: Using knowledge graphs for image classification. In *CVPR*.

Dai Quoc Nguyen, Thanh Vu, Tu Dinh Nguyen, Dat Quoc Nguyen, and Dinh Q. Phung. 2019. A capsule network-based embedding model for knowledge graph completion and search personalization. In *NAACL*.

Maximilian Nickel, Volker Tresp, and Hans-Peter Kriegel. 2011. A three-way model for collective learning on multi-relational data. In *ICML*.

Sara Sabour, Nicholas Frosst, and Geoffrey E. Hinton. 2017. Dynamic routing between capsules. In *NeurIPS*.

Haohai Sun, Jialun Zhong, Yunpu Ma, Zhen Han, and Kun He. 2021. TimeTraveler: Reinforcement learning for temporal knowledge graph forecasting. In *EMNLP*.

Rakshit Trivedi, Hanjun Dai, Yichen Wang, and Le Song. 2017. Know-evolve: Deep reasoning in temporal knowledge graphs. In *ICML*.

Yao-Hung Hubert Tsai, Nitish Srivastava, Hanlin Goh, and Ruslan Salakhutdinov. 2020. Capsules with inverted dot-product attention routing. In *ICLR*.

Petar Velickovic, Guillem Cucurull, Arantxa Casanova, Adriana Romero, Pietro Liò, and Yoshua Bengio. 2018. Graph attention networks. In *ICLR*.

Zhen Wang, Jianwen Zhang, Jianlin Feng, and Zheng Chen. 2014. Knowledge graph embedding by translating on hyperplanes. In *AAAI*.

Keyulu Xu, Weihua Hu, Jure Leskovec, and Stefanie Jegelka. 2019. How powerful are graph neural networks? In *ICLR*.

Bishan Yang, Wen-tau Yih, Xiaodong He, Jianfeng Gao, and Li Deng. 2015. Embedding entities and relations for learning and inference in knowledge bases. In *ICLR*.

Fei Yu, Jiji Tang, Weichong Yin, Yu Sun, Hao Tian, Hua Wu, and Haifeng Wang. 2021. Ernie-vil: Knowledge enhanced vision-language representations through scene graphs. In *AAAI*.

Cunchao Zhu, Muhao Chen, Changjun Fan, Guangquan Cheng, and Yan Zhang. 2021. Learning from history: Modeling temporal knowledge graphs with sequential copy-generation networks. In *AAAI*.

SlotGAN: Detecting Mentions in Text via Adversarial Distant Learning

Daniel Daza[1,2,3], **Michael Cochez**[1,3], **Paul Groth**[2,3]
[1]Vrije Universiteit Amsterdam
[2]University of Amsterdam
[3]Discovery Lab, Elsevier, The Netherlands
d.dazacruz@vu.nl, m.cochez@vu.nl, p.groth@uva.nl

Abstract

We present SlotGAN, a framework for training a mention detection model that only requires unlabeled text and a gazetteer. It consists of a generator trained to extract spans from an input sentence, and a discriminator trained to determine whether a span comes from the generator, or from the gazetteer. We evaluate the method on English newswire data and compare it against supervised, weakly-supervised, and unsupervised methods. We find that the performance of the method is lower than these baselines, because it tends to generate more and longer spans, and in some cases it relies only on capitalization. In other cases, it generates spans that are valid but differ from the benchmark. When evaluated with metrics based on overlap, we find that SlotGAN performs within 95% of the precision of a supervised method, and 84% of its recall. Our results suggest that the model can generate spans that overlap well, but an additional filtering mechanism is required.

1 Introduction

Detecting mentions of entities in text is an important step towards the extraction of structured information from natural language sources. Mention Detection (MD) components can be found frequently in systems for Named Entity Recognition (NER) (Straková et al., 2019; Wang et al., 2021), entity linking (Wu et al., 2020; Cao et al., 2021), relationship extraction (Katiyar and Cardie, 2017; Zhong and Chen, 2021), and coreference resolution (Joshi et al., 2019; Xu and Choi, 2020; Kirstain et al., 2021), where accurately modeling mentions is crucial for downstream performance.

The MD task is often subsumed under NER, where most effective approaches employ supervised learning with exhaustively annotated datasets. These methods become less feasible in cases where we need to rapidly build MD systems, for example, when moving to a domain with incompatible NER classes; or when there are not enough resources to create a labeled dataset. In contrast, we assume that we have access to an unlabeled corpus, and a list of known entity names (i.e. a *gazetteer*). We propose SlotGAN– a framework for detecting mentions that uses a generator to extract spans conditioned on some input text, and a discriminator that determines whether a span comes from the generator, or from the gazetteer (see Fig. 1). In contrast with distant supervision methods that require training with false negatives (Ratner et al., 2016; Giannakopoulos et al., 2017; Shang et al., 2018), SlotGAN relies on the discriminator to learn patterns that are *not* likely to be names of entities (such as verb phrases, or very long spans, which rarely occur in a gazzetteer), thereby improving the generator's ability to detect valid mentions.

We evaluate the method in a MD task using the CoNLL 2003 English dataset (Tjong Kim Sang and De Meulder, 2003). We observe that the absence of strong supervision in SlotGAN results in different, yet valid notions of what constitutes an entity. For instance, while in the sentence *"On the road to Tripoli airport..."* the word *Tripoli* is selected as a gold mention, SlotGAN selects *Tripoli airport*. In this case, exact match metrics for NER underestimate performance, assigning zero precision and recall. To account for this, we introduce overlap-based metrics into the evaluation.

When using exact boundary match metrics, SlotGAN exhibits lower performance compared to different baselines. When evaluating overlap, precision (how much of the predicted span overlaps with the gold span) is within 95% of the performance of the supervised baseline, while recall (how much of the gold span is actually predicted) is within 84%. We observe that SlotGAN tends to generate more and longer spans than those in the benchmark, and in some cases it relies only on capitalization.

Our contributions are the following: 1) A framework towards distantly-supervised MD that avoids explicit training with false negatives, and an imple-

Proceedings of the Sixth Workshop on Structured Prediction for NLP, pages 32 - 39

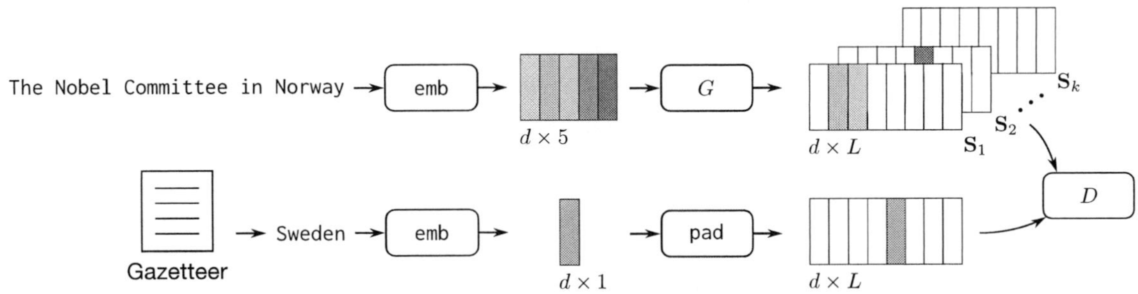

Figure 1: SlotGAN consists of a generator G trained to extract spans from an input sentence. We represent spans as matrices containing embeddings of words in a span, padded with zeros to a fixed length L. True spans are generated from a gazetteer. A discriminator D is trained to determine if a span was generated from G or from the gazetteer.

mentation via an end-to-end differentiable architecture for extracting distinct spans; 2) Evidence for the use of overlap-based metrics into the evaluation of MD methods to account for ambiguous cases in gold annotations; 3) An analysis of the performance of SlotGAN, identifying its failure modes and outlining directions of improvement.

2 SlotGAN

In the MD task, we are given a sentence from a corpus as a sequence of words $(w_1, w_2, ..., w_n)$. The output of the system is a set of spans that contain a mention, and each span is a tuple (i_s, i_e) where i_s is an integer indicating the position where the span starts, and i_e the position where it ends. Additionally, we have access to a gazetteer $E = (e_1, e_2, ..., e_N)$ containing names of entities relevant to a particular domain.

SlotGAN is a method for MD based on Generative Adversarial Networks (Goodfellow et al., 2014; Mirza and Osindero, 2014). It consists of a generator trained to extract spans from a sentence, and a discriminator that determines whether a span comes from the generator or from the gazetteer.

We define the embedding of a sentence $w = (w_1, ..., w_n)$ as a matrix $\mathsf{emb}(w) \in \mathbb{R}^{d \times n}$, where emb is a function that maps words to d-dimensional pretrained embeddings (for example, from the input embedding layer of BERT (Devlin et al., 2019)).

We represent each mention span in a sequence as a matrix in a space $\mathcal{S} = \mathbb{R}^{d \times L}$, where L is the length of the sequence. For a span (i_s, i_e), the matrix contains the embeddings of the words within the span, from column i_s to column i_e, and is zero in the remaining columns.

The generator takes as input the embedding matrix $\mathsf{emb}(w)$ of a sentence, and assigns each of its columns to one of k *slots*. The output is a sequence of k span representations $(\mathbf{S}_i)_{i=1}^k$ with $\mathbf{S}_i \in \mathcal{S}$, such that the j-th column of $\mathbf{S}_i$ contains the j-th column of the input matrix, if it was assigned to slot i. Unused columns of $\mathbf{S}_i$ are filled with zeros.

When sampling a name e of an entity in the gazetteer, we embed it as $\mathsf{emb}(e)$ and then add zero padding via a pad function until reaching a maximum length L, to obtain a span representation in $\mathcal{S}$. The amount of padding is added randomly to both sides of an entity name, with the purpose of emulating how in a sentence, a mention can appear at an arbitrary position. The discriminator takes as input span representations in $\mathcal{S}$, and outputs a score that should be high for samples from the gazetteer, and low for samples from the generator.

Denoting as p_w the distribution used to sample sentences from the corpus, and as p_e the distribution for sampling names from the gazetteer, the generator and discriminator are trained via gradient descent using the W-GAN (Arjovsky et al., 2017) minimax optimization objective:

$$\min_G \max_D \mathbb{E}_{e \sim p_e}[D(\mathsf{pad}(\mathsf{emb}(e)))] - \mathbb{E}_{w \sim p_w}\left[\sum_{i=1}^{k} D(G(\mathsf{emb}(w))_i)\right], \quad (1)$$

where we have denoted as $G(\mathsf{emb}(w))_i$ the i-th span representation produced by the generator.

To allow also *not* extracting any mentions when not required, we randomly introduce empty spans in the gazetteer, and we reformulate the generator objective with an equality constraint. Following Bastings et al. (2019), we define the constraint in terms of a differentiable function C such that $C(G(\mathsf{emb}(w)_i)$ counts the number of transitions from zero to non-zero, and vice versa, in a span representation. For valid spans, this should be equal to 2. We solve the problem introducing a Lagrange multiplier λ, and the term in Eq. 1 that depends on the generator becomes

$$\min_{\lambda,G} \mathbb{E}_{w\sim p_w}\left[\sum_{i=1}^{k} -D(\mathbf{S}_i(w)) - \lambda(2 - C(\mathbf{S}_i(w))\right], \quad (2)$$

where $\mathbf{S}_i(w)$ is a shorthand for $G(\mathtt{emb}(w))_i$. This constraint prevents the generator from producing only empty spans.

At test time, we can use the spans produced by the generator as predictions for mentions. Alternatively, we can balance precision and recall by leveraging the discriminator, by only keeping spans with a score $D(\mathbf{S}_i(w)) > t$ where t is a threshold.

We implement the generator using BERT (Devlin et al., 2019), followed by a modified Slot Attention layer (Locatello et al., 2020) to model discrete selections of distinct spans. The discriminator is a temporal CNN. For more details on the architecture, we refer the reader to Appendix A.

3 Related Work

The task of MD has been addressed under NER effectively via supervised learning (Devlin et al., 2019; Straková et al., 2019; Peters et al., 2018; Yu et al., 2020; Wang et al., 2021). Some works address the lack of labeled data in a target domain by applying adaptation techniques from a source domain with labeled data (Zhou et al., 2019; Li et al., 2019; Zhang et al., 2021). In this work we focus on the case where annotations are not available.

Closer to our work are methods for weakly or distantly supervised learning, where heuristics and domain-specific rules are used to generate a noisy training set, often using external sources like gazetteers (Safranchik et al., 2020; Lison et al., 2020; Zhao et al., 2021; Ratner et al., 2016; Shang et al., 2018; Li et al., 2021a). These methods are limited by false negatives that reduce recall in MD. Furthermore, even though rules can be used to annotate a dataset at a large scale, the process of devising these rules in the first place can be tedious, and might require domain expert knowledge.

Luo et al. (2020) recently introduced a fully unsupervised method for NER that uses a pipeline of clustering over word embeddings, a generative model, and reinforcement learning to solve the NER task without any labels or external sources. These elements are optimized separately, whereas SlotGAN provides an end-to-end architecture.

4 Experiments

Datasets We evaluate MD performance using the CoNLL 2003 English dataset for NER (Tjong Kim Sang and De Meulder, 2003). For methods that require a dictionary of entity types or a gazetteer, we build it using the annotations in the training set. We also explore a pretraining strategy for SlotGAN, where we sample sentences from Wikipedia articles, and names of entities from Wikidata. Both are obtained from the July 2019 dumps.

Experimental setup We evaluate the performance of SlotGAN when trained with the CoNLL 2003 data only, and when pretraining with Wikipedia and Wikidata. We apply a threshold to all spans based on the discriminator score, selected using the validation set. Training and hyperparameter details can be found in Appendix B. Our implementation is available online[1].

Baselines We consider a string matching baseline where we label all spans present in the gazetteer, giving precedence to longer spans. We also compare with methods ranging from supervised, weakly supervised, to unsupervised. ACE (Wang et al., 2021) is a state-of-the-art method for supervised NER. AutoNER (Shang et al., 2018) is a weakly supervised method that requires a type dictionary. Lastly, we compare with the unsupervised method of Luo et al. (2020)[2].

Evaluation Recent works have highlighted the presence of unlabeled mentions in the CoNLL dataset, which has a negative effect when training and evaluating models based on exact match (Jie et al., 2019; Li et al., 2021b). Exact match metrics also penalize more strongly models that do not match boundaries exactly, than a model that does not predict a span at all (Manning, 2006; Esuli and Sebastiani, 2010). With this motivation, we also report overlap[3] by computing the intersection between gold and predicted spans. Precision is defined as the length of the intersection divided by the length of the predicted span, and recall is the length of the intersection divided by the length of the gold span. We denote these as OP and OR, respectively. Overlap F1 (OF1) is the harmonic mean of OP and OR. We report the average over all gold spans.

[1] `https://github.com/dfdazac/slotgan`

[2] Their implementation is not available. Results for P, R, and F1 from their paper.

[3] Partial matches have been considered by Segura-Bedmar et al. (2013), though not taking span lengths into account.

Method	Data	P	R	F1	OP	OR	OF1
String matching	Gazetteer	76.2	54.0	63.2	57.4	61.3	58.6
ACE (Wang et al., 2021)	Gold labels	96.0	97.1	96.5	98.3	98.1	98.1
AutoNER (Shang et al., 2018)	Type dictionary	88.4	94.2	91.2	97.4	97.2	96.9
Unsupervised (Luo et al., 2020)	Domain concepts	80.0	72.0	76.0	—	—	—
SlotGAN - no pretraining	Gazetteer	55.9	66.1	60.6	82.9	79.5	82.9
SlotGAN - pretrained		60.1	71.1	65.2	93.2	83.0	84.7

Table 1: Mention detection results evaluated via exact match precision (P), recall (R), and F1 score; and overlap metrics (preceded with O). The "Data" column indicates what is required to train the model in addition to a corpus.

Gold	on the road to **[Tripoli]** airport
Predicted	on the road to **[Tripoli airport]**
Gold	**[Belgian]** police said on Saturday
Predicted	**[Belgian police]** said on Saturday
Gold	**[JOHNSON]** WINS UNANIMOUS POINTS VERDICT
Predicted	**[JOHNSON WINS UNANIMOUS POINTS VERDICT]**
Gold	BASKETBALL - **[BENETTON]** BEAT **[DINAMO]** 92 - 81
Predicted	**[BASKETBALL]** - **[BENETTON BEAT DINAMO]** 92 - 81

Table 2: Comparison of gold spans and spans predicted by SlotGAN.

Results We present MD results in Table 1. We observe that pretraining with Wikipedia and Wikidata entity names helps to improve the performance over a version trained with the CoNLL 2003 data only. The higher recall of SlotGAN in comparison with the string matching baseline shows that the generator is not simply memorizing the gazetteer and can thus detect mentions not seen during training. However, its precision and recall are low compared to other systems. We attribute this partly to the lack of strong supervision of the generator, which results in boundaries that differ from gold spans, and detection of more mentions than those present in the dataset. The overlap-based metrics show that on average, predicted spans overlap 93% and gold spans overlap 83% with the intersection. This indicates that extra words are added to predicted spans, and boundary mismatch, though these values of precision and recall are within 95% and 84% of the supervised baseline, respectively.

A closer analysis of the length of overlapping spans shows that in 69.4% of the cases the length is the same as gold spans, in 21.1% the predicted span is longer, and in 9.5% it is shorter. This often leads to mentions that are actually correct, as shown in Table 2. However, SlotGAN also produces spans that do not overlap with any gold span. This can be observed by plotting the average number of words assigned to a mention by the model versus the gold annotations, as shown in Fig 2. We see that across different numbers of mention words for the gold annotations, SlotGAN produces a higher number in average. We also find cases where it relies on capitalization only, which becomes problematic in upper case sentences: for regular sentences, there is no exact boundary match in 11% of the cases. For sentences in upper case, this increases to 23%.

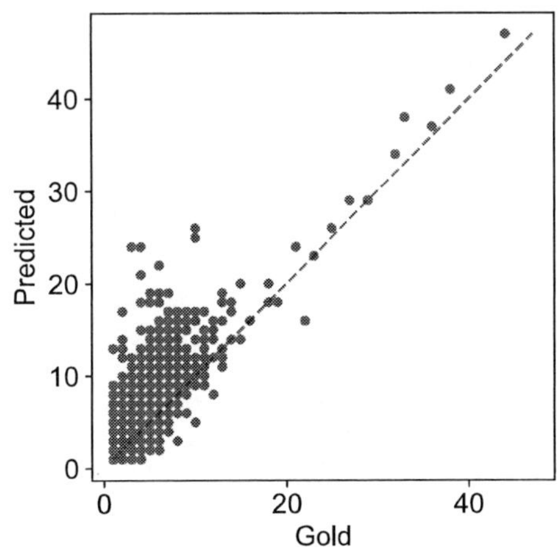

Figure 2: Number of words assigned to a mention per sentence, computed over gold and predicted spans.

5 Conclusion

We have presented SlotGAN, a method for training a mention detector that only requires unlabeled text and a list of entity names, that relies on implicit supervision provided by a discriminator that is also optimized during training. This results in spans that overlap well with gold spans, but also a tendency towards generating more and longer spans, and relying on capitalization only. This suggests that spans predicted by SlotGAN are likely to be correct, but an additional mechanism is needed to filter them. This can be enforced via tighter constraints on generated spans, or a stronger discriminator.

Even though its performance is close to a supervised model according to overlap-based metrics, it cannot match other methods that also use a gazetteer or are unsupervised. In spite of this, we consider SlotGAN a promising framework for other IE tasks with less supervision, for example, where relations between slots could be induced. The end-to-end architecture also presents an opportunity for fine-tuning with gold labels, which we plan to explore in future work.

Acknowledgments

This project was funded by Elsevier's Discovery Lab.

References

Martín Arjovsky, Soumith Chintala, and Léon Bottou. 2017. Wasserstein generative adversarial networks. In *Proceedings of the 34th International Conference on Machine Learning, ICML 2017, Sydney, NSW, Australia, 6-11 August 2017*, volume 70 of *Proceedings of Machine Learning Research*, pages 214–223. PMLR.

Jasmijn Bastings, Wilker Aziz, and Ivan Titov. 2019. Interpretable neural predictions with differentiable binary variables. In *Proceedings of the 57th Annual Meeting of the Association for Computational Linguistics*, pages 2963–2977, Florence, Italy. Association for Computational Linguistics.

Nicola De Cao, Gautier Izacard, Sebastian Riedel, and Fabio Petroni. 2021. Autoregressive entity retrieval. In *9th International Conference on Learning Representations, ICLR 2021, Virtual Event, Austria, May 3-7, 2021*. OpenReview.net.

Jacob Devlin, Ming-Wei Chang, Kenton Lee, and Kristina Toutanova. 2019. BERT: pre-training of deep bidirectional transformers for language understanding. In *Proceedings of the 2019 Conference of the North American Chapter of the Association for Computational Linguistics: Human Language Technologies, NAACL-HLT 2019, Minneapolis, MN, USA, June 2-7, 2019, Volume 1 (Long and Short Papers)*, pages 4171–4186. Association for Computational Linguistics.

Andrea Esuli and Fabrizio Sebastiani. 2010. Evaluating information extraction. In *Multilingual and Multimodal Information Access Evaluation, International Conference of the Cross-Language Evaluation Forum, CLEF 2010, Padua, Italy, September 20-23, 2010. Proceedings*, volume 6360 of *Lecture Notes in Computer Science*, pages 100–111. Springer.

Athanasios Giannakopoulos, Claudiu Musat, Andreea Hossmann, and Michael Baeriswyl. 2017. Unsupervised aspect term extraction with B-LSTM & CRF using automatically labelled datasets. In *Proceedings of the 8th Workshop on Computational Approaches to Subjectivity, Sentiment and Social Media Analysis*, pages 180–188, Copenhagen, Denmark. Association for Computational Linguistics.

Ian J. Goodfellow, Jean Pouget-Abadie, Mehdi Mirza, Bing Xu, David Warde-Farley, Sherjil Ozair, Aaron C. Courville, and Yoshua Bengio. 2014. Generative adversarial nets. In *Advances in Neural Information Processing Systems 27: Annual Conference on Neural Information Processing Systems 2014, December 8-13 2014, Montreal, Quebec, Canada*, pages 2672–2680.

Ishaan Gulrajani, Faruk Ahmed, Martín Arjovsky, Vincent Dumoulin, and Aaron C. Courville. 2017. Improved training of wasserstein gans. In *Advances in Neural Information Processing Systems 30: Annual Conference on Neural Information Processing Systems 2017, December 4-9, 2017, Long Beach, CA, USA*, pages 5767–5777.

Zhanming Jie, Pengjun Xie, Wei Lu, Ruixue Ding, and Linlin Li. 2019. Better modeling of incomplete annotations for named entity recognition. In *Proceedings of the 2019 Conference of the North American Chapter of the Association for Computational Linguistics: Human Language Technologies, Volume 1 (Long and Short Papers)*, pages 729–734, Minneapolis, Minnesota. Association for Computational Linguistics.

Mandar Joshi, Omer Levy, Luke Zettlemoyer, and Daniel Weld. 2019. BERT for coreference resolution: Baselines and analysis. In *Proceedings of the 2019 Conference on Empirical Methods in Natural Language Processing and the 9th International Joint Conference on Natural Language Processing (EMNLP-IJCNLP)*, pages 5803–5808, Hong Kong, China. Association for Computational Linguistics.

Arzoo Katiyar and Claire Cardie. 2017. Going out on a limb: Joint extraction of entity mentions and relations without dependency trees. In *Proceedings of the 55th Annual Meeting of the Association for Computational Linguistics (Volume 1: Long Papers)*, pages 917–928, Vancouver, Canada. Association for Computational Linguistics.

Yuval Kirstain, Ori Ram, and Omer Levy. 2021. Coreference resolution without span representations. In *Proceedings of the 59th Annual Meeting of the Association for Computational Linguistics and the 11th International Joint Conference on Natural Language Processing (Volume 2: Short Papers)*, pages 14–19, Online. Association for Computational Linguistics.

Jiacheng Li, Haibo Ding, Jingbo Shang, Julian McAuley, and Zhe Feng. 2021a. Weakly supervised named entity tagging with learnable logical rules. In *Proceedings of the 59th Annual Meeting of the Association for Computational Linguistics and the 11th International*

Joint Conference on Natural Language Processing (Volume 1: Long Papers), pages 4568–4581, Online. Association for Computational Linguistics.

Jing Li, Deheng Ye, and Shuo Shang. 2019. Adversarial transfer for named entity boundary detection with pointer networks. In *Proceedings of the Twenty-Eighth International Joint Conference on Artificial Intelligence, IJCAI 2019, Macao, China, August 10-16, 2019*, pages 5053–5059. ijcai.org.

Yangming Li, Lemao Liu, and Shuming Shi. 2021b. Empirical analysis of unlabeled entity problem in named entity recognition. In *9th International Conference on Learning Representations, ICLR 2021, Virtual Event, Austria, May 3-7, 2021*. OpenReview.net.

Pierre Lison, Jeremy Barnes, Aliaksandr Hubin, and Samia Touileb. 2020. Named entity recognition without labelled data: A weak supervision approach. In *Proceedings of the 58th Annual Meeting of the Association for Computational Linguistics*, pages 1518–1533, Online. Association for Computational Linguistics.

Francesco Locatello, Dirk Weissenborn, Thomas Unterthiner, Aravindh Mahendran, Georg Heigold, Jakob Uszkoreit, Alexey Dosovitskiy, and Thomas Kipf. 2020. Object-centric learning with slot attention. In *Advances in Neural Information Processing Systems 33: Annual Conference on Neural Information Processing Systems 2020, NeurIPS 2020, December 6-12, 2020, virtual*.

Ying Luo, Hai Zhao, and Junlang Zhan. 2020. Named entity recognition only from word embeddings. In *Proceedings of the 2020 Conference on Empirical Methods in Natural Language Processing, EMNLP 2020, Online, November 16-20, 2020*, pages 8995–9005. Association for Computational Linguistics.

Christopher Manning. 2006. Doing named entity recognition? don't optimize for F1. *NLPers Blog*, 25. Accessed on November, 2021.

Mehdi Mirza and Simon Osindero. 2014. Conditional generative adversarial nets. *CoRR*, abs/1411.1784.

Matthew E. Peters, Mark Neumann, Mohit Iyyer, Matt Gardner, Christopher Clark, Kenton Lee, and Luke Zettlemoyer. 2018. Deep contextualized word representations. In *Proceedings of the 2018 Conference of the North American Chapter of the Association for Computational Linguistics: Human Language Technologies, Volume 1 (Long Papers)*, pages 2227–2237, New Orleans, Louisiana. Association for Computational Linguistics.

John C. Platt and Alan H. Barr. 1987. Constrained differential optimization. In *Neural Information Processing Systems, Denver, Colorado, USA, 1987*, pages 612–621. American Institue of Physics.

Alexander J. Ratner, Christopher De Sa, Sen Wu, Daniel Selsam, and Christopher Ré. 2016. Data programming: Creating large training sets, quickly. In *Advances in Neural Information Processing Systems 29: Annual Conference on Neural Information Processing Systems 2016, December 5-10, 2016, Barcelona, Spain*, pages 3567–3575.

Esteban Safranchik, Shiying Luo, and Stephen H. Bach. 2020. Weakly supervised sequence tagging from noisy rules. In *The Thirty-Fourth AAAI Conference on Artificial Intelligence, AAAI 2020, The Thirty-Second Innovative Applications of Artificial Intelligence Conference, IAAI 2020, The Tenth AAAI Symposium on Educational Advances in Artificial Intelligence, EAAI 2020, New York, NY, USA, February 7-12, 2020*, pages 5570–5578. AAAI Press.

Isabel Segura-Bedmar, Paloma Martínez, and María Herrero-Zazo. 2013. SemEval-2013 task 9 : Extraction of drug-drug interactions from biomedical texts (DDIExtraction 2013). In *Second Joint Conference on Lexical and Computational Semantics (*SEM), Volume 2: Proceedings of the Seventh International Workshop on Semantic Evaluation (SemEval 2013)*, pages 341–350, Atlanta, Georgia, USA. Association for Computational Linguistics.

Jingbo Shang, Liyuan Liu, Xiaotao Gu, Xiang Ren, Teng Ren, and Jiawei Han. 2018. Learning named entity tagger using domain-specific dictionary. In *Proceedings of the 2018 Conference on Empirical Methods in Natural Language Processing*, pages 2054–2064, Brussels, Belgium. Association for Computational Linguistics.

Jana Straková, Milan Straka, and Jan Hajic. 2019. Neural architectures for nested NER through linearization. In *Proceedings of the 57th Annual Meeting of the Association for Computational Linguistics*, pages 5326–5331, Florence, Italy. Association for Computational Linguistics.

Erik F. Tjong Kim Sang and Fien De Meulder. 2003. Introduction to the CoNLL-2003 shared task: Language-independent named entity recognition. In *Proceedings of the Seventh Conference on Natural Language Learning at HLT-NAACL 2003*, pages 142–147.

Xinyu Wang, Yong Jiang, Nguyen Bach, Tao Wang, Zhongqiang Huang, Fei Huang, and Kewei Tu. 2021. Automated concatenation of embeddings for structured prediction. In *Proceedings of the 59th Annual Meeting of the Association for Computational Linguistics and the 11th International Joint Conference on Natural Language Processing, ACL/IJCNLP 2021, (Volume 1: Long Papers), Virtual Event, August 1-6, 2021*, pages 2643–2660. Association for Computational Linguistics.

Thomas Wolf, Lysandre Debut, Victor Sanh, Julien Chaumond, Clement Delangue, Anthony Moi, Pierric Cistac, Tim Rault, Rémi Louf, Morgan Funtowicz, and Jamie Brew. 2019. Huggingface's transformers: State-of-the-art natural language processing. *CoRR*, abs/1910.03771.

Ledell Wu, Fabio Petroni, Martin Josifoski, Sebastian Riedel, and Luke Zettlemoyer. 2020. Scalable zero-shot entity linking with dense entity retrieval. In *Proceedings of the 2020 Conference on Empirical Methods in Natural Language Processing (EMNLP)*, pages 6397–6407, Online. Association for Computational Linguistics.

Liyan Xu and Jinho D. Choi. 2020. Revealing the myth of higher-order inference in coreference resolution. In *Proceedings of the 2020 Conference on Empirical Methods in Natural Language Processing (EMNLP)*, pages 8527–8533, Online. Association for Computational Linguistics.

Juntao Yu, Bernd Bohnet, and Massimo Poesio. 2020. Neural mention detection. In *Proceedings of the 12th Language Resources and Evaluation Conference*, pages 1–10, Marseille, France. European Language Resources Association.

Tao Zhang, Congying Xia, Philip S. Yu, Zhiwei Liu, and Shu Zhao. 2021. PDALN: Progressive domain adaptation over a pre-trained model for low-resource cross-domain named entity recognition. In *Proceedings of the 2021 Conference on Empirical Methods in Natural Language Processing*, pages 5441–5451, Online and Punta Cana, Dominican Republic. Association for Computational Linguistics.

Xinyan Zhao, Haibo Ding, and Zhe Feng. 2021. GLaRA: Graph-based labeling rule augmentation for weakly supervised named entity recognition. In *Proceedings of the 16th Conference of the European Chapter of the Association for Computational Linguistics: Main Volume*, pages 3636–3649, Online. Association for Computational Linguistics.

Zexuan Zhong and Danqi Chen. 2021. A frustratingly easy approach for entity and relation extraction. In *Proceedings of the 2021 Conference of the North American Chapter of the Association for Computational Linguistics: Human Language Technologies*, pages 50–61, Online. Association for Computational Linguistics.

Joey Tianyi Zhou, Hao Zhang, Di Jin, Hongyuan Zhu, Meng Fang, Rick Siow Mong Goh, and Kenneth Kwok. 2019. Dual adversarial neural transfer for low-resource named entity recognition. In *Proceedings of the 57th Annual Meeting of the Association for Computational Linguistics*, pages 3461–3471, Florence, Italy. Association for Computational Linguistics.

A Architectures

In our implementation of SlotGAN, the embedding function $\texttt{emb}(w)$ used to obtain embeddings of sentences and names in the gazetteer uses the pretrained WordPiece embeddings from the input layer of BERT (Devlin et al., 2019).

The generator consists of BERT, which for an input sentence of length n, outputs a matrix $\mathbf{H} \in \mathbb{R}^{d \times n}$ where d is the dimension of the output layer of BERT, equal to 768. We use the `bert-base-cased` implementation in HuggingFace's Transformer library (Wolf et al., 2019).

Layer	Output features	Activation
3×3 Conv	128	ReLU
3×3 Conv	64	ReLU
3×3 Conv	64	ReLU
3×3 Conv	64	—
Flatten		—
Linear	32	ReLU
Linear	1	—

Table 3: Architecture of the discriminator used in our experiments.

The output matrix is passed to a modified Slot Attention layer (Locatello et al., 2020), which we use as a differentiable mechanism to assign n input embeddings to k slots. In the original implementation, Slot Attention would assign each of the n outputs in the columns of $\mathbf{H}$ to k slots, by using a differentiable clustering algorithm. This algorithm works for a variable number of slots, by sampling k initial slot representations from a Gaussian distribution. In our experiments we use $k = 10$, and the number of iterations of the clustering algorithm is set to 3.

In the MD case, for words that do not belong to any mention, we want the generator to be able to assign them to a "default" slot. We achieve this by introducing an extra slot, whose representation, instead of sampled, is a single vector with a learned representation. Slot Attention in the generator thus contains $k+1$ slots, but the default slot is discarded when passing generated spans to the discriminator.

After discarding the default slot, the result is an attention mask $\mathbf{M} \in \mathbb{R}^{k \times n}$ where the m_{ij} entry indicates the fraction of input j assigned to slot i, and each column is normalized to 1. The i-th span representation is then obtained as

$$\mathbf{S}_i = \texttt{emb}(w) \odot \mathbf{M}_{i:}, \tag{3}$$

where $\mathbf{M}_{i:}$ is the i-th row of $\mathbf{M}$, and $\odot$ is broadcast element-wise multiplication.

For the discriminator we use a temporal CNN, where convolutions are applied along the sequence axis. The input is a matrix of span representations of shape $d \times L$, and the output is a scalar. The architecture is described in Table 3.

B Training Procedure

We train SlotGAN with mini-batches of 32 sentences. We update the generator once for every 5 updates of the discriminator. To let the discriminator accept empty spans as valid, we replace names from the gazetteer with an empty span with a probability of 0.5. We use a gradient penalty coefficient (Gulrajani et al., 2017) of 10 when computing the discriminator loss.

We use a learning rate of 2×10^{-5}, with a linear warm-up schedule for the first 10% of epochs. For the Lagrange multiplier, we use the Modified Differential Method of Multipliers (Platt and Barr, 1987) with a constant learning rate of 1×10^{-3}.

We run our experiments in a workstation with an Intel Xeon processor, 1 NVIDIA GeForce GTX 1080 Ti GPU with 11GB of memory, and 60GB of RAM. When pretraining with Wikipedia and Wikidata, we train SlotGAN with 20,000 updates of the generator, and 5,000 when training with the CoNLL 2003 dataset.

A Joint Learning Approach for Semi-supervised Neural Topic Modeling

Jeffrey Chiu* **Rajat Mittal*** **Neehal Tumma*** **Abhishek Sharma** **Finale Doshi-Velez**
Harvard University, Cambridge, MA

Abstract

Topic models are some of the most popular ways to represent textual data in an interpretable manner. Recently, advances in deep generative models, specifically auto-encoding variational Bayes (AEVB), have led to the introduction of unsupervised neural topic models, which leverage deep generative models as opposed to traditional statistics-based topic models. We extend upon these neural topic models by introducing the *Label-Indexed Neural Topic Model (LI-NTM)*, which is, to the extent of our knowledge, the first effective upstream semi-supervised neural topic model. We find that LI-NTM outperforms existing neural topic models in document reconstruction benchmarks, with the most notable results in low labeled data regimes and for data-sets with informative labels; furthermore, our jointly learned classifier outperforms baseline classifiers in ablation studies.

1 Introduction

Topic models are one of the most widely used and studied text modeling techniques, both because of their intuitive generative process and interpretable results (Blei, 2012). Though topic models are mostly used on textual data (Rosen-Zvi et al., 2012; Yan et al., 2013), use cases have since expanded to areas such as genomics modeling (Liu et al., 2016) and molecular modeling (Schneider et al., 2017).

Recently, neural topic models, which leverage deep generative models have been used successfully for learning these probabilistic models. A lot of this success is due to the development of variational autoencoders (Rezende et al., 2014; Kingma and Welling, 2014) which allow for inference of intractable distributions over latent variables through a back-propagation over an inference network. Furthermore, recent research shows promising results for Neural Topic Models compared to traditional topic models due to the added expressivity from neural representations; specifically, we see significant improvements in low data regimes (Srivastava and Sutton, 2017; Iwata, 2021).

Joint learning of topics and other tasks have been researched in the past, specifically through supervised topic models (Blei and McAuliffe, 2010; Huh and Fienberg, 2012; Cao et al., 2015; Wang and Yang, 2020). These works are centered around the idea of a prediction task using a topic model as a dimensionality reduction tool. Fundamentally, they follow a downstream task setting (Figure 1), where the label is assumed to be generated from the latent variable (topics). On the other hand, an upstream setting would be when the input (document) is generated from a combination of the latent variable (topics) and label, which has the benefit of better directly modeling how the label affects the document, resulting in topic with additional information being injected from the label information. Upstream variants of supervised topic models are much less common, with, to the extent of our knowledge, no neural architectures to this date. (Ramage et al., 2009; Lacoste-Julien et al., 2008).

Our model, the *Label-Indexed Neural Topic Model (LI-NTM)* stands uniquely with respect to all existing topic models. We combine the benefits of an *upstream generative processes* (Figure 1), *label-indexed* topics, and a topic model capable of *semi-supervised learning* and *neural topic modeling* to jointly learn a topic model and label classifier. Our main contributions are:

1. The introduction of the first upstream semi-supervised neural topic model.

2. A label-indexed topic model that allows more cohesive and diverse topics by allowing the label of a document to supervise the learned topics in a semi-supervised manner.

3. A joint training framework that allows for users to tune the trade-off between document

*Equal contribution

Proceedings of the Sixth Workshop on Structured Prediction for NLP, pages 40 - 51

classifier and topic quality which results in a classifier that outperforms same classifier trained in an isolated setting for certain hyper-parameters.

2 Related Work

2.1 Neural Topic Models

Most past work in neural topic models focused on designing inference networks with better model specification in the unsupervised setting. One line of recent research attempts to improve topic model performance by modifying the inference network through changes to the topic priors or regularization over the latent space (Miao et al., 2016; Srivastava and Sutton, 2017; Nan et al., 2019). Another line of research looks towards incorporating the expressivity of word embeddings to topic models (Dieng et al., 2019a,b).

In contrast to existing work on neural topic models, our approach does not mainly focus on model specification; rather, we create a broader architecture into which neural topic models of all specifications can be trained in an upstream, semi-supervised setting. We believe that our architecture will enable existing neural topic models to be used in a wider range of real-word scenarios where we leverage labeled data alongside unlabeled data and use the knowledge present in document labels to further supervise topic models. Moreover, by directly tying our topic distributions to the labels through label-indexing, we create topics that are specific to labels, making these topics more interpretable as users are directly able to glean what types of documents each of the topics are summarizing.

2.2 Downstream Supervised Topic Models

Most supervised topic models follow the downstream supervised framework introduced in s-LDA (Blei and McAuliffe, 2010). This framework assumes a two-stage setting in which a topic model is trained and then a predictive model for the document labels is trained independently of the topic model. Neural topic models following this framework have also been developed, with the predictive model being a discriminative layer attached to the learned topics, essentially treating topic modeling as a dimensionality reduction tool (Wang and Yang, 2020; Cao et al., 2015; Huh and Fienberg, 2012).

In contrast to existing work, *LI-NTM* is an upstream generative model (Figure 2, Figure 3) following a *prediction-constrained* framework. The upstream setting allows us to implicitly train our classifier and topic model in a *one-stage setting* that is end-to-end. This has the benefit of allowing us to tune the trade-off between our classifier and topic model performance in a *prediction-constrained* framework, which has been shown to achieve better empirical results when latent variable models are used as a dimensionality reduction tool (Hughes et al., 2018; Hope et al.; Sharma et al., 2021). Furthermore, the upstream setting allows us to introduce the document label classifier as a latent variable, enabling our model to work in semi-supervised settings.

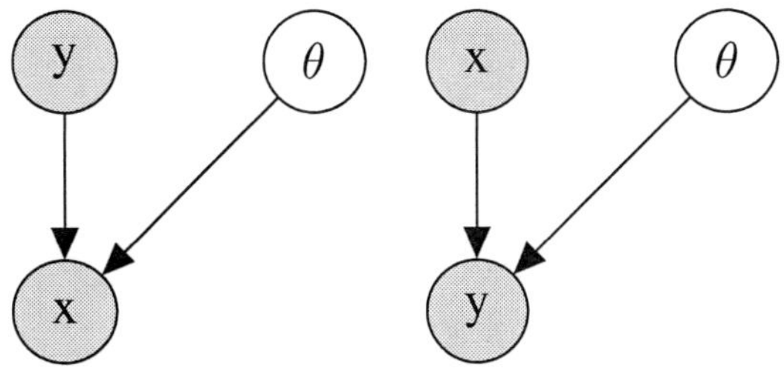

(a) Upstream Generative (b) Downstream Generative

Figure 1: Generative process for downstream vs upstream supervision. Note that in upstream supervision, the label, y, supervises the document, x, whereas in downstream supervision the document supervises the label. θ is an arbitrary latent variable, in our case representing topic proportions.

3 Background

LI-NTM extends upon two core ideas: Latent Dirichlet Allocation (LDA) and deep generative models. For the rest of the paper, we assume a setting where we have a document corpus of D documents, a vocabulary with V unique words, and each document having a label from the L possible labels. Furthermore let us represent w_{dn} as the n-th word in the d-th document.

3.1 Latent Dirichlet Allocation (LDA)

LDA is a probabilistic generative model for topic modeling (Blei et al., 2003; Blei and McAuliffe, 2010). Through the process of estimation and inference, LDA learns K topics $\beta_{1:K}$. The generative process of LDA posits that each document is a mixture of topics with the topics being global to the entire corpus. For each document, the generative process is listed below:

1. Draw topic proportions $\theta_d \sim \text{Dirichlet}(\alpha_\theta)$

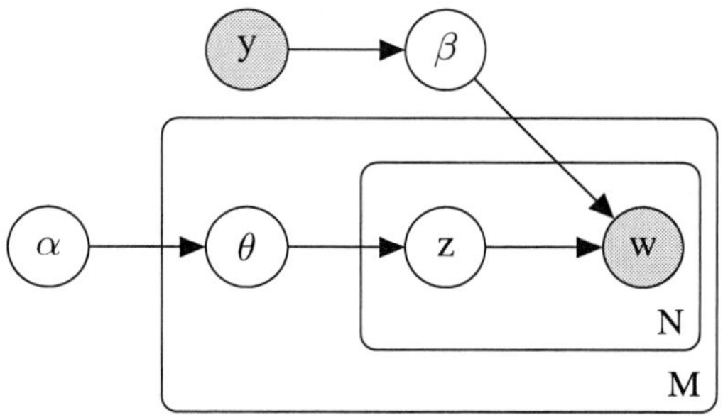

Figure 2: Generative Process for LI-NTM: The label y indexes into our label-topic-word matrix β, which is "upstream" of the observed words in the document w.

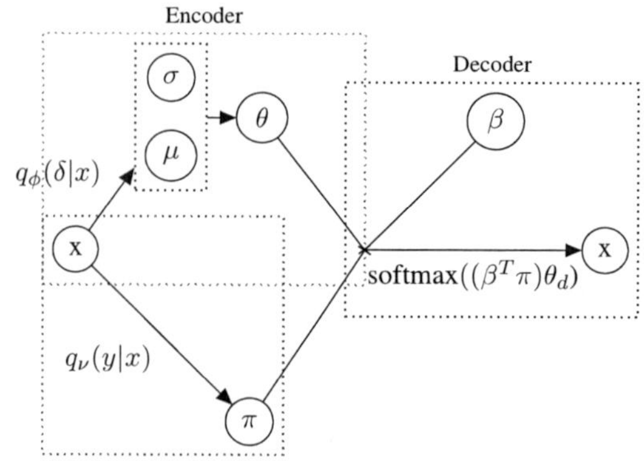

Figure 3: Architecture for LI-NTM in the un-labeled setting. y is used instead of obtaining a probability distribution π from the classifier in the labeled setting. $q(\cdot|x)$ are distributions parameterized by neural networks. Note that we can optimize the classifier, encoder, and decoder in one backwards pass.

2. For each word w in document:
   (a) Draw topic assignment $z_{dn} \sim \text{Cat}(\theta_d)$
   (b) Draw word $w_{dn} \sim \text{Cat}(\beta z_{dn})$
3. Draw responses $y|z_{1:N}, \eta, \sigma^2 \sim \mathcal{N}(\eta^T \bar{z}, \sigma^2)$ *(if supervised)*

where $\bar{z} := \frac{1}{N}\sum_{i=1}^{N} z_n$ and the parameters η, σ^2 are estimated during inference. α_θ is a hyperparameter that serves as a prior for topic mixture proportions. In addition we also have hyperparameter α_β that we use to place a dirichlet prior on our topics, $\beta_k \sim \text{Dirichlet}(\alpha_\beta)$.

3.2 Deep Generative Models

Deep Generative Models serve as the bridge between probabilistic models and neural networks. Specifically, deep generative models treat the parameters of distributions within probabilistic models as outputs of neural networks. Deep generative models fundamentally work because of the *re-parameterization trick* that allows for backpropogation through Monte-Carlo samples of distributions from the location-scale family. Specifically, for any distribution $g(\cdot)$ from the location-scale family, we have that

$$z \sim g(\mu, \sigma^2) \iff z = \mu + \sigma \cdot \epsilon, \epsilon \sim g(0, 1)$$

thus allowing differentiation with respect to μ, σ^2.

The Variational Auto-encoder is the simplest deep generative model (Kingma and Welling, 2014) and it's generative process is as follows:

$$p_\theta(x, z) = p_\theta(x|z)p(z)$$
$$p_\theta(x|z) \sim \mathcal{N}(\mu_\theta(z), \Sigma_\theta(z))$$
$$p(z) \sim \mathcal{N}(0, \mathcal{I})$$

where $\mu_\theta(z), \Sigma_\theta(z)$ are both parameterized by neural networks with variational parameters θ. Inference on a variational autoencoder is done through approximating the true posterior $p(z|x)$ which is often intractable with an approximation $q_\phi(z|x)$ that is parametrized by a neural network.

The M2 model is the semi-supervised extension of the variational auto-encoder where the input is modeled as being generated by both a continuous latent variable z and the class label y as a latent variable (Kingma et al., 2014). It follows the generative process below:

$$p_\theta(x, z, y) = p_\theta(x|y, z)p(y)p(z)$$
$$p_\theta(x|y, z) \sim \mathcal{N}(\mu_\theta(y, z), \Sigma_\theta(y, z))$$
$$p(y) \sim Cat(y|\pi)$$
$$p(z) \sim \mathcal{N}(0, \mathcal{I})$$

where π is parameterizing the distribution on y and $\mu_\theta(y, z), \Sigma_\theta(y, z)$ are both parameterized by neural networks. We then approximate the true posterior $p(y, z|x)$ using by saying

$$p(y, z|x) \approx q_\phi(z|y, x)q_\phi(y|x)$$

where $q_\phi(y|x)$ is a classifier that's used in the unlabeled case and $q_\phi(z|y, x)$ is a neural network that takes in the true labels if available and the outputted labels from $q_\phi(y|x)$ if unavailable.

4 The Label-Indexed Neural Topic Model

LI-NTM is a neural topic model that leverages the labels y as a latent variable alongside the topic proportions θ in generating the document x.

Notationally, let us denote the bag of words representation of a document as $x \in \mathbb{R}^V$ and the one-hot encoded document label as $y \in \mathbb{R}^L$. Furthermore, we denote our latent topic proportions as $\theta_d \in \mathbb{R}^K$ and our topics are represented using a three dimensional matrix $\beta \in \mathbb{R}^{L \times K \times V}$.

Under the LI-NTM, the generative process (also depicted in Figure 2) of the d-th document x_d is the following:

1. Draw topic proportions $\theta_d \sim \mathcal{LN}(0, \mathbb{I})$
2. Draw document label $y_d \sim \pi$
3. For each word w in document:
   (a) Draw topic assignment $z_{dn} \sim \text{Cat}(\theta_d)$
   (b) Draw word $w_{dn} \sim \text{Cat}(\beta_{y_d, z_{dn}})$

In Step 1, we draw from the Logistic-Normal $\mathcal{LN}(\cdot)$ to approximate the Dirichlet Distribution while remaining in the location-scale family necessary for re-parameterization (Blei et al., 2003). This is done obtained through:

$$\delta_d \sim \mathcal{N}(0, \mathbb{I}), \theta_d = softmax(\delta_d)$$

Note that since we sample from the Logistic-Normal, we do not require the Dirichlet prior hyper-parameter α.

Step 2 is unique for LI-NTM , in the unlabeled case, we sample a label y_d from π, which is the output of our classifier. In the labeled scenario, we skip step 2 and simply pass in the document label for our y_d. Step 3 is typical of traditional LDA, but one key difference is that in step 3b we also index by the β by y_d instead of just z_{dn}. This step is motivated by how the M2 model extended variational autoencoders to a semi-supervised setting (Kingma et al., 2014).

A key contribution of our model is the idea of label-indexing. We introduce the supervision of the document labels by having different topics for different labels. Specifically, we have $L \times K$ different topics and we denote the k-th topic for label l as the V dimensional vector, $\beta_{l,k}$. Under this setting, we can envision LI-NTM as running a separate LDA for each label once we index our corpus by document labels.

Label-indexing allows us to effectively train our model in a semi-supervised setting. In the unlabeled data setting, our jointly-learned classifier, $q_\phi(y|x)$, outputs a distribution over the labels, π. By computing the dot-product between π and our topic matrix β, this allows us to partially index into each label's topic proportional to the classifier's confidence and update the topics based on the unlabeled examples we are currently training on.

Algorithm 1 Topic Modeling with LI-NTM

```
Initialize model and variational parameters
for iteration i = 1, 2, ... do
    for each document c in c_1, c_2, ..., c_d do
        Get normalized bag-of-word representation x_d
        Compute μ_d = NN_encoder(x_d | φ_μ)
        Compute Σ_d = NN_encoder(x_d | φ_Σ)
        if labeled then
            π = y_d
        else
            π = NN_classifier(x_d | ν)
        end if
        Sample θ_d ~ LN(μ_d, Σ_d)
        for each word in the document do
            p(w_dn | θ_d, π) = softmax(β)^T π θ_d
        end for
    end for
    Compute the ELBO and its gradient (backprop.)
    Update model parameters β
    Update variational parameters (φ_μ, φ_Σ, ν)
end for
```

5 Inference and Estimation

Given a corpus of normalized bag-of-word representation of documents $x_1, x_2, \cdots, x_d$ we aim to fit LI-NTM using variational inference in order to approximate intractable posteriors in maximum likelihood estimation (Jordan et al., 1999). Furthermore, we amortize the loss to allow for joint learning of the classifier and the topic model.

5.1 Variational Inference

We begin first by looking at a family of variational distributions $q_\phi(\delta_d|x_d)$ in modeling the untransformed topic proportions and $q_\nu(y_d|x_d)$ in modeling the classifier. More specifically, $q_\phi(\delta_d|x_d)$ is a Gaussian whose mean and variance are parameterized by neural networks with parameter ϕ and $q_\nu(y_d|x_d)$ is a distribution over the labels parameterized by a MLP with parameter ν (Kingma and Welling, 2014; Kingma et al., 2014).

We use this family of variational distributions alongside our classifier to lower-bound the marginal likelihood. The evidence lower bound (ELBO) is a function of model and variational parameters and provides a lower bound for the complete data log-likelihood. We derive two ELBO-based loss functions: one for the labeled case and one for the unlabeled case and we compute a linear interpolation of the two for our overall loss function.

$$\mathcal{L}_u = \sum_{d=1}^{D}\sum_{n=1}^{N_d} \mathbb{E}_q[\log p(w_{dn}|\delta_d, q_\nu(y_d|x_d)] - \tau KL(q_\phi(\delta_d|x_d)||p(\delta_d)) \quad (1)$$

$$\mathcal{L}_l = \sum_{d=1}^{D}\sum_{n=1}^{N_d} \mathbb{E}_q[\log p(w_{dn}|\delta_d, q_\nu(y_d|x_d)] - \tau KL(q_\phi(\delta_d|x_d)||p(\delta_d)) + \rho\mathcal{H}(y_d, q_\nu(y_d|x_d)) \quad (2)$$

where Equation 1 serves as our unlabeled loss and Equation 2 serves as our labeled loss. $\mathcal{H}(\cdot,\cdot)$ is the cross-entropy function. τ and ρ are hyper-parameters on the KL and cross-entropy terms in the loss respectively.

These hyper-parameters are well motivated. τ is seen to be a hyper-parameter that tempers our posterior distribution over weights, which has been well-studied and shown to increase robustness to model mis-specification (Mandt et al., 2016; Wenzel et al., 2020). Lower values τ would result in posterior distributions with higher probability densities around the modes of the posterior. Furthermore, the ρ hyperparameter in our unlabeled loss is the core hyperparameter that makes our model fit the *prediction-constrained* framework, essentially allowing us to trade-off the between classifier and topic modeling performance (Hughes et al., 2018). Increasing values of ρ corresponds to emphasizing classifier performance over topic modeling performance.

We treat our overall loss as a combination of our labeled and unlabeled loss with $\lambda \in (0, 1)$ being a hyper-parameter weighing the labeled and unlabeled loss. λ allows us weigh how heavily we want our unlabeled data to influence our models. Example cases where we may want high values of λ are when we have poor classifier performance or a disproportionate amount of unlabeled data compared to label data, causing the unlabeled loss to completely outweigh the labeled loss.

$$\mathcal{L} = \lambda\mathcal{L}_l + (1-\lambda)\mathcal{L}_u \quad (3)$$

We optimize our loss with respect to both the model and variational parameters and leverage the *reparameterization trick* to perform stochastic optimization (Kingma and Welling, 2014). The training procedure is shown in Algorithm 1 and a visualization of a forward pass is given in Figure 3. This loss function allows us to jointly learn our classification and topic modeling elements and we hypothesize that the implicit regularization from joint learning will increase performance for both elements as seen in previous research studies (Zweig and Weinshall, 2013).

6 Experimental Setup

We perform an empirical evaluation of LI-NTM with two corpora: a synthetic dataset and *AG News*.

6.1 Baselines

We compare our topic model to the Embedded Topic Model (ETM), which is the current state of the art neural topic model that leverages word embeddings alongside variational autoencoders for unsupervised topic modeling (Dieng et al., 2019a). Further details about ETM are shown in the appendix (subsection A.2). Furthermore, our baseline for our jointly trained classifier is a classifier with the same architecture outside of our jointly trained setting.

6.2 Synthetic Dataset

We constructed our synthetic data to evaluate LI-NTM in ideal and worst-case settings.

- **Ideal Setting**: An ideal setting for LI-NTM consists of a corpus with similar word distributions for documents with the same label and very dissimilar word distributions for documents with different labels

- **Worst Case Setting** worst-case setting for LI-NTM consists of a corpus where the label has little to no correlation with the distribution of words in a document.

Since the labels are a fundamental aspect of LI-NTM we wanted to investigate how robust LI-NTM is in a real-word setting, specifically looking at how robust it was to certain types of mis-labeled data points. By jointly training our classifier with our topic model, we hope that by properly trading off topic quality and classification quality, our model will be more robust to mis-labeled data since we are able to manually tune how much we want to depend on the data labels.

We use the same distributions to generate the documents for both the ideal and worst-case data. In particular, we consider a vocabulary with $V =$

20 words, and a task with $L = 2$ labels. Documents are generated from one of two distributions, $\mathcal{D}_1$ and $\mathcal{D}_2$. $\mathcal{D}_1$ generates documents which have many occurrences of the first 10 words in the vocabulary (and very few occurrences of the last 10 words), while $\mathcal{D}_2$ does the opposite, generating documents which have many occurrences of the last 10 words in the vocabulary (and very few occurrences of the first 10 words). The distributions $\mathcal{D}_1$ and $\mathcal{D}_2$ have parameters which are generated randomly for each trial, although the shape of the distributions is largely the same from trial to trial.

In the ideal case, the label corresponds directly to the distribution from which the document was generated. For the worst-case data, the label is 0 if the number of words in the document is an even number, and 1 otherwise, ensuring there is little to no correlation between label and word distributions in a document. Note that in our synthetic data experiments, all of the data is labeled. The effectiveness of LI-NTM in semi-supervised domains is evaluated in our *AG News* experiments.

6.3 AG News Dataset

The *AG News* dataset is a collection of news articles collected from more than 2,000 news sources by ComeToMyHead, an academic news search engine. This dataset includes 118,000 training samples and 7,600 test samples. Each sample is a short text with a single four-class label (one of world, business, sports and science/technology).

6.4 Evaluation Metrics

To evaluate our models, we used accuracy as a metric to gauge the quality of the classifier and perplexity to gauge the quality of the model as a whole. We opted to use perplexity as it is a measure for how well the model generalizes to unseen test data.

7 Synthetic Data Experimental Results

We used our synthetic dataset to examine the performance of LI-NTM relative to ETM in a setting where the label strongly partitions our dataset into subsets that have distinct topics to investigate the effect and robustness of label indexing.

LI-NTM was trained on the fully labeled version of the both the ideal and worse case label synthetic dataset and ETM was trained on the same dataset with the label excluded, as ETM is a unsupervised method. We varied the number of topics in both LI-

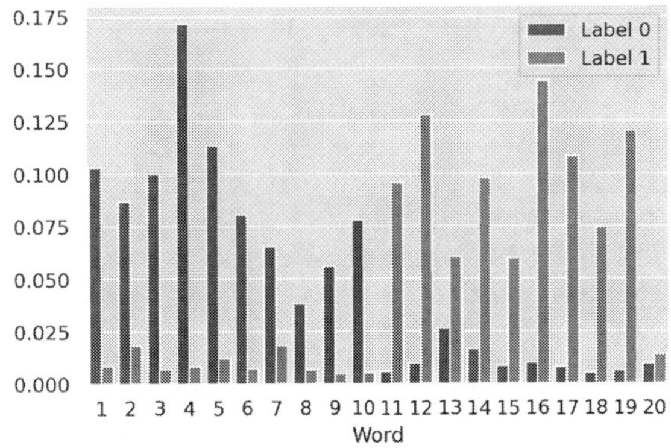

Figure 4: Topic-word probability distribution visualization for LI-NTM on ideal case synthetic dataset with one topic per label. We observe that we learn topics that are strongly label partitioned.

NTM and ETM to explore realistic settings $K = 2, 8$ and the extreme setting $K = 20$.

7.1 Effect of Number of Topics

Takeaway: More topics lead to better performance, especially when the label is uninformative.

First, we note that as we increase the number of topics, the performance of LI-NTM on ideal case labels, LI-NTM on worst case labels, and ETM improves as shown in Table 1. This is expected as having more topics gives the model the capacity to learn more diverse topic-word distributions which leads to an improved reconstruction. However, we note that LI-NTM trained on the worst-case labels benefits most from the increase in the number of topics.

7.2 Informative Labels

Takeaway: Label Indexing is highly effective when labels partition the dataset well.

Next, we note that LI-NTM trained on the ideal case label synthetic dataset outperforms ETM with respect to perplexity (see Table 1). This result can be attributed to the fact that LI-NTM leverages label indexing to learn the label-topic-word distribution. Since the ideal case label version of the dataset was constructed such that the label strongly partitions the dataset into two groups (each of which has a very distinct topic-word distribution), and since we had perfect classifier accuracy (the ideal case label dataset was constructed such that the classification problem was trivial), LI-NTM is able to use the output

Total Num. Topics	ETM	Ideal LI-NTM	WC LI-NTM (V1)	WC LI-NTM (V2)	Perplexity Lower Bound
2	11.78	11.42	19.71	18.70	–
8	11.27	10.72	12.83	10.90	–
20	10.88	10.50	11.20	10.77	9.50

Table 1: Perplexities of LI-NTM (ideal and worst case synthetic data) compared to ETM for a varied number of topics. WC LI-NTM (V1) corresponds to training the model normally in the worst case setting, while WC LI-NTM (V2) corresponds to training with $\rho = 0$. Note that LI-NTM is able to outperform ETM in both the ideal and worst case scenarios.

Total Num. Topics	Worst Case Labels	Ideal Case Labels
2	50.2 ± 0.6	54.2 ± 2.0
8	50.4 ± 0.5	84.3 ± 8.8
20	50.4 ± 0.2	93.7 ± 6.2

Table 2: Accuracies of classifier LI-NTM (V2) on ideal case and worst case labels. LI-NTM (V2) is trained only on worst-case labels but evaluated on both worst case and ideal case label test sets. Note that even though $\alpha = 0$ and the training set is only worst case labels, the reconstruction loss distantly supervises the classifier to learn the true ideal case labels.

from the classifier to index into the topic-word distribution with 100% accuracy.

If we denote the topic-word distribution corresponding to label 0 by β_0 and the topic-word distribution corresponding to label 1 by β_1, we note that LI-NTM is able to leverage β_0 to specialize in generating the words for the documents corresponding to label 0 while using β_1 to specialize in generating the words for the documents corresponding to label 1 (see Figure 4). Overall, this result suggests that LI-NTM performs well in settings when the dataset exhibits strong label partitioning.

7.3 Uninformative Labels

Takeaway: With proper hyperparameters, LI-NTM is able to achieve good topic model performance even when we have uninformative labels.

We now move to examining the results produced by LI-NTM trained on the worst-case labels. In this data setting, we investigated the robustness of the LI-NTM architecture. Specifically, we looked at a worst-case dataset, where we have labels that are uninformative and are thus not good at partitioning the dataset into subsets that have distinct topics.

In the worst-case setting, we define the following two instances of the LI-NTM model.

- **LI-NTM (V1)** This model refers to the normal ($\rho \neq 0$) version of the model trained in the worst case setting.
- **LI-NTM (V2)** This model refers to a LI-NTM model with zero-ed out classification loss ($\rho = 0$), essentially pushing the model to only accurately reconstruct the original data.

For LI-NTM (V1), we did see decreases in performance; namely, that V1 has a worse perplexity than both ETM and ideal case LI-NTM. This aligns with our expectation that having a label with very low correlation to the topic-word distributions in the document results in poor performance in LI-NTM. This can be attributed to the failure of LI-NTM to adequately label-index in cases where this occurs.

However, for LI-NTM (V2) we found that we were actually able to achieve lower perplexity than ETM when the model was told to produce more than 2 topics, even with uninformative labels. To understand why this was happening, we analyzed the accuracy of the original classifier in LI-NTM (V2) on both the worst-case labels (which it was trained on) and the ideal-case labels (which it was not trained on). We report our results in Table 2. The key takeaway is that we observed a much higher accuracy on the ideal labels compared to the worst-case labels. This suggests that when $\rho = 0$ the classifier *implicitly* learns the ideal labels that are necessary to learn a good reconstruction of the data, even when the provided labels are heavily *uninformative or misspecified.* This shows the benefit

Data Regime	ETM Perplexity	LI-NTM Perplexity	LI-NTM Accuracy	Baseline Accuracy
5% labeled, 5% unlabeled	**205.93**	210.76 ± 2.17	86.3%	86.2%
5% labeled, 15% unlabeled	190.10	$\mathbf{187.66 \pm 2.23}$	86.3%	86.2%
5% labeled, 55% unlabeled	177.71	$\mathbf{175.43 \pm 5.01}$	86.8%	86.2%
5% labeled, 95% unlabeled	177.34	$\mathbf{169.40 \pm 4.08}$	87.2%	86.2%

Table 3: The results from ETM, LI-NTM, and a baseline classifier for the AG News dataset. The baseline classifier was the same for each data regime, hence the duplicate values. Note that in the high data settings, LI-NTM outperformed ETM in terms of perplexity, although in the lowest data setting, the lack of data hurt LI-NTM since it further partitions the topics by labels. Accuracy increased near linearly as unlabeled data increased.

Sports	Science/Technology	World	Business
series	web	minister	stocks
game	search	prime	oil
red	google	palestinian	prices
boston	new	gaza	reuters
run	online	israel	company
night	site	leader	shares
league	internet	arafat	inc
yankees	engine	said	percent
new	com	yasser	yesterday
york	yahoo	sharon	percent

Table 4: Example topics (top ten words) corresponding to each label from LI-NTM run on the AG-News Dataset. Each topic is assigned a label and it is clear that the distribution of words for each topic depends on the label.

of label-indexing and of jointly learning our topic model and classifier in a semi-supervised fashion. Even in cases with uninformative data points, by setting $\rho = 0$, the joint learning setting of our classifier and topic model pushes the classifier, through the need for successful document reconstruction, to generate a probability distribution over labels that is close to the true, ideal-case labels despite only being given uninformative or mis-labeled data.

8 AG News Experimental Results

We used the AG News dataset to evaluate the performance of LI-NTM in the semi-supervised setting. Specifically, we aimed to analyze the extent to which unlabeled data can improve the performance of *both* the classifier and topic model in the LI-NTM architecture. Ideally, in the unlabeled case, the distant supervision provided to the classifier from the reconstruction loss would align with the task of predicting correct labels.

We ran four experiments on ETM and LI-NTM in which the amount of unlabeled data was gradually increased, while the amount of labeled data was kept fixed. In each of the experiments, 5% of the dataset was considered labeled, while 5%, 15%, 55%, and 95% of the whole dataset was considered unlabeled in each of the four experiments respectively.

8.1 Semi-Supervised Learning: Topic Model Performance

Takeaway: Combining label-indexing with semi-supervised learning increases topic model performance.

In Table 3 we observe that perplexity decreases as the model sees more unlabeled data. We also note that LI-NTM has a lower perplexity than ETM in higher data settings, supporting the hypothesis that guiding the reconstruction of a document exclusively via label-specific topics makes reconstruction an easier task. In the lowest data regime (5% labeled, 5% unlabeled), LI-NTM performs worse than ETM. This suggests that while in high-data settings, LI-NTM is able to effectively leverage $L = 4$ sets of topics, in low-data settings there are not enough documents to learn sufficient structure.

8.2 Semi-Supervised Learning: Classifier Performance

Takeaway: Topic modeling supervises the classifier, resulting in better classification performance.

Jointly learning the classifier and topic model also seem to benefit the classifier; Table 3 shows classification performance increases linearly with the amount of unlabeled data. The accuracy increase suggest the task of reconstructing the bag of words is helpful in news article classification.

Select topics learned from LI-NTM on the AG News Dataset are presented in Table 4 and the distributions are visualized in the appendix Figure A1.

9 Conclusion

In this paper, we introduced the LI-NTM, which, to the extent of our knowledge, is the first upstream neural topic model with applications to a semi-supervised data setting. Our results show that when applied to both a synthetic dataset and AG News, LI-NTM outperforms ETM with respect to perplexity. Furthermore, we found that the classifier in LI-NTM was able to outperform a baseline that doesn't leverage any unlabeled data. Even more promising is the fact that the classifier in LI-NTM continued to experience gains in accuracy when increasing the proportion of unlabeled data. While we aim to iterate upon our results, our current findings indicate that LI-NTM is comparable with current state-of-the-art models while being applicable in a wider range of real-world settings.

In future work, we hope to further experiment with the idea of label-indexing. While in LI-NTM every topic is label-specific, real datasets have some common words and topics that are label-agnostic. Future work could augment the existing LI-NTM framework with additional label-agnostic global topics which prevent identical topics from being learned across multiple labels. We are also interested in extending our semi-supervised, upstream paradigm to a semi-parametric setting in which the number of topics we learn is not a predefined hyperparameter but rather something that is learned.

10 Acknowledgements

AS is supported by R01MH123804, and FDV is supported by NSF IIS-1750358. All authors acknowledge insightful feedback from members of CS282 Fall 2021.

References

David M Blei. 2012. Probabilistic topic models. *Communications of the ACM*, 55(4):77–84.

David M Blei, Thomas L Griffiths, Michael I Jordan, Joshua B Tenenbaum, et al. Hierarchical topic models and the nested chinese restaurant process.

David M Blei and John D Lafferty. 2007. A correlated topic model of science. *The annals of applied statistics*, 1(1):17–35.

David M. Blei and Jon D. McAuliffe. 2010. Supervised topic models.

David M Blei, Andrew Y Ng, and Michael I Jordan. 2003. Latent dirichlet allocation. *the Journal of machine Learning research*, 3:993–1022.

Ziqiang Cao, Sujian Li, Yang Liu, Wenjie Li, and Heng Ji. 2015. A novel neural topic model and its supervised extension. In *Proceedings of the AAAI Conference on Artificial Intelligence*, volume 29.

Adji B. Dieng, Francisco J. R. Ruiz, and David M. Blei. 2019a. Topic modeling in embedding spaces.

Adji B Dieng, Francisco JR Ruiz, and David M Blei. 2019b. The dynamic embedded topic model. *arXiv preprint arXiv:1907.05545*.

Caitlin Doogan and Wray Buntine. 2021. Topic model or topic twaddle? re-evaluating semantic interpretability measures. In *Proceedings of the 2021 Conference of the North American Chapter of the Association for Computational Linguistics: Human Language Technologies*, pages 3824–3848, Online. Association for Computational Linguistics.

Gabriel Hope, Michael C Hughes, Finale Doshi-Velez, and Erik B Sudderth. Prediction-constrained hidden markov models for semi-supervised classification.

Alexander Hoyle, Pranav Goel, Andrew Hian-Cheong, Denis Peskov, Jordan Boyd-Graber, and Philip Resnik. 2021. Is automated topic model evaluation broken? the incoherence of coherence. *Advances in Neural Information Processing Systems*, 34.

Michael Hughes, Gabriel Hope, Leah Weiner, Thomas McCoy, Roy Perlis, Erik Sudderth, and Finale Doshi-Velez. 2018. Semi-supervised prediction-constrained topic models. In *Proceedings of the Twenty-First International Conference on Artificial Intelligence and Statistics*, volume 84 of *Proceedings of Machine Learning Research*, pages 1067–1076. PMLR.

Seungil Huh and Stephen E Fienberg. 2012. Discriminative topic modeling based on manifold learning. *ACM Transactions on Knowledge Discovery from Data (TKDD)*, 5(4):1–25.

Tomoharu Iwata. 2021. Few-shot learning for topic modeling. *arXiv preprint arXiv:2104.09011*.

Michael I Jordan, Zoubin Ghahramani, Tommi S Jaakkola, and Lawrence K Saul. 1999. An introduction to variational methods for graphical models. *Machine learning*, 37(2):183–233.

Diederik P. Kingma, Danilo J. Rezende, Shakir Mohamed, and Max Welling. 2014. Semi-supervised learning with deep generative models.

Diederik P Kingma and Max Welling. 2014. Auto-encoding variational bayes.

Durk P Kingma, Tim Salimans, and Max Welling. 2015. Variational dropout and the local reparameterization trick. *Advances in neural information processing systems*, 28.

Simon Lacoste-Julien, Fei Sha, and Michael Jordan. 2008. Disclda: Discriminative learning for dimensionality reduction and classification. *Advances in neural information processing systems*, 21.

Lin Liu, Lin Tang, Wen Dong, Shaowen Yao, and Wei Zhou. 2016. An overview of topic modeling and its current applications in bioinformatics. *SpringerPlus*, 5(1):1–22.

Stephan Mandt, James McInerney, Farhan Abrol, Rajesh Ranganath, and David Blei. 2016. Variational tempering. In *Artificial intelligence and statistics*, pages 704–712. PMLR.

Xianling Mao, Zhaoyan Ming, Tat-Seng Chua, Si Li, Hongfei Yan, and Xiaoming Li. 2012. Sshlda: A semi-supervised hierarchical topic model. In *EMNLP-CoNLL*, pages 800–809.

Yishu Miao, Lei Yu, and Phil Blunsom. 2016. Neural variational inference for text processing.

Feng Nan, Ran Ding, Ramesh Nallapati, and Bing Xiang. 2019. Topic modeling with wasserstein autoencoders.

Yves Petinot, Kathleen McKeown, and Kapil Thadani. 2011. A hierarchical model of web summaries. In *Proceedings of the 49th Annual Meeting of the Association for Computational Linguistics: Human Language Technologies*, pages 670–675, Portland, Oregon, USA. Association for Computational Linguistics.

Daniel Ramage, David Hall, Ramesh Nallapati, and Christopher D. Manning. 2009. Labeled lda: A supervised topic model for credit attribution in multi-labeled corpora. In *Proceedings of the 2009 Conference on Empirical Methods in Natural Language Processing: Volume 1 - Volume 1*, EMNLP '09, page 248–256, USA. Association for Computational Linguistics.

Jason Ren, Russell Kunes, and Finale Doshi-Velez. 2020. Prediction focused topic models via feature selection. In *International Conference on Artificial Intelligence and Statistics*, pages 4420–4429. PMLR.

Danilo Jimenez Rezende, Shakir Mohamed, and Daan Wierstra. 2014. Stochastic backpropagation and approximate inference in deep generative models. In *International conference on machine learning*, pages 1278–1286. PMLR.

Michal Rosen-Zvi, Thomas Griffiths, Mark Steyvers, and Padhraic Smyth. 2012. The author-topic model for authors and documents. *arXiv preprint arXiv:1207.4169*.

Nadine Schneider, Nikolas Fechner, Gregory A. Landrum, and Nikolaus Stiefl. 2017. Chemical topic modeling: Exploring molecular data sets using a common text-mining approach. *Journal of Chemical Information and Modeling*, 57(8):1816–1831. PMID: 28715190.

Abhishek Sharma, Catherine Zeng, Sanjana Narayanan, Sonali Parbhoo, and Finale Doshi-Velez. 2021. On learning prediction-focused mixtures. *arXiv preprint arXiv:2110.13221*.

Akash Srivastava and Charles Sutton. 2017. Autoencoding variational inference for topic models.

Xinyi Wang and Yi Yang. 2020. Neural topic model with attention for supervised learning. In *International Conference on Artificial Intelligence and Statistics*, pages 1147–1156. PMLR.

Florian Wenzel, Kevin Roth, Bastiaan Veeling, Jakub Swiatkowski, Linh Tran, Stephan Mandt, Jasper Snoek, Tim Salimans, Rodolphe Jenatton, and Sebastian Nowozin. 2020. How good is the bayes posterior in deep neural networks really? In *International Conference on Machine Learning*, pages 10248–10259. PMLR.

Xiaohui Yan, Jiafeng Guo, Yanyan Lan, and Xueqi Cheng. 2013. A biterm topic model for short texts. In *Proceedings of the 22nd international conference on World Wide Web*, pages 1445–1456.

Alon Zweig and Daphna Weinshall. 2013. Hierarchical regularization cascade for joint learning. In *International Conference on Machine Learning*, pages 37–45. PMLR.

A Appendix

A.1 Optimization Procedure

During optimization, there are three components of LI-NTM that are being trained: the encoder neural network, β (the word distributions per label and topic), and the classifier neural network. We found randomly initializing all three trainable components and training them together lead to undesirable local minima (both perplexity and classification accuracy were undesirable). Instead, we consistently achieved our best results by first training the classifier normally on the task before training all three components together. All experimental results shown used this optimization procedure.

A.2 Embedded Topic Model (ETM)

Please find the generative process for ETM below (Dieng et al., 2019a). Note that ETM has two latent dimensions. There is the L-dimensional embedding space which the vocabulary is embedded into and each document is represented by K latent topics. Furthermore, note that in ETM, each topic is represented by a vector $\alpha_k \in \mathbb{R}^L$ which is the embedded representation of the topic in embedding space. Furthermore, ETM defines an embedding matrix ρ with dimension $L \times K$ where the column ρ_v is the embedding of word v.

1. Draw topic proportions $\theta_d \sim \mathcal{LN}(0, I)$
2. For each word n in document:
   (a) Draw topic assignment $z_{dn} \sim \text{Cat}(\theta_d)$
   (b) Draw word $w_{dn} \sim \text{softmax}(\rho^T \alpha_{z_{dn}})$

A.3 Visualization of Topics

See Figure A1

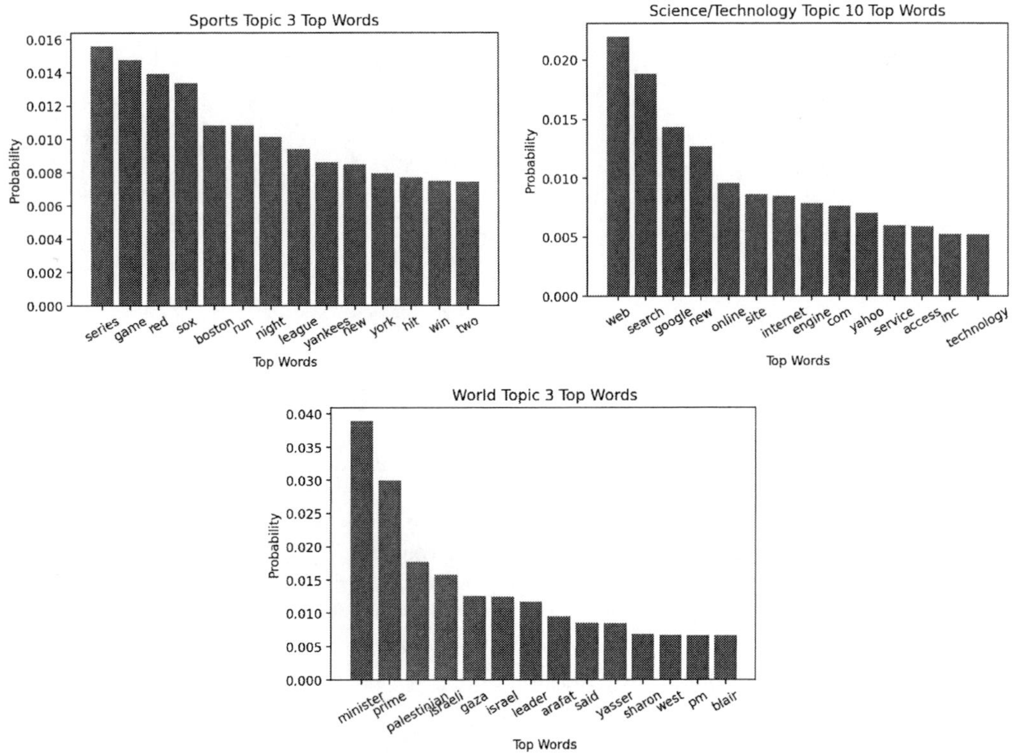

Figure A1: The probabilities of the top words from 5 selected topics from LINT-m. Note that LINT-m has the nice property that topics are naturally sorted by label unlike ETM. The first topic, with words like "series", "yankees", "red", "sox", corresponds to baseball. Note that perplexity will still be high even if this topic is correctly given a high proportion in a baseball-themed news article since there are many potential baseball teams and baseball terminology that the article could be referencing. The second topic corresponds to search engines, and the third corresponds to the Israeli–Palestinian conflict.

Neural String Edit Distance

Jindřich Libovický[1] and **Alexander Fraser**[2]
[1]Faculty of Mathematics and Physics, Charles University, Prague, Czech Republic
[2]Center for Information and Language Processing, LMU Munich, Germany
libovicky@ufal.mff.cuni.cz fraser@cis.lmu.de

Abstract

We propose the *neural string edit distance* model for string-pair matching and string transduction based on learnable string edit distance. We modify the original expectation-maximization learned edit distance algorithm into a differentiable loss function, allowing us to integrate it into a neural network providing a contextual representation of the input. We evaluate on cognate detection, transliteration, and grapheme-to-phoneme conversion, and show that we can trade off between performance and interpretability in a single framework. Using contextual representations, which are difficult to interpret, we match the performance of state-of-the-art string-pair matching models. Using static embeddings and a slightly different loss function, we force interpretability, at the expense of an accuracy drop.

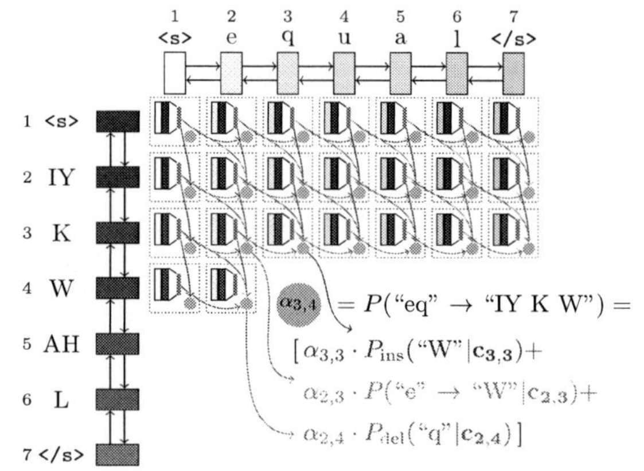

Figure 1: An example of applying the dynamic programming algorithm used to compute the edit probability score. It gradually fills the table of probabilities that prefixes of the word "equal" transcribe into prefixes of phoneme sequence "IY K W AH L". The probability (gray circles) depends on the probabilities of the prefixes and probabilities of plausible edit operations: insert (blue arrows), substitute (green arrows) and delete (red arrows).

1 Introduction

State-of-the-art models for string-pair classification and string transduction employ powerful neural architectures that lack interpretability. For example, BERT (Devlin et al., 2019) compares all input symbols with each other via 96 attention heads, whose functions are difficult to interpret. Moreover, attention itself can be hard to interpret (Jain and Wallace, 2019; Wiegreffe and Pinter, 2019).

In many tasks, such as in transliteration, a relation between two strings can be interpreted more simply as edit operations (Levenshtein, 1966). The edit operations define the alignment between the strings and provide an interpretation of how one string is transcribed into another. Learnable edit distance (Ristad and Yianilos, 1998) allows learning the weights of edit operations from data using the expectation-maximization (EM) algorithm. Unlike post-hoc analysis of black-box models, which depends on human qualitative judgment (Adadi and Berrada, 2018; Hoover et al., 2020; Lipton, 2018), the restricted set of edit operations allows direct interpretation. Unlike hard attention (Mnih et al., 2014; Indurthi et al., 2019) which also provides a discrete alignment between input and output, edit distance explicitly says how the input symbols are processed. Also, unlike models like Levenshtein Transformer (Gu et al., 2019), which does not explicitly align source and target uses edit operations to model intermediate generation steps only within the target string, learnable edit distance considers both source and target symbols to be a subject of the edit operations.

We reformulate the EM training used to train learnable edit distance as a differentiable loss function that can be used in a neural network. We propose two variants of models based on *neural string edit distance*: a bidirectional model for string-pair matching and a conditional model for string transduction. We evaluate on cognate detection, transliteration, and grapheme-to-phoneme (G2P) conver-

Proceedings of the Sixth Workshop on Structured Prediction for NLP, pages 52 - 66
May 27, 2022 ©2022 Association for Computational Linguistics

sion. The model jointly learns to perform the task and to generate a latent sequence of edit operations explaining the output. Our approach can flexibly trade off performance and intepretability by using input representations with various degrees of contextualization and outperforms methods that offer a similar degree of interpretability (Tam et al., 2019).

2 Learnable Edit Distance

Edit distance (Levenshtein, 1966) formalizes transcription of a string $\mathbf{s} = (s_1, \ldots, s_n)$ of n symbols from alphabet $\mathcal{S}$ into a string $\mathbf{t} = (t_1, \ldots, t_m)$ of m symbols from alphabet $\mathcal{T}$ as a sequence of operations: delete, insert and substitute, which have different costs.

Ristad and Yianilos (1998) reformulated operations as random events drawn from a distribution of all possible operations: deleting any $s \in \mathcal{S}$, inserting any $t \in \mathcal{T}$, and substituting any pair of symbols from $\mathcal{S} \times \mathcal{T}$. The probability $\mathrm{P}(\mathbf{s}, \mathbf{t}) = \alpha_{n,m}$ of $\mathbf{t}$ being edited from $\mathbf{s}$ can be expressed recursively:

$$\begin{aligned} \alpha_{n,m} &= \alpha_{n,m-1} \cdot \mathrm{P}_{\text{ins}}(t_m) + \\ &\quad \alpha_{n-1,m} \cdot \mathrm{P}_{\text{del}}(s_n) + \\ &\quad \alpha_{n-1,m-1} \cdot \mathrm{P}_{\text{subs}}(s_n, t_m) \end{aligned} \tag{1}$$

This can be computed using the dynamic programming algorithm of Wagner and Fischer (1974), which also computes values of $\alpha_{i,j}$ for all prefixes $\mathbf{s}_{:i}$ and $\mathbf{t}_{:j}$. The operation probabilities only depend on the individual pairs of symbols at positions i, j, so the same dynamic programming algorithm is used for computing the *suffix-pair* transcription probabilities $\beta_{i,j}$ (the backward probabilities).

With a training corpus of pairs of matching strings, the operation probabilities can be estimated using the EM algorithm. In the expectation step, expected counts of all edit operations are estimated for the current parameters using the training data. Each pair of symbols s_i and t_j contribute to the expected counts of the operations:

$$E_{\text{subs}}(s_i, t_j) \mathrel{+}= \alpha_{i-1,j-1} \mathrm{P}_{\text{subs}}(s_i, t_j) \beta_{i,j} / \alpha_{n,m} \tag{2}$$

and analogically for the delete and insert operations. In the maximization step, operation probabilities are estimated by normalizing the expected counts. See Algorithms 1–5 in Ristad and Yianilos (1998) for more details.

3 Neural String Edit Distance Model

In our model, we replace the discrete table of operation probabilities with a probability estimation based on a continuous representation of the input, which brings in the challenge of changing the EM training into a differentiable loss function that can be back-propagated into the representation.

Computation of the transcription probability is shown in Figure 1. We use the same dynamic programming algorithm (Equation 1 and Algorithm 2 in Appendix A) that gradually fills a table of probabilities row by row. The input symbols are represented by learned, possibly contextual embeddings (yellow and blue boxes in Figure 1) which are used to compute a representation of symbol pairs with a small feed-forward network. The symbol pair representation is used to estimate the probabilities of insert, delete and substitute operations (blue, red and green arrows in Figure 1).

Formally, we embed the source sequence $\mathbf{s}$ of length n into a matrix $\mathbf{h}^{\mathbf{s}} \in \mathbb{R}^{n \times d}$ and analogically $\mathbf{t}$ into $\mathbf{h}^{\mathbf{t}} \in \mathbb{R}^{m \times d}$ (yellow and blue boxes in Figure 1). We represent the symbol-pair contexts as a function of the respective symbol representations (small gray rectangles in Figure 1) as a function of repspective symbol representation $\mathbf{c}_{i,j} = f(\mathbf{h}^s_i, \mathbf{h}^t_j)$ depending on the task.

The logits (i.e., the probability scores before normalization) for the edit operations are obtained by concatenation of the following vectors (corresponds to red, green and blue arrows in Figure 1):

- $\mathbf{z}^{i,j}_{\text{del}} = \mathrm{Linear}(\mathbf{c}_{i-1,j}) \in \mathbb{R}^{d_{\text{del}}}$,
- $\mathbf{z}^{i,j}_{\text{ins}} = \mathrm{Linear}(\mathbf{c}_{i,j-1}) \in \mathbb{R}^{d_{\text{ins}}}$,
- $\mathbf{z}^{i,j}_{\text{subs}} = \mathrm{Linear}(\mathbf{c}_{i-1,j-1}) \in \mathbb{R}^{d_{\text{subs}}}$,

where $\mathrm{Linear}(\mathbf{x}) = \mathbf{W}\mathbf{x} + \mathbf{b}$ where $\mathbf{W}$ and $\mathbf{b}$ are trainable parameters of a linear projection and d_{del}, d_{ins} and d_{subs} are the numbers of possible delete, insert and substitute operations given the vocabularies. The distribution $\mathrm{P}_{i,j} \in \mathbb{R}^{d_{\text{del}}+d_{\text{ins}}+d_{\text{subs}}}$ over operations that lead to prefix pair $\mathbf{s}_{:i}$ and $\mathbf{t}_{:j}$ in a single derivation step is

$$\mathrm{P}_{i,j} = \mathrm{softmax}(\mathbf{z}^{i,j}_{\text{del}} \oplus \mathbf{z}^{i,j}_{\text{ins}} \oplus \mathbf{z}^{i,j}_{\text{subs}}).i, j \tag{3}$$

The probabilities $\mathrm{P}^{i,j}_{\text{del}}$, $\mathrm{P}^{i,j}_{\text{ins}}$ and $\mathrm{P}^{i,j}_{\text{subs}}$ are obtained by taking the respective values from the distribution corresponding to the logits.[1] Note that $\mathrm{P}_{i,j}$ only depends on (possibly contextual) input embeddings $\mathbf{h}^s_i$, $\mathbf{h}^s_{i-1}$, $\mathbf{h}^t_j$, and $\mathbf{h}^t_{j-1}$, but not on the derivation of prefix $\mathbf{t}_{:j}$ from $\mathbf{s}_{:i}$.

[1]Using Python-like notation $\mathrm{P}^{i,j}_{\text{del}} = \mathrm{P}_{i,j}[\,:d_{\text{del}}]$, $\mathrm{P}^{i,j}_{\text{ins}} = \mathrm{P}_{i,j}[d_{\text{del}} : d_{\text{del}}+d_{\text{ins}}]$, $\mathrm{P}^{i,j}_{\text{subs}} = \mathrm{P}_{i,j}[d_{\text{del}}+d_{\text{ins}} :\,]$.

Algorithm 1 Expectation-Maximization Loss

1: $\mathcal{L}_{\text{EM}} \leftarrow 0$
2: **for** $i = 1 \ldots n$ **do**
3:   **for** $j = 1 \ldots m$ **do**
4:     plausible $\leftarrow \mathbf{0}$ ▷ Indication vector
5:     ▷ I.e., operations that can be used given s_i and t_j
6:     **if** $j > 1$ **then** ▷ Insertion is plausible
7:       plausible $\mathrel{+}= \mathbb{1}(\text{insert } t_j)$
8:       $E^{\text{ins}}_{i,j} \leftarrow \alpha_{i,j-1} \cdot \mathrm{P}_{\text{ins}}(\bullet|\mathbf{c}_{i,j-1}) \cdot \beta_{i,j}$
9:     **if** $i > 1$ **then** ▷ Deletion is plausible
10:       plausible $\mathrel{+}= \mathbb{1}(\text{delete } s_i)$
11:       $E^{\text{del}}_{i,j} \leftarrow \alpha_{i-1,j} \mathrm{P}_{\text{del}}(\bullet|\mathbf{c}_{i-1,j}) \beta_{i,j}$
12:     **if** $i > 1$ and $j > 1$ **then** ▷ Subs. is plausible
13:       plausible $\mathrel{+}= \mathbb{1}(\text{substitute } s_i \rightarrow t_j)$
14:       $E^{\text{subs}}_{i,j} \leftarrow \alpha_{i-1,j-1} \cdot \mathrm{P}_{\text{subs}}(\bullet|\mathbf{c}_{i-1,j-1}) \cdot \beta_{i,j}$
15:     expected $\leftarrow$ normalize(plausible $\odot$
16:       $[E^{\text{ins}}_{i,j} \oplus E^{\text{del}}_{i,j} \oplus E^{\text{subs}}_{i,j}]$)
17:     ▷ Expected distr. can only contain plausible ops.
18:     $\mathcal{L}_{\text{EM}} \mathrel{+}= \mathrm{KL}(\mathrm{P}_{i,j} || \text{ expected})$
19: **return** $\mathcal{L}_{\text{EM}}$

The transduction probability $\alpha_{i,j}$, i.e., a probability that $\mathbf{s}_{:i}$ transcribes to $\mathbf{t}_{:j}$ (gray circles in Figure 1) is computed in the same way as in Equation 1.

The same algorithm with the reversed order of iteration can be used to compute probabilities $\beta_{i,j}$, the probability that suffix $\mathbf{s}_{i:}$ transcribes to $\mathbf{t}_{j:}$. The complete transduction probability is the same, i.e., $\beta_{1,1} = \alpha_{n,m}$. Tables α and β are used to compute the EM training loss $\mathcal{L}_{\text{EM}}$ (Algorithm 1) which is then optimized using gradient-based optimization. Symbol $\bullet$ in the probability stands for all possible operations (the operations that the model can assign a probability score to), "normalize"' means scale the values such that they sum up to one.

Unlike the statistical model that uses a single discrete multinomial distribution and stores the probabilities in a table, in our neural model the operation probabilities are conditioned on continuous vectors. For each operation type, we compute the expected distribution given the α and β tables (line 6–14). From this distribution, we only select operations that are plausible given the context (line 15), i.e., we zero out the probability of all operations that do not involve symbols s_i and t_j. Finally (line 18), we measure the KL divergence of the predicted operation distribution $\mathrm{P}_{i,j}$ (Equation 3) from the expected distribution, which is the loss function $\mathcal{L}_{\text{EM}}$.

With a trained model, we can estimate the probability of $\mathbf{t}$ being a good transcription of $\mathbf{s}$. Also, by replacing the summation in Equation 1 by the max operation, we can obtain the most probable operation sequence of operation transcribing $\mathbf{s}$ to $\mathbf{t}$ using the Viterbi (1967) algorithm.

Note that the interpretability of our model depends on how contextualized the input representations $\mathbf{h}^s$ and $\mathbf{h}^t$ are. The degree of contextualization spans from static symbol embeddings with the same strong interpretability as statistical models, to Transformers with richly contextualized representations, which, however, makes our model more similar to standard black-box models.

3.1 String-Pair Matching

Here, our goal is to train a binary classifier deciding if strings $\mathbf{t}$ and $\mathbf{s}$ match. We consider strings matching if $\mathbf{t}$ can be obtained by editing $\mathbf{s}$, with the probability $\mathrm{P}(\mathbf{s}, \mathbf{t}) = \alpha_{n,m}$ higher than a threshold. The model needs to learn to assign a high probability to derivations of matching the source string to the target string and low probability to derivations matching different target strings.

The symbol-pair context $\mathbf{c}_{i,j}$ is computed as

$$\mathrm{LN}\left(\mathrm{ReLU}\left(\mathrm{Linear}(\mathbf{h}^s_i \oplus \mathbf{h}^t_j)\right)\right) \in \mathbb{R}^d, \quad (4)$$

where LN stands for layer normalization and $\oplus$ means concatenation.

The statistical model assumes a single multinomial table over edit operations. A non-matching string pair gets little probability because all derivations (i.e., sequence of edit operations) of non-matching string pairs consist of low-probability operations and high probability is assigned to operations that are not plausible. In the neural model, the same information can be kept in model parameters and we can thus simplify the output space of the model (see Appendix B for thought experiments justifying the design choices).

We no longer need to explicitly model the probability of implausible operations and can only use *a single class* for each type of edit operation (insert, delete, substitute) and one additional *non-match* option that stands for the case when the inputs strings do not match and none of the plausible edit operations is probable (corresponding to the sum of probabilities of the implausible operations in the statistical model).

The value of $\mathrm{P}(\mathbf{s}, \mathbf{t}) = \alpha_{m,n}$ serves as a classification threshold for the binary classification. As additional training signal, we also explicitly optimize the probability using the binary cross-entropy as an auxiliary loss, pushing the value towards 1 for positive examples and towards 0 for negative examples. We set the classification threshold dynamically to maximize the validation F_1-score.

3.2 String Transduction

In the second use case, we use neural string edit distance as a string transduction model: given a source string, edit operations are applied to generate a target string. Unlike classification, we model the transcription process with vocabulary-specific-operations, but still use only a single class for deletion. For the insertion and substitution operation, we use $|\mathcal{T}|$ classes corresponding to the target string alphabet. Unlike classification, we do not add the non-match class. To better contextualize the generation, we add attention to the symbol-pair representation $\mathbf{c}_{i,j}$:

$$\mathrm{LN}\left(\mathrm{ReLU}\left(\mathrm{Linear}(\mathbf{h}_i^s \oplus \mathbf{h}_j^t)\right) \oplus \mathrm{Att}\left(\mathbf{h}_j^t, \mathbf{h}^s\right)\right) \tag{5}$$

of dimension $2d$, where $\mathrm{Att}(\mathbf{q}, \mathbf{v})$ is a multihead attention with queries $\mathbf{q}$ and keys and values $\mathbf{v}$.

While generating the string left-to-right, the only way a symbol can be generated is either by inserting it or by substituting a source symbol. Therefore, we estimate the probability of inserting symbol t_{j+1} given a target prefix $\mathbf{t}_{:j}$ from the probabilities of inserting a symbol after t_j or substituting any s_i by t_{j+1} (i.e., averaging over a row in Figure 1):

$$P(t_{j+1}|\hat{\mathbf{t}}_{:j}, \mathbf{s}) = \sum_{j=1}^{|S|} \alpha_{i,j} \mathrm{P}_{\text{ins}}(t_{j+1}|\mathbf{c}_{i,j}) + \sum_{j=2}^{|S|} \alpha_{i,j} \mathrm{P}_{\text{subs}}(s_i, t_{j+1}|\mathbf{c}_{i,j}). \tag{6}$$

Probabilities P_{ins} and P_{subs} are respective parts of the distribution $\mathrm{P}_{i,j}$ (Equation 3). Probablity P_{del} is unkown at this point because computing it would be computed based on state $\mathbf{c}_{i,j+1}$ which is impossible without what the $(j+1)$-th target symbol is, where logits for P_{ins} and P_{subs} use $\mathbf{c}_{i,j}$ and $\mathbf{c}_{i-1,j}$. Therefore, we approximate Equation 3 as

$$\hat{\mathrm{P}}_{i,j} = \mathrm{softmax}\left(\mathbf{z}_{\text{ins}}^{i,j} \oplus \mathbf{z}_{\text{subs}}^{i,j}\right). \tag{7}$$

At inference time, we decide the next symbol $\hat{t}_j$ based on $\hat{P}_{i,j}$. Knowing the symbol allows computing the $\mathrm{P}_{i,j}$ distribution and values $\alpha_{\bullet,j}$ that are used in the next step of inference. The inference can be done using the beam search algorithm as is done with sequence-to-sequence (S2S) models.

We also use the probability distribution $\hat{P}$ to define an additional training objective which is the *negative log-likelihood* of the ground truth output with respect to this distribution, analogically to training S2S models,

$$\mathcal{L}_{\text{NLL}} = -\sum_{j=0}^{|\mathbf{t}|} \log \sum_{i=0}^{|\mathbf{s}|} \hat{\mathrm{P}}_{i,j} / |\mathbf{s}|. \tag{8}$$

3.3 Interpretability Loss

In our preliminary experiments with Viterbi decoding, we noticed that the model tends to avoid the substitute operation and chose an order of insert and delete operations that is not interpretable. To prevent this behavior, we introduce an additional regularization loss. To decrease the values of α that are further from the diagonal, we add the term $\sum_{i=1}^{n} \sum_{j=1}^{m} |i-j| \cdot \alpha_{i,j}$ to the loss function. Note that this formulation assumes that the source and target sequence have similar lengths. For tasks where the sequence lengths vary significantly, we would need to consider the sequence length in the loss function.

In the string transduction model, optimization of this term can lead to a degenerate solution by flattening all distributions and thus lowering all values in table α. We thus compensate for this loss by adding the $-\log \alpha_{n,m}$ term to the loss function which enforces increasing the α values.

4 Experiments

We evaluate the string-pair matching model on cognate detection, and the string transduction model on Arabic-to-English transliteration and English grapheme-to-phoneme conversion.

In all tasks, we study four ways of representing the input symbols with different degrees of contextualization. The interpretable context-free (unigram) encoder uses symbol embeddings summed with learned position embeddings. We use a 1-D convolutional neural network (CNN) for locally contexualized representation where hidden states correspond to consecutive input n-grams. We use bidirectional recurrent networks (RNNs) and Transformers (Vaswani et al., 2017) for fully contextualized input representations.

Architectural details and hyperparameters are listed in Appendix C. All hyperparameters are set manually based on preliminary experiments. Further hyperparameter tuning can likely lead to better accuracy of both baselines and our model.

	Method	# Param.	Indo-European			Austro-Asiatic		
			Plain	+ Int. loss	Time	Plain	+ Int. loss	Time
	Learnable edit distance	0.2M	32.8 ±1.8	—	0.4h	10.3 ±0.5	—	0.2h
	Transformer [CLS]	2.7M	93.5 ±2.1	—	0.7h	78.5 ±0.8	—	0.6h
STANCE	unigram	0.5M	46.2 ±4.9	—	0.2h	16.6 ±0.3	—	0.1h
STANCE	RNN	1.9M	80.6 ±1.2	—	0.3h	15.9 ±0.2	—	0.2h
STANCE	Transformer	2.7M	76.7 ±1.3	—	0.3h	16.7 ±0.3	—	0.2h
ours	unigram	0.5M	78.5 ±1.0	80.1 ±0.8	1.5h	47.8 ±0.7	48.4 ±0.6	0.7h
ours	CNN (3-gram)	0.7M	94.0 ±0.7	93.9 ±0.8	0.9h	77.9 ±1.5	76.2 ±1.9	0.5h
ours	RNN	1.9M	96.9 ±0.6	**97.1 ±0.6**	1.9h	**84.0 ±0.4**	83.7 ±0.5	1.2h
ours	Transformer	2.7M	87.2 ±1.6	87.3 ±1.8	1.6h	69.9 ±1.0	70.7 ±1.1	1.0h

Table 1: F_1 and training time for cognate detection. F_1 on validation is in Table 6 in the Appendix.

However, preliminary experiments showed that increasing the model size only has a small effect on model accuracy. We run every experiment 5 times and report the mean performance and the standard deviation to control for training stability. The source code for the experiments is available at https://github.com/jlibovicky/neural-string-edit-distance.

Cognate Detection. Cognate detection is the task of detecting if words in different languages have the same origin. We experiment with Austro-Asiatic languages (Sidwell, 2015) and Indo-European languages (Dunn, 2012) normalized into the international phonetic alphabet as provided by Rama et al. (2018).[2]

For Indo-European languages, we have 9,855 words (after excluding singleton-class words) from 43 languages forming 2,158 cognate classes. For Austro-Asiatic languages, the dataset contains 11,828 words of 59 languages, forming only 98 cognate classes without singletons. We generate classification pairs from these datasets by randomly sampling 10 negative examples for each true cognate pair. We use 20k pairs for validation and testing, leaving 1.5M training examples for Indo-European and 80M for Austro-Asiatic languages.

Many cognate detection methods are unsupervised and are evaluated by comparison of a clustering from the method with true cognate classes. We train a supervised classifier, so we use F_1-score on our splits of the dataset.

Because the input and the output are from the same alphabet, we share the parameters of the encoders of the source and target sequences.

As a baseline we use the original statistical learnable edit distance (Ristad and Yianilos, 1998). The well-performing black-box model used as another baseline for comparison with our model is a Transformer processing a concatenation of the two input strings. Similar to BERT (Devlin et al., 2019), we use the representation of the first technical symbol as an input to a linear classifier. We also compare our results with the STANCE model (Tam et al., 2019), a neural model utilizing optimal-transport-based alignment over input text representation which makes similar claims about interpretability as we do. Similar to our model, we experiment with various degrees of representation contextualization.

Transliteration and G2P Conversion. For string transduction, we test our model on two tasks: Arabic-to-English transliteration (Rosca and Breuel, 2016)[3] and English G2P conversion using the CMUDict dataset (Weide, 2017)[4].

The Arabic-to-English transliteration dataset consists of 12,877 pairs for training, 1,431 for validation, and 1,590 for testing. The source-side alphabet uses 47 different symbols; the target side uses 39. The CMUDict dataset contains 108,952 training, 5,447 validation, and 12,855 test examples, 10,999 unique. The dataset uses 27 different graphemes and 39 phonemes.

We evaluate the output strings using Character Error Rate (CER): the standard edit distance between the generated hypotheses and the ground truth string divided by the ground-truth string length; and Word Error Rate (WER): the proportion of words that were transcribed incorrectly. The CMUDict dataset contains multiple transcriptions

[2]https://www.aclweb.org/anthology/attachments/N18-2063.Datasets.zip

[3]https://github.com/google/transliteration

[4]https://github.com/microsoft/CNTK/tree/master/Examples/SequenceToSequence/CMUDict/Data

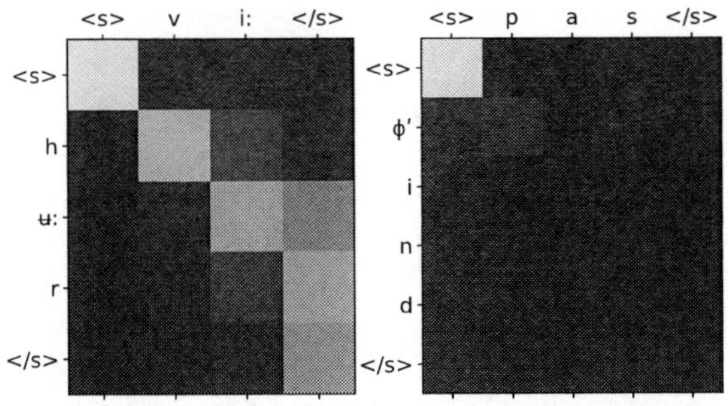

Figure 2: Visualization of the α table (0 is dark blue, 1 is yellow) for cognate detection using a unigram model. Left: A *cognate* pair, Right: a *non-cognate* pair

Loss functions	F_1
Complete loss	97.1 ±0.6
— binary XENT for $\alpha_{m,n}$	96.1 ±0.3
— expectation-maximization (Alg. 1)	96.3 ±0.7

Table 2: Ablation study for loss function on Cognate classification with a model with RNN contextualizer.

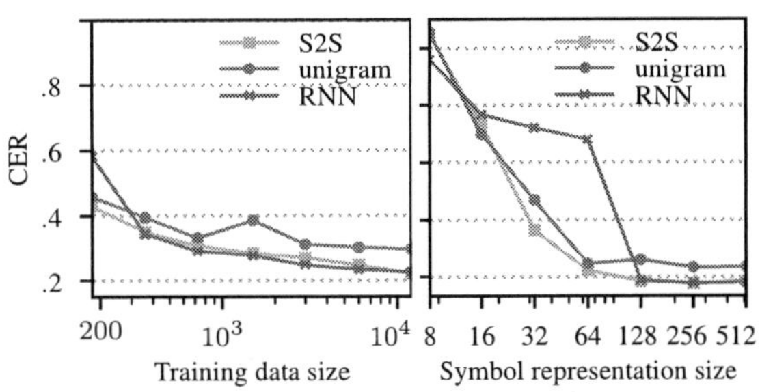

Figure 3: Character Error Rate for Arabic transliteration into English for *various training data sizes* (left) and *various representation sizes* (right).

for some words, as is usually done we select the transcription with the lowest CER as a reference.

Unlike the string-matching task, the future target symbols are unknown. Therefore, when using the contextual representations, we encode the target string using a single-direction RNN and using a masked Transformer, respectively.

To evaluate our model under low-resource conditions, we conduct two sets of additional experiments with the transliteration of Arabic. We compare our unigram and RNN-based models with the RNN-based S2S model trained on smaller subsets of training data (6k, 3k, 1.5k, 750, 360, 180, and 60 training examples) and different embedding and hidden state size (8, 16, ..., 512).

For the G2P task, where the source and target symbols can be approximately aligned, we further quantitatively assess the model's interpretability by measuring how well it captures alignment between the source and target string. We consider the substitutions in the Viterbi decoding to be aligned symbols. We compare this alignment with statistical word alignment and report the F_1 score. We obtain the source-target strings alignment using Efmaral (Östling and Tiedemann, 2016), a state-of-the-art word aligner, by running the aligner on the entire CMUDict dataset. We use grow-diagonal for alignment symmetrization.

The baseline models are RNN-based (Bahdanau et al., 2015) and Transformer-based (Vaswani et al., 2017) S2S models.

5 Results

Cognate Detection. The results of cognate detection are presented in Table 1 (learning curves are in Figure 5 in Appendix). In cognate detection, our model significantly outperforms both the statistical baseline and the STANCE model. The F_1-score achieved by the unigram model is worse than the Transformer classifier by a large margin. Local representation contextualization with CNN reaches similar performance as the black-box Transformer classifier while retaining a similar strong interpretability to the static embeddings. Models with RNN encoders outperform the baseline classifier, whereas the Transformer encoder yields slightly worse results. Detecting cognates seems to be more difficult in Austro-Asiatic languages than in Indo-European languages. The training usually converges before finishing a single epoch of the training data. An example of how the α captures the prefix-pair probabilities is shown in Figure 2. The interpretability loss only has a negligible (although mostly slightly negative) influence on the accuracy, within the variance of training runs. The ablation study on loss functions (Table 2) shows that the binary cross-entropy plays a more important role. The EM loss alone works remarkably well given that it was trained on positive examples only.

Transliteration and G2P Conversion. The results for the two transduction tasks are presented in Table 3 (learning curves are in Figure 5 in Appendix). Our transliteration baseline slightly outperforms the baseline presented with the dataset (Rosca and Breuel, 2016, 22.4% CER, 77.1% WER). Our baselines for the G2P conversion perform slightly worse than the best models by

Method		# Param.	Arabic → English					CMUDict						
			Plain		+ Interpret. loss		Time	Plain			+ Interpret. loss			Time
			CER	WER	CER	WER		CER	WER	Align.	CER	WER	Align.	
RNN Seq2seq		3.3M	22.0 ±0.2	75.8 ±0.6	—	—	12m	5.8 ±0.1	23.6 ±0.9	24.5	—	—	—	1.8h
Transformer		3.1M	22.9 ±0.2	78.5 ±0.4	—	—	11m	6.5 ±0.1	26.6 ±0.3	33.2	—	—	—	1.1h
ours	unigram	0.7M	31.7 ±1.8	85.2 ±0.9	31.2 ±1.4	85.0 ±0.5	36m	20.9 ±0.3	67.5 ±1.0	55.7	20.6 ±0.3	66.3 ±0.2	59.5	2.4h
ours	CNN (3-gram)	1.1M	24.6 ±0.6	80.5 ±0.3	24.5 ±0.9	80.1 ±0.9	41m	12.8 ±1.0	48.4 ±3.1	35.4	12.8 ±0.2	48.4 ±0.6	38.1	2.5h
ours	Deep CNN	3.0M	24.4 ±0.5	80.0 ±0.7	23.8 ±0.3	79.3 ±0.1	52m	10.8 ±0.5	41.4 ±1.9	23.3	10.8 ±0.5	42.1 ±1.6	28.8	2.5h
ours	RNN	2.9M	24.1 ±0.2	77.0 ±2.0	22.0 ±0.3	77.4 ±0.8	60m	7.8 ±0.3	31.9 ±1.3	44.7	7.3 ±0.4	33.3 ±1.5	48.9	2.3h
ours	Transformer	3.2M	24.3 ±0.9	79.0 ±0.7	23.9 ±1.6	78.6 ±1.3	1.2h	10.7 ±1.0	41.8 ±3.1	33.3	10.2 ±1.1	43.6 ±3.2	37.9	2.3h

Table 3: Model error rates for Arabic-to-English transliteration and English G2P generation and respective training times. For the second data set, we also report the alignment F_1 scores (Align.). Our best models are in bold. The error rates on the validation data are in Table 7 in the Appendix.

Loss functions	CER	WER
Complete loss	22.5 ±0.3	77.4 ±0.8
— expectation maximization	68.2 ±7.4	93.5 ±1.0
— next symbol NLL	27.2 ±1.4	81.1 ±2.2
— $\alpha_{m,n}$ maximization	23.5 ±1.3	79.2 ±2.5

Table 4: Ablation study for loss function on Arabic-to-English transliteration using RNN and the underlying representation.

Yolchuyeva et al. (2019), which had 5.4% CER and 22.1% WER with a twice as large model, and 6.5% CER and 23.9% WER with a similarly sized one.

The transliteration of Arabic appears to be a simpler problem than G2P conversion. The performance matches S2S, has fast training times, and there is a smaller gap between the error rates of the context-free and contextualized models.

The training time of our transduction models is 2–3× higher than with the baseline S2S models because the baseline models use builtin PyTorch functions, whereas our model is implemented using loops using TorchScript[5] (15% faster than plain Python). The performance under low data conditions and with small model capacity is in Figure 3.

Models that use static symbol embeddings as the input perform worse than the black-box S2S models in both tasks. Local contextualization with CNN improves the performance over static symbol embeddings. Using the fully contextualized input representation narrows the performance gap between S2S models and neural string edit distance models at the expense of decreased interpretability because all input states can, in theory, contain information about the entire input sequence. The ability to preserve source-target alignment is highest when the input is represented by embeddings only. RNN models not only have the best accuracy, but also capture quite well the source-target alignment. We hypothesize that RNNs work well because of their inductive bias towards sequence processing, which might be hard to learn from position embeddings given the task dataset sizes.

Including the interpretability loss usually slightly improves the accuracy and improves the alignment between the source and target strings. It manifests both qualitatively (Table 5) and quantitatively in the increased alignment accuracy.

Compared to S2S models, beam search decoding leads to much higher accuracy gains, with beam search 5 reaching around 2× error reduction compared to greedy decoding. For all input representations except the static embeddings, length normalization does not improve decoding. Unlike machine translation models, accuracy doesn't degrade with increasing beam size. See Figure 4 in Appendix.

The ablation study on loss functions (Table 4) shows that all loss functions contribute to the final accuracy. The EM loss is most important, direct optimization of the likelihood is second.

6 Related Work

Weighted finite-state transducers. Rastogi et al. (2016) use a weighted-finite state transducer (WFST) with neural scoring function to model sequence transduction. As in our model, they back-propagate the error via a dynamic program. Our model is stronger because, in the WFST, the output symbol generation only depends on the contextualized source symbol embedding, disregarding the string generated so far.

Lin et al. (2019) extend the model by including contextualized target string representation and edit operation history. This makes their model more powerful than ours, but the loss function cannot be exactly computed by dynamic programming and

[5]https://pytorch.org/docs/stable/jit.html

graphemes	phonemes	edit operations
GOELLER	G OW L ER	G→G -O -E -L L→OW +L -E R→ER G→G O→OW -E -L L→L -E R→ER
VOGAN	V OW G AH N	V→V -O G→OW +G +AH -A N→N V→V +OW -O G→G -A N→N
FLAGSHIPS	F L AE G SH IH P S	F→F L→L -A -G S→AE +G -H +SH -I P→IH +P +S F→F L→L +AE -A G→G -S H→SH +IH -I P→P S→S
ENDLER	EH N D L ER	+EH -E N→N D→D L→L -E R→ER E→EH N→N D→D L→L -E R→ER
SWOOPED	S W UW P T	S→S W→W +UW -O -O P→P -E D→T S→S W→W -O O→UW P→P -E D→T

Table 5: Edit operations predicted by RNN-based model for grapheme (blue) to phoneme (green) conversion with and without the interpretability loss (when provided ground-truth target). Green boxes are insertions, blue boxes deletions, yellow boxes substitutions.

requires sampling possible operation sequences.

Segment to Segment Neural Transduction. Yu et al. (2016) use two operation algorithm (shift and emit) for string transduction. Unlike our model directly, it models independently the operation type and target symbols and lacks the concept of symbol substitution.

Neural sequence matching. Several neural sequence-matching methods utilize a scoring function similar to symbol-pair representation. Cuturi and Blondel (2017) propose integrating alignment between two sequences into a loss function that eventually leads to finding alignment between the sequences. The STANCE model (Tam et al., 2019), which we compare results with, first computes the alignment as an optimal transfer problem between the source and target representation. In the second step, they assign a score using a convolutional neural network applied to a soft-alignment matrix. We showed that our model reaches better accuracy with the same input representation. Similar to our model, these approaches provide interpretability via alignment. They allow many-to-many alignments, but cannot enforce a monotonic sequence of operations unlike WFSTs and our model.

Learnable edit distance. McCallum et al. (2005) used trainable edit distance in combination with CRFs for string matching. Recently, Riley and Gildea (2020) integrated the statistical learnable edit distance within a pipeline for unsupervised bilingual lexicon induction. As far as we know, our work is the first using neural networks directly in dynamic programming for edit distance.

Edit distance in deep learning. LaserTagger (Malmi et al., 2019) and EditNTS (Dong et al., 2019) formulate sequence generation as tagging of the source text with edit operations. They use standard edit distance to pre-process the data (so, unlike our model cannot work with different alphabets) and then learn to predict the edit operations. Levenshtein Transformer (Gu et al., 2019) is a partially non-autoregressive S2S model generating the output iteratively via insert and delete operations. It delivers a good trade-off of decoding speed and translation quality, but is not interpretable.

Dynamic programming in deep learning. Combining dynamic programming and neural-network-based estimators is a common technique, especially in sequence modeling. Connectionist Temporal Classification (CTC; Graves et al., 2006) uses the forward-backward algorithm to estimate the loss of assigning labels to a sequence with implicit alignment. The loss function of a linear-chain conditional random field propagated into a neural network (Do and Artieres, 2010) became the state-of-the-art for tasks like named entity recognition (Lample et al., 2016). Loss functions based on dynamic programming are also used in non-autoregressive neural machine translation (Libovický and Helcl, 2018; Saharia et al., 2020).

Cognate detection. Due to the limited amount of annotated data, cognate detection is usually approached using unsupervised methods. Strings are compared using measures such as pointwise mutual information (Jäger, 2014) or LexStat similarity (List, 2012), which are used as an input to a distance-based clustering algorithm (List et al.,

2016). Jäger et al. (2017) used a supervised SVM classifier trained on one language family using features that were previously used for clustering and applied the classifier to other language families.

Transliteration. Standard S2S models (Bahdanau et al., 2015; Gehring et al., 2017; Vaswani et al., 2017) or CTC-based sequence-labeling (Graves et al., 2006) are the state of the art for both transliteration (Rosca and Breuel, 2016; Kundu et al., 2018) and G2P conversion (Yao and Zweig, 2015; Peters et al., 2017; Yolchuyeva et al., 2019).

7 Conclusions

We introduced neural string edit distance, a neural model of string transduction based on string edit distance. Our novel formulation of neural string edit distance critically depends on a differentiable loss. When used with context-free representations, it offers a direct interpretability via insert, delete and substitute operations, unlike widely used S2S models. Using input representations with differing amounts of contextualization, we can trade off interpretability for better performance. Our experimental results on cognate detection, Arabic-to-English transliteration and grapheme-to-phoneme conversion show that with contextualized input representations, the proposed model is able to match the performance of standard black-box models. We hope that our approach will help motivate more work on this type of interpretable model and that our framework will be useful in such future work.

Acknowledgments

The work at LMU Munich was supported by was supported by the European Research Council (ERC) under the European Union's Horizon 2020 research and innovation programme (No. 640550) and by the German Research Foundation (DFG; grant FR 2829/4-1). The work at CUNI was supported by the European Commission via its Horizon 2020 research and innovation programme (No. 870930).

References

Amina Adadi and Mohammed Berrada. 2018. Peeking inside the black-box: A survey on explainable artificial intelligence (xai). *IEEE Access*, 6:52138–52160.

Lei Jimmy Ba, Jamie Ryan Kiros, and Geoffrey E. Hinton. 2016. Layer normalization. *CoRR*, abs/1607.06450.

Dzmitry Bahdanau, Kyunghyun Cho, and Yoshua Bengio. 2015. Neural machine translation by jointly learning to align and translate. In *3rd International Conference on Learning Representations, ICLR 2015, San Diego, CA, USA, May 7-9, 2015, Conference Track Proceedings*.

Mia Xu Chen, Orhan Firat, Ankur Bapna, Melvin Johnson, Wolfgang Macherey, George Foster, Llion Jones, Mike Schuster, Noam Shazeer, Niki Parmar, Ashish Vaswani, Jakob Uszkoreit, Lukasz Kaiser, Zhifeng Chen, Yonghui Wu, and Macduff Hughes. 2018. The best of both worlds: Combining recent advances in neural machine translation. In *Proceedings of the 56th Annual Meeting of the Association for Computational Linguistics (Volume 1: Long Papers)*, pages 76–86, Melbourne, Australia. Association for Computational Linguistics.

Kyunghyun Cho, Bart van Merriënboer, Caglar Gulcehre, Dzmitry Bahdanau, Fethi Bougares, Holger Schwenk, and Yoshua Bengio. 2014. Learning phrase representations using RNN encoder–decoder for statistical machine translation. In *Proceedings of the 2014 Conference on Empirical Methods in Natural Language Processing (EMNLP)*, pages 1724–1734, Doha, Qatar. Association for Computational Linguistics.

Marco Cuturi and Mathieu Blondel. 2017. Soft-DTW: a differentiable loss function for time-series. volume 70 of *Proceedings of Machine Learning Research*, pages 894–903, International Convention Centre, Sydney, Australia. PMLR.

Yann N. Dauphin, Angela Fan, Michael Auli, and David Grangier. 2017. Language modeling with gated convolutional networks. In *Proceedings of the 34th International Conference on Machine Learning, ICML 2017, Sydney, NSW, Australia, 6-11 August 2017*, volume 70 of *Proceedings of Machine Learning Research*, pages 933–941. PMLR.

Jacob Devlin, Ming-Wei Chang, Kenton Lee, and Kristina Toutanova. 2019. BERT: Pre-training of deep bidirectional transformers for language understanding. In *Proceedings of the 2019 Conference of the North American Chapter of the Association for Computational Linguistics: Human Language Technologies, Volume 1 (Long and Short Papers)*, pages 4171–4186, Minneapolis, Minnesota. Association for Computational Linguistics.

Trinh–Minh–Tri Do and Thierry Artieres. 2010. Neural conditional random fields. In *Proceedings of the Thirteenth International Conference on Artificial Intelligence and Statistics*, volume 9 of *Proceedings of Machine Learning Research*, pages 177–184, Chia Laguna Resort, Sardinia, Italy. PMLR.

Yue Dong, Zichao Li, Mehdi Rezagholizadeh, and Jackie Chi Kit Cheung. 2019. EditNTS: An neural programmer-interpreter model for sentence simplification through explicit editing. In *Proceedings of the 57th Annual Meeting of the Association for Computational Linguistics*, pages 3393–3402, Florence, Italy. Association for Computational Linguistics.

Michael Dunn. 2012. Indo-European lexical cognacy database (IELex). Nijmegen, The Netherlands. Max Planck Institute for Psycholinguistics.

Jonas Gehring, Michael Auli, David Grangier, Denis Yarats, and Yann N. Dauphin. 2017. Convolutional sequence to sequence learning. In *Proceedings of the 34th International Conference on Machine Learning, ICML 2017, Sydney, NSW, Australia, 6-11 August 2017*, volume 70 of *Proceedings of Machine Learning Research*, pages 1243–1252. PMLR.

Alex Graves, Santiago Fernández, Faustino Gomez, and Jürgen Schmidhuber. 2006. Connectionist temporal classification: labelling unsegmented sequence data with recurrent neural networks. In *Proceedings of the 23rd international conference on Machine learning*, pages 369–376. ACM.

Jiatao Gu, Changhan Wang, and Junbo Zhao. 2019. Levenshtein transformer. In *Advances in Neural Information Processing Systems*, pages 11179–11189.

Kaiming He, Xiangyu Zhang, Shaoqing Ren, and Jian Sun. 2016. Deep residual learning for image recognition. In *2016 IEEE Conference on Computer Vision and Pattern Recognition, CVPR 2016, Las Vegas, NV, USA, June 27-30, 2016*, pages 770–778. IEEE Computer Society.

Benjamin Hoover, Hendrik Strobelt, and Sebastian Gehrmann. 2020. exBERT: A Visual Analysis Tool to Explore Learned Representations in Transformer Models. In *Proceedings of the 58th Annual Meeting of the Association for Computational Linguistics: System Demonstrations*, pages 187–196, Online. Association for Computational Linguistics.

Sathish Reddy Indurthi, Insoo Chung, and Sangha Kim. 2019. Look harder: A neural machine translation model with hard attention. In *Proceedings of the 57th Annual Meeting of the Association for Computational Linguistics*, pages 3037–3043, Florence, Italy. Association for Computational Linguistics.

Gerhard Jäger. 2014. Phylogenetic inference from word lists using weighted alignment with empirically determined weights. In *Quantifying Language Dynamics*, pages 155–204. Brill.

Gerhard Jäger, Johann-Mattis List, and Pavel Sofroniev. 2017. Using support vector machines and state-of-the-art algorithms for phonetic alignment to identify cognates in multi-lingual wordlists. In *Proceedings of the 15th Conference of the European Chapter of the Association for Computational Linguistics: Volume 1, Long Papers*, pages 1205–1216, Valencia, Spain. Association for Computational Linguistics.

Sarthak Jain and Byron C. Wallace. 2019. Attention is not Explanation. In *Proceedings of the 2019 Conference of the North American Chapter of the Association for Computational Linguistics: Human Language Technologies, Volume 1 (Long and Short Papers)*, pages 3543–3556, Minneapolis, Minnesota. Association for Computational Linguistics.

Diederik P. Kingma and Jimmy Ba. 2015. Adam: A method for stochastic optimization. In *3rd International Conference on Learning Representations, ICLR 2015, San Diego, CA, USA, May 7-9, 2015, Conference Track Proceedings*.

Soumyadeep Kundu, Sayantan Paul, and Santanu Pal. 2018. A deep learning based approach to transliteration. In *Proceedings of the Seventh Named Entities Workshop*, pages 79–83, Melbourne, Australia. Association for Computational Linguistics.

Guillaume Lample, Miguel Ballesteros, Sandeep Subramanian, Kazuya Kawakami, and Chris Dyer. 2016. Neural architectures for named entity recognition. In *Proceedings of the 2016 Conference of the North American Chapter of the Association for Computational Linguistics: Human Language Technologies*, pages 260–270, San Diego, California. Association for Computational Linguistics.

Vladimir I Levenshtein. 1966. Binary codes capable of correcting deletions, insertions, and reversals. In *Soviet physics doklady*, volume 10, pages 707–710.

Jindřich Libovický and Jindřich Helcl. 2018. End-to-end non-autoregressive neural machine translation with connectionist temporal classification. In *Proceedings of the 2018 Conference on Empirical Methods in Natural Language Processing*, pages 3016–3021, Brussels, Belgium. Association for Computational Linguistics.

Chu-Cheng Lin, Hao Zhu, Matthew R. Gormley, and Jason Eisner. 2019. Neural finite-state transducers: Beyond rational relations. In *Proceedings of the 2019 Conference of the North American Chapter of the Association for Computational Linguistics: Human Language Technologies, Volume 1 (Long and Short Papers)*, pages 272–283, Minneapolis, Minnesota. Association for Computational Linguistics.

Zachary C. Lipton. 2018. The mythos of model interpretability. *Queue*, 16(3):31–57.

Johann-Mattis List. 2012. LexStat: Automatic detection of cognates in multilingual wordlists. In *Proceedings of the EACL 2012 Joint Workshop of LINGVIS & UNCLH*, pages 117–125, Avignon, France. Association for Computational Linguistics.

Johann-Mattis List, Philippe Lopez, and Eric Bapteste. 2016. Using sequence similarity networks to identify partial cognates in multilingual wordlists. In *Proceedings of the 54th Annual Meeting of the Association for Computational Linguistics (Volume 2: Short Papers)*, pages 599–605, Berlin, Germany. Association for Computational Linguistics.

Eric Malmi, Sebastian Krause, Sascha Rothe, Daniil Mirylenka, and Aliaksei Severyn. 2019. Encode, tag, realize: High-precision text editing. In *Proceedings of the 2019 Conference on Empirical Methods in Natural Language Processing and the 9th International Joint Conference on Natural Language Processing (EMNLP-IJCNLP)*, pages 5054–5065, Hong Kong, China. Association for Computational Linguistics.

Andrew McCallum, Kedar Bellare, and Fernando C. N. Pereira. 2005. A conditional random field for discriminatively-trained finite-state string edit distance. In *UAI '05, Proceedings of the 21st Conference in Uncertainty in Artificial Intelligence, Edinburgh, Scotland, July 26-29, 2005*, pages 388–395. AUAI Press.

Volodymyr Mnih, Nicolas Heess, Alex Graves, and Koray Kavukcuoglu. 2014. Recurrent models of visual attention. In *Advances in Neural Information Processing Systems 27: Annual Conference on Neural Information Processing Systems 2014, December 8-13 2014, Montreal, Quebec, Canada*, pages 2204–2212.

Robert Östling and Jörg Tiedemann. 2016. Efficient word alignment with Markov Chain Monte Carlo. *Prague Bulletin of Mathematical Linguistics*, 106:125–146.

Ben Peters, Jon Dehdari, and Josef van Genabith. 2017. Massively multilingual neural grapheme-to-phoneme conversion. In *Proceedings of the First Workshop on Building Linguistically Generalizable NLP Systems*, pages 19–26, Copenhagen, Denmark. Association for Computational Linguistics.

Taraka Rama, Johann-Mattis List, Johannes Wahle, and Gerhard Jäger. 2018. Are automatic methods for cognate detection good enough for phylogenetic reconstruction in historical linguistics? In *Proceedings of the 2018 Conference of the North American Chapter of the Association for Computational Linguistics: Human Language Technologies, Volume 2 (Short Papers)*, pages 393–400, New Orleans, Louisiana. Association for Computational Linguistics.

Pushpendre Rastogi, Ryan Cotterell, and Jason Eisner. 2016. Weighting finite-state transductions with neural context. In *Proceedings of the 2016 Conference of the North American Chapter of the Association for Computational Linguistics: Human Language Technologies*, pages 623–633, San Diego, California. Association for Computational Linguistics.

Parker Riley and Daniel Gildea. 2020. Unsupervised bilingual lexicon induction across writing systems. *CoRR*, abs/2002.00037.

Eric Sven Ristad and Peter N. Yianilos. 1998. Learning string-edit distance. *IEEE Trans. Pattern Anal. Mach. Intell.*, 20(5):522–532.

Mihaela Rosca and Thomas Breuel. 2016. Sequence-to-sequence neural network models for transliteration. *CoRR*, abs/1610.09565.

Chitwan Saharia, William Chan, Saurabh Saxena, and Mohammad Norouzi. 2020. Non-autoregressive machine translation with latent alignments. In *Proceedings of the 2020 Conference on Empirical Methods in Natural Language Processing (EMNLP)*, pages 1098–1108, Online. Association for Computational Linguistics.

Paul Sidwell. 2015. Austroasiatic dataset for phylogenetic analysis: 2015 version. *Mon-Khmer Studies (Notes, Reviews, Data-Papers)*, 44:lxviii–ccclvii.

Derek Tam, Nicholas Monath, Ari Kobren, Aaron Traylor, Rajarshi Das, and Andrew McCallum. 2019. Optimal transport-based alignment of learned character representations for string similarity. In *Proceedings of the 57th Annual Meeting of the Association for Computational Linguistics*, pages 5907–5917, Florence, Italy. Association for Computational Linguistics.

Ashish Vaswani, Noam Shazeer, Niki Parmar, Jakob Uszkoreit, Llion Jones, Aidan N. Gomez, Lukasz Kaiser, and Illia Polosukhin. 2017. Attention is all you need. In *Advances in Neural Information Processing Systems 30: Annual Conference on Neural Information Processing Systems 2017, 4-9 December 2017, Long Beach, CA, USA*, pages 5998–6008.

Andrew J. Viterbi. 1967. Error bounds for convolutional codes and an asymptotically optimum decoding algorithm. *IEEE Trans. Inf. Theory*, 13(2):260–269.

Robert A. Wagner and Michael J. Fischer. 1974. The string-to-string correction problem. *J. ACM*, 21(1):168–173.

Robert Weide. 2017. The Carnegie-Mellon pronouncing dictionary [cmudict. 0.7]. Pittsburgh, PA, USA. Carnegie Mellon University.

Sarah Wiegreffe and Yuval Pinter. 2019. Attention is not not explanation. In *Proceedings of the 2019 Conference on Empirical Methods in Natural Language Processing and the 9th International Joint Conference on Natural Language Processing (EMNLP-IJCNLP)*, pages 11–20, Hong Kong, China. Association for Computational Linguistics.

Thomas Wolf, Lysandre Debut, Victor Sanh, Julien Chaumond, Clement Delangue, Anthony Moi, Pierric Cistac, Tim Rault, Remi Louf, Morgan Funtowicz, Joe Davison, Sam Shleifer, Patrick von Platen, Clara Ma, Yacine Jernite, Julien Plu, Canwen Xu, Teven Le Scao, Sylvain Gugger, Mariama Drame, Quentin Lhoest, and Alexander Rush. 2020. Transformers: State-of-the-art natural language processing. In *Proceedings of the 2020 Conference on Empirical Methods in Natural Language Processing: System Demonstrations*, pages 38–45, Online. Association for Computational Linguistics.

Kaisheng Yao and Geoffrey Zweig. 2015. Sequence-to-sequence neural net models for grapheme-to-phoneme conversion. In *INTERSPEECH 2015, 16th Annual Conference of the International Speech Communication Association, Dresden, Germany, September 6-10, 2015*, pages 3330–3334. ISCA.

Sevinj Yolchuyeva, Géza Németh, and Bálint Gyires-Tóth. 2019. Transformer based grapheme-to-phoneme conversion. In *Interspeech 2019, 20th Annual Conference of the International Speech Communication Association, Graz, Austria, 15-19 September 2019*, pages 2095–2099. ISCA.

Lei Yu, Jan Buys, and Phil Blunsom. 2016. Online segment to segment neural transduction. In *Proceedings of the 2016 Conference on Empirical Methods in Natural Language Processing*, pages 1307–1316, Austin, Texas. Association for Computational Linguistics.

A Inference algorithm

Algorithm 2 is a procedural implementation of Equation 1. In the Viterbi decoding used for obtaining the alignment, the summation on line 6, 8 and 10 is replaced by taking the maximum.

Algorithm 2 Forward evaluation

1: $\alpha \in \mathbb{R}^{n \times m} \leftarrow \mathbf{0}$
2: $\alpha_{0,0} \leftarrow 1$
3: **for** $i = 1 \ldots n$ **do**
4:     **for** $j = 1 \ldots m$ **do**
5:         **if** $j > 0$ **then**
6:             $\alpha_{i,j} \mathrel{+}= \mathrm{P}_{\text{ins}}(t_j | \mathbf{c}_{i,j-1}) \cdot \alpha_{i,j-1}$
7:         **if** $i > 0$ **then**
8:             $\alpha_{i,j} \mathrel{+}= \mathrm{P}_{\text{del}}(s_i | \mathbf{c}_{i-1,j}) \cdot \alpha_{i-1,j}$
9:         **if** $i > 0$ and $j > 0$ **then**
10:             $\alpha_{i,j} \mathrel{+}= \mathrm{P}_{\text{subs}}(s_i \rightarrow t_j | \mathbf{c}_{i-1,j-1}) \cdot \alpha_{i-1,j-1}$

B Motivation for design choices in the string-matching model

Let us assume a toy example transliteration. The source alphabet is {A, B, C}, the target alphabet is {a, b, c}, the transcription rules are:

1. If B is at the beginning of the string, delete it.
2. Multiple As rewrite to a single a.
3. Rewrite B to b and C to c.

The statistical learnable edit distance would not be capable of properly learning rules 1 and 2 because it would not know that B was at the beginning of the string and if an occurrence of A is the first A. This problem gets resolved by introducing a contextualized representation of the input.

The original statistical EM algorithm only needs positive examples to learn the operation distribution. For instance, rewriting B to c will end up as improbable due to the inherent limitation of a single sharing static probability table. Using a single table regardless of the context means that if some operations become more probable, the others must become less probable. A neural network does not have such limitations. A neural model can in theory find solutions that maximize the probability of the training data, however, do not correspond to the original set of rules by finding a highly probable sequence of operations for any string pair. For instance, it can learn to count the positions in the string:

1′. Whatever symbols at the same position i (s_i and t_i) are, substitute s_i with t_j with the probability of 1.

2′. If $i < j$, assign probability of 1 to deleting s_i.

3′. If $i > j$, assign probability of 1 to inserting t_j.

For this reason, we introduce the binary cross-entropy as an additional loss function. This should steer the model away from degenerate solutions assigning a high probability score to any input string pair.

But our ablation study in Table 2 showed that even without the binary cross-entropy loss, the model converges to a good non-degenerate solution.

This thought experiment shows keeping the full table of possible model outcomes is no longer crucial for the modeling strength. Let us assume that the output distribution of the neural model contains all possible edit operations as they are in the static probability tables of the statistical model. The model can learn to rely on the position information only and select the correct symbols in the output probability distribution ignoring the actual content of the symbols, using their embeddings as a key to identify the correct item from the output distribution. The model can thus learn to ignore the function the full probability table had in the statistical model. Also, given the inputs, it is always clear what the plausible operations are, it is easy for the model not to assign any probability to the implausible operations (unlike the statistical model).

These thoughts lead us to the conclusion that there is no need to keep the full output distribution and we only can use four target classes: one for insertion, one for deletion, one for substitution, and one special class that would get the part of probability mass that would be assigned to implausible operations in the statistical model. We call the last one the *non-match* option.

C Model Hyperparameters

Following Gehring et al. (2017), the CNN uses gated linear units as non-linearity (Dauphin et al., 2017), layer normalization (Ba et al., 2016) and residual connections (He et al., 2016). The symbol embeddings are summed with learnable position embeddings before the convolution.

The RNN uses gated recurrent units (Cho et al., 2014) and follows the scheme of Chen et al. (2018), which includes residual connections (He et al., 2016), layer normalization (Ba et al., 2016), and multi-headed scaled dot-product attention (Vaswani et al., 2017).

The Transformers follow the architecture decisions of BERT (Devlin et al., 2019) as implemented in the Transformers library (Wolf et al., 2020).

All hyperparameters are set manually based on preliminary experiments. For all experiments, we use embedding size of 256. The CNN encoder uses a single layer with kernel size 3 and ReLU non-linearity. For both the RNN and Transformer models, we use 2 layers with 256 hidden units. The Transformer uses 4 attention heads of dimension 64 in the self-attention. The same configuration is used for the encoder-decoder attention for both RNN and Transformer. We use the same hyperparameters also for the baselines.

We include all main loss functions with weight 1.0, i.e., for string-pair matching: the EM loss, non-matching negative log-likelihood and binary cross-entropy; for string transduction: the EM loss and next symbol negative log-likelihood. We test each model with and without the interpretability loss, which is included with weight 0.1.

We optimize the models using the Adam optimizer (Kingma and Ba, 2015) with an initial learning rate of 10^{-4}, and batch size of 512. We validate the models every 50 training steps. We decrease the learning rate by a factor of 0.7 if the validation performance does not increase in two consecutive validations. We stop the training after the learning rate decreases 10 times.

D Notes on Reproducibility

The training times were measured on machines with GeForce GTX 1080 Ti GPUs and with Intel Xeon E5–2630v4 CPUs (2.20GHz). We report average wall time of training including data preprocessing, validation and testing. The measured time might be influenced by other processes running on the machines.

Validation scores are provided in Tables 6 and 7.

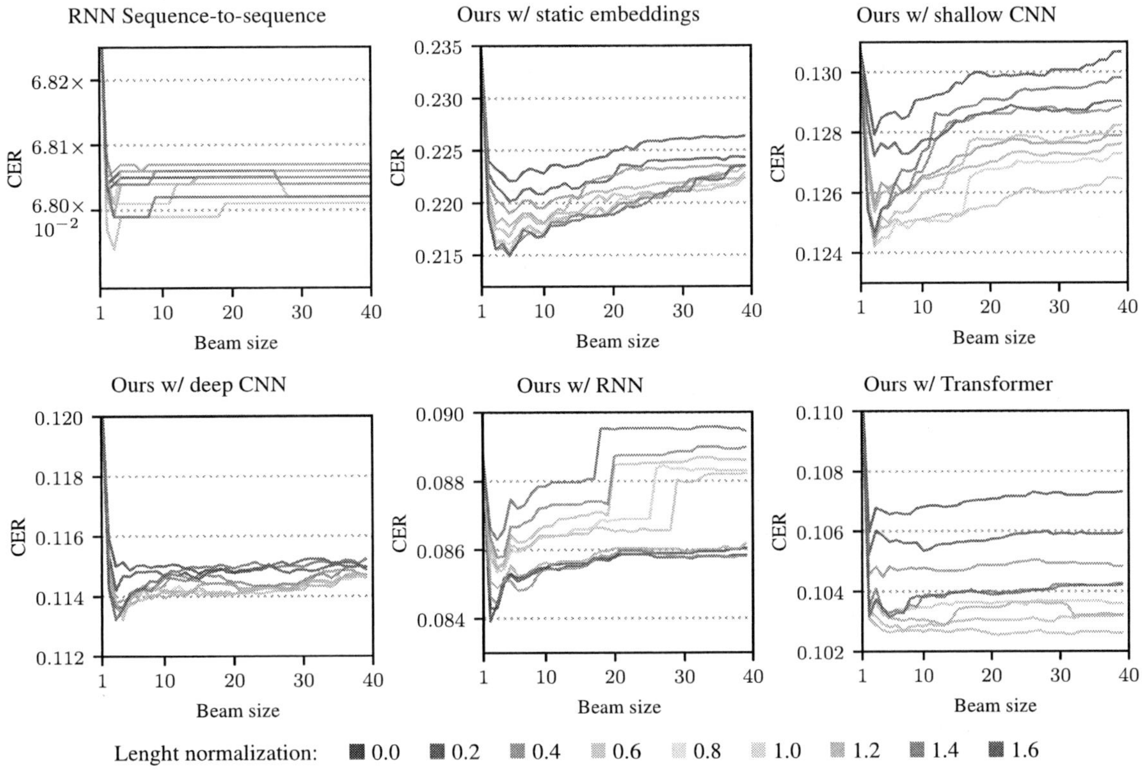

Figure 4: Effect of beam search on test data for grapheme-to-phoneme conversion.

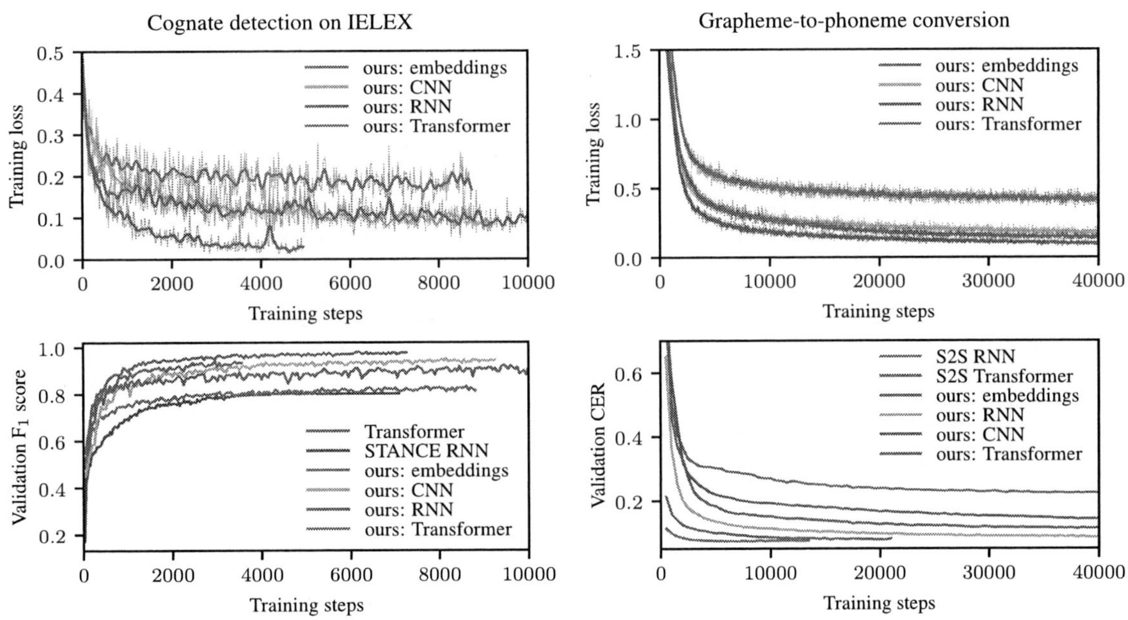

Figure 5: Learning curves for Cognate classification for Indo-European languages (left) and for grapheme-to-phoneme conversion (right).

Method		Indo-European		Austro-Asiatic	
		Base	+ Int. loss	Base	+ Int. loss
Transformer `[CLS]`		91.4 ±2.8	—	78.8 ±0.8	—
STANCE	unigram	46.5 ±4.7	—	16.5 ±0.4	—
STANCE	RNN	80.4 ±1.6	—	16.5 ±0.1	—
STANCE	Transformer	76.8 ±1.3	—	17.2 ±0.2	—
ours	unigram	81.2 ±1.0	82.0 ±0.5	52.6 ±0.8	53.9 ±0.6
ours	CNN (3-gram)	95.2 ±0.6	94.9 ±0.7	78.9 ±0.8	78.1 ±1.7
ours	RNN	97.2 ±0.2	88.8 ±1.1	82.8 ±0.6	83.1 ±0.7
ours	Transformer	88.8 ±1.6	88.7 ±1.1	71.5 ±1.1	71.5 ±1.1

Table 6: F_1-score for cognate detection on the *validation* data.

Method		Arabic → English				CMUDict			
		Base		+ Int. loss		Base		+ Int. loss	
		CER	WER	CER	WER	CER	WER	CER	WER
RNN Seq2seq		21.7 ±0.1	75.0 ±0.6	—	—	7.4 ±0.0	31.5 ±0.1	—	—
Transformer		22.8 ±0.2	77.7 ±0.6	—	—	7.8 ±0.1	32.7 ±0.3	—	—
ours	unigram	28.4 ±0.7	84.1 ±0.8	28.3 ±0.5	84.3 ±0.7	21.2 ±1.0	66.4 ±1.9	21.5 ±0.8	68.0 ±2.1
ours	CNN (3-gram)	34.4 ±1.1	86.5 ±0.8	32.2 ±1.1	86.5 ±0.8	36.0 ±5.7	80.9 ±3.2	33.8 ±3.5	79.0 ±2.8
ours	RNN	42.4 ±9.0	90.9 ±5.4	45.2 ±2.6	90.9 ±1.8	59.1 ±2.5	96.2 ±0.7	43.6 ±5.6	80.5 ±5.6
ours	Transformer	41.2 ±9.1	91.7 ±4.4	47.7 ±3.6	92.5 ±2.4	24.6 ±4.3	73.8 ±6.1	43.5 ±3.6	84.9 ±2.5

Table 7: Model error-rates for Arabic-to-English transliteration and English G2P generation on *validation* data.

Predicting Attention Sparsity in Transformers

Marcos Treviso[1,2] **António Góis**[5*] **Patrick Fernandes**[1,2,3]
Erick Fonseca[6*] **André F. T. Martins**[1,2,4]

[1]Instituto de Telecomunicações, Lisbon, Portugal
[2]Instituto Superior Técnico & LUMLIS (Lisbon ELLIS Unit), Lisbon, Portugal
[3]Language Technologies Institute, Carnegie Mellon University, Pittsburgh, PA
[4]Unbabel, Lisbon, Portugal
[5]Mila, Université de Montréal, Canada
[6]Kaufland e-commerce, Cologne, Germany

Abstract

Transformers' quadratic complexity with respect to the input sequence length has motivated a body of work on efficient sparse *approximations* to softmax. An alternative path, used by entmax transformers, consists of having built-in *exact* sparse attention; however this approach still requires quadratic computation. In this paper, we propose *Sparsefinder*, a simple model trained to *identify* the sparsity pattern of entmax attention before computing it. We experiment with three variants of our method, based on distances, quantization, and clustering, on two tasks: machine translation (attention in the decoder) and masked language modeling (encoder-only). Our work provides a new angle to study model efficiency by doing extensive analysis of the tradeoff between the sparsity and recall of the predicted attention graph. This allows for detailed comparison between different models along their Pareto curves, important to guide future benchmarks for sparse attention models.

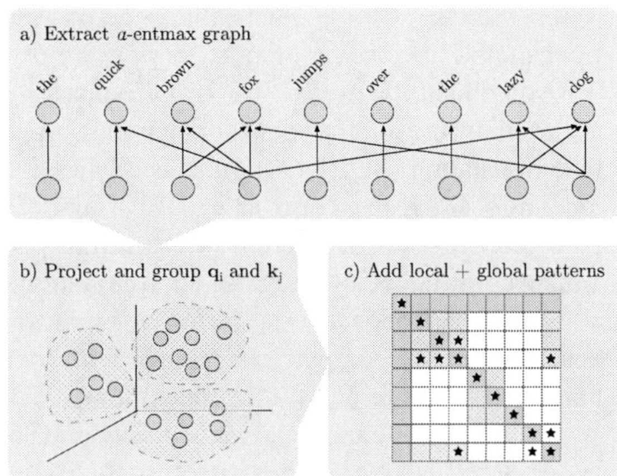

Figure 1: (a) Extract sparse attention graphs from a pretrained α-entmax transformer; (b) Project query and key vectors to a smaller and appropriated space such that similar points are likely to fall in the same vicinity; (c) Additionally, we can combine window and global patterns (green blocks) with the learned pattern (yellow blocks) to increase the recall in recovering ground-truth edges from the sparse graph at the top (starred blocks).

1 Introduction

Transformer-based architectures have achieved remarkable results in many NLP tasks (Vaswani et al., 2017; Devlin et al., 2019; Brown et al., 2020). However, they also bring important computational and environmental concerns, caused by their quadratic time and memory computation requirements with respect to the sequence length. This comes in addition to the difficulty of interpreting their inner workings, caused by their overparametrization and large number of attention heads.

There is a large body of work developing ways to "sparsify" the computation in transformers, either by imposing local or fixed attention patterns (Child et al., 2019; Tay et al., 2020; Zaheer et al., 2020), by applying low-rank kernel approximations to softmax (Wang et al., 2020; Choromanski et al., 2021), or by learning which queries and keys should be grouped together (Kitaev et al., 2019; Daras et al., 2020; Roy et al., 2021; Wang et al., 2021). Most of the existing work seeks to *approximate* softmax-based attention by ignoring the (predicted) tails of the distribution, which can lead to performance degradation. An exception is transformers with **entmax-based sparse attention** (Correia et al., 2019), a content-based approach which is natively sparse – this approach has the ability to let each attention head learn from data how sparse it should be, eliminating the need for heuristics or approximations. The disadvantage of this approach is that it still requires a quadratic computation to determine the sparsity pattern, failing to take computational advantage of attention sparsity.

In this paper, we propose **Sparsefinder**, which fills the gap above by making entmax attention more efficient (§4). Namely, we investigate three

*Work done at Instituto de Telecomunicações. Correspondence to marcos.treviso@tecnico.ulisboa.pt

Proceedings of the Sixth Workshop on Structured Prediction for NLP, pages 67 - 81

methods to predict the sparsity pattern of entmax without having to compute it: one based on metric learning, which is still quadratic but with a better constant (§4.3), one based on quantization (§4.4), and another based on clustering (§4.5). In all cases, the predictors are trained offline on ground-truth sparse attention graphs from an entmax transformer, seeking high recall in their predicted edges without compromising the total amount of sparsity. Figure 1 illustrates our method.

More precisely, to evaluate the effectiveness of our method across different scenarios, we perform experiments on two NLP tasks, encompassing encoder-only and decoder-only configurations: machine translation (MT, §5) and masked language modeling (MLM, §6), doing an extensive analysis of the tradeoff between sparsity and recall (i.e., performance on the attention graph approximation), and sparsity and accuracy (performance on downstream tasks). We compare our method with four alternative solutions based on efficient transformers: Longformer (Beltagy et al., 2020), Bigbird (Zaheer et al., 2020), Reformer (Kitaev et al., 2020), and Routing Transformer (Roy et al., 2021), along their entire Pareto curves. We complement these experiments by analyzing qualitatively what is selected by the different attention heads at the several layers and represented in different clusters/buckets. Overall, our contributions are:[1]

- We propose a simple method that exploits learnable sparsity patterns to efficiently compute multi-head attention (§4).
- We do an extensive analysis of the tradeoff between sparsity and recall, and sparsity and accuracy in MT (§5) and MLM (§6), showing that there is clear room for improvement in the design of efficient transformers.
- We qualitatively analyze what is selected by the different attention heads at various layers and represented in different clusters/buckets.

2 Related Work

Interpreting multi-head attention. Several works analyze the functionalities learned by different attention heads, such as positional and local context patterns (Raganato and Tiedemann, 2018; Voita et al., 2019). Building upon prior work on sparse attention mechanisms (Peters et al., 2019), Correia et al. (2019) constrain the attention heads to induce sparse selections individually for each head, bringing interpretability without post-hoc manipulation. Related approaches include the explicit sparse transformer (Zhao et al., 2019) and rectified linear attention (Zhang et al., 2021), which drops the normalization constraint. Raganato et al. (2020) show that it is possible to fix attention patterns based on previously known behavior (e.g. focusing on previous token) while improving translation quality. However, a procedure that exploits learnable sparsity patterns to accelerate multi-head attention is still missing.

Low-rank softmax approximations. Methods based on low-rank approximation to the softmax such as Linearized Attention (Katharopoulos et al., 2020), Linformer (Wang et al., 2020), and Performer (Choromanski et al., 2021) reduce both speed and memory complexity of the attention mechanism from quadratic to linear, but make interpretability more challenging because the scores are not computed explicitly. On the other hand, methods that focus on inducing sparse patterns provide interpretable alignments and also have performance gains in terms of speed and memory.

Fixed attention patterns. Among fixed pattern methods, Sparse Transformer (Child et al., 2019) and LongFormer (Beltagy et al., 2020) attend to fixed positions by using strided/dilated sliding windows. BigBird uses random and two fixed patterns (global and window) to build a block sparse matrix representation (Zaheer et al., 2020), taking advantage of block matrix operations to accelerate GPU computations. In contrast, we replace the random pattern with a learned pattern that mimics pretrained α-entmax sparse attention graphs.

Learnable attention patterns. Learnable pattern methods usually have to deal with assignment decisions within the multi-head attention mechanism. Clustered Attention (Vyas et al., 2020) groups query tokens into clusters and computes dot-products only with centroids. Reformer (Kitaev et al., 2020) and SMYRF (Daras et al., 2020) use locality-sensitive hashing to efficiently group tokens in buckets. More similar to our work, Routing Transformer (Roy et al., 2021) and Cluster-Former (Wang et al., 2021) cluster queries and keys with online k-means and compute dot-products over the top-k cluster points. Some queries and

[1] https://github.com/deep-spin/sparsefinder

keys are discarded due to this filtering, which affects the overall recall of the method (as we show in §5 and §6). The ability of Routing Transformer to benefit from contextual information has been analyzed by Sun et al. (2021). In contrast, Sparsefinder learns to cluster based on sparsity patterns from attention graphs generated by α-entmax.

3 Background

3.1 Transformers

The main component of transformers is the **multi-head attention** mechanism (Vaswani et al., 2017). Given as input a matrix $\mathbf{Q} \in \mathbb{R}^{n \times d}$ containing d-dimensional representations for n queries, and matrices $\mathbf{K}, \mathbf{V} \in \mathbb{R}^{m \times d}$ for m keys and values, the *scaled dot-product attention* at a single head is computed in the following way:

$$\text{att}(\mathbf{Q}, \mathbf{K}, \mathbf{V}) = \pi \underbrace{\left(\frac{\mathbf{Q}\mathbf{K}^\top}{\sqrt{d}} \right)}_{\mathbf{Z} \in \mathbb{R}^{n \times m}} \mathbf{V} \in \mathbb{R}^{n \times d}. \quad (1)$$

The π transformation maps rows to distributions, with softmax being the most common choice, $\pi(\mathbf{Z})_{ij} = \text{softmax}(\mathbf{z}_i)_j$. Multi-head attention is computed by evoking Eq. 1 in parallel for each head h:

$$\text{head}_h(\mathbf{Q}, \mathbf{K}, \mathbf{V}) = \text{att}(\mathbf{Q}\mathbf{W}_h^Q, \mathbf{K}\mathbf{W}_h^K, \mathbf{V}\mathbf{W}_h^V),$$

where $\mathbf{W}_h^Q$, $\mathbf{W}_h^K$, $\mathbf{W}_h^V$ are learned linear transformations. This way, heads are able to learn specialized phenomena. According to the nature of the input, transformers have three types of multi-head attention mechanism: encoder self-attention (source-to-source), decoder self-attention (target-to-target), and decoder cross-attention (target-to-source). While there are no restrictions to which elements can be attended to in the encoder, elements in position $j > i$ in the decoder self-attention are masked at timestep i ("causal mask").

3.2 Extmax Transformers and Learned Sparsity

The main computational bottleneck in transformers is the matrix multiplication $\mathbf{Q}\mathbf{K}^\top$ in Eq. 1, which costs $\mathcal{O}(nmd)$ time and can be impractical when n and m are large. Many approaches, discussed in §2, approximate Eq. 1 by ignoring entries far from the main diagonal or computing only some blocks of this matrix, with various heuristics. By doing so, the result will be an *approximation* of the softmax attention in Eq. 1. This is because the original softmax-based attention is *dense*, i.e., it puts *some* probability mass on all tokens – not only a computational disadvantage, but also making interpretation harder, as it has been observed that only a small fraction of attention heads capture relevant information (Voita et al., 2019).

An alternative to softmax is the **α-entmax transformation** (Peters et al., 2019; Correia et al., 2019), which leads to sparse patterns directly, *without any approximation*:

$$\alpha\text{-entmax}(\mathbf{z}) = [(\alpha - 1)\mathbf{z} - \tau(\mathbf{z})\mathbf{1}]_+^{1/\alpha - 1}, \quad (2)$$

where $[\cdot]_+$ is the positive part (ReLU) function, and $\tau : \mathbb{R}^n \to \mathbb{R}$ is a normalizing function satisfying $\sum_j [(\alpha - 1)z_j - \tau(\mathbf{z})]_+^{1/\alpha - 1} = 1$ for any $\mathbf{z}$. That is, entries with score $z_j \leq \tau(\mathbf{z})/\alpha - 1$ get exactly zero probability. In the limit $\alpha \to 1$, α-entmax recovers the softmax function, while for any value of $\alpha > 1$ this transformation can return sparse probability vectors (as the value of α increases, the induced probability distribution becomes more sparse). When $\alpha = 2$, we recover sparsemax (Martins and Astudillo, 2016). In this paper, we use $\alpha = 1.5$, which works well in practice and has a specialized fast algorithm (Peters et al., 2019).

Although sparse attention improves interpretability and head diversity when compared to dense alternatives (Correia et al., 2019), the learned sparsity patterns cannot be trivially exploited to reduce the quadratic burden of self-attention, since we still need to compute dot-products between all queries and keys ($\mathbf{Q}\mathbf{K}^\top$) before applying the α-entmax transformation. In the next section (§4), we propose a simple method that learns to *identify* these sparsity patterns beforehand, avoiding the full matrix multiplication.

4 Sparsefinder

We now propose our method to extract sparse attention graphs and learn where to attend by exploiting a special property of α-entmax: *sparse-consistency* (§4.1). We design three variants of Sparsefinder to that end, based on metric learning (§4.3), quantization (§4.4), and clustering (§4.5).

4.1 Attention graph and sparse-consistency

For each attention head h, we define its **attention graph** as $\mathcal{G}_h = \{(\mathbf{q}_i, \mathbf{k}_j) \mid p_{i,j} > 0\}$, a bipartite graph connecting query and key pairs $\mathbf{q}_i, \mathbf{k}_j \in \mathbb{R}^d$

for which the α-entmax probability $p_{i,j}$ is nonzero. An example of attention graph is shown in Figure 1. We denote by $|\mathcal{G}_h|$ the total size of an attention graph, i.e., its number of edges. With α-entmax with $\alpha = 1.5$ we typically have $|\mathcal{G}_h| \ll nm$. In contrast, softmax attention always leads to a complete graph, $|\mathcal{G}_h| = nm$.

Problem statement. Our goal is to build a model – which we call *Sparsefinder* – that predicts $\hat{\mathcal{G}}_h \approx \mathcal{G}_h$ without having to perform all pairwise comparisons between queries and keys. This enables the complexity of evaluating Eq. 1 to be reduced from $\mathcal{O}(nmd)$ to $\mathcal{O}(|\hat{\mathcal{G}}_h|d)$, effectively taking advantage of the sparsity of α-entmax. In order to learn such a model, we first extract a dataset of sparse attention graphs $\{\mathcal{G}_h\}$ from a pretrained entmax-based transformer, which acts as a teacher. Then, the student learns where to pay attention based on this information. This procedure is motivated by the following **sparse-consistency** property of α-entmax:

Proposition 1 (Sparse-consistency property). *Let* $\mathbf{b}$ *be a binary vector such that* $b_j = 1$ *if* $p_j^\star > 0$, *and* $b_j = 0$ *otherwise. For any binary mask vector* $\mathbf{m}$ *"dominated" by* $\mathbf{b}$ *(i.e.* $\mathbf{m} \odot \mathbf{b} = \mathbf{b}$*), we have*

$$\alpha\text{-}entmax(\mathbf{z}) = \alpha\text{-}entmax(\mathbf{z}|_{\mathbf{m}}), \tag{3}$$

where $z_j|_{\mathbf{m}} = z_j$ *if* $m_j = 1$ *and* $-\infty$ *if* $m_j = 0$.

Proof. See §A in the supplemental material. □

This property ensures that, if $\hat{\mathcal{G}}_h$ is such that $\mathcal{G}_h \subseteq \hat{\mathcal{G}}_h$, then we obtain *exactly* the same result as with the original entmax attention. Therefore, we are interested in having high recall,

$$\text{recall}(\hat{\mathcal{G}}_h; \mathcal{G}_h) = \frac{|\hat{\mathcal{G}}_h \cap \mathcal{G}_h|}{|\mathcal{G}_h|}, \tag{4}$$

meaning that our method is nearly exact, and high sparsity,

$$\text{sparsity}(\hat{\mathcal{G}}_h) = 1 - \frac{|\hat{\mathcal{G}}_h|}{nm}, \tag{5}$$

which indicates that computation can be made efficient.[2] Although a high sparsity may indicate that many computations can be ignored, converting this theoretical result into efficient computation is not trivial and potentially hardware-dependent. In this paper, rather than proposing a practical computational efficient method, we focus on showing that such methods do exist and that they can be designed to outperform fixed and learned pattern methods while retaining a high amount of sparsity when compared to the ground-truth graph.

Our strategies. We teach the student model to predict $\hat{\mathcal{G}}_h \approx \mathcal{G}_h$ by taking inspiration from the Reformer model (Kitaev et al., 2020) and the Routing Transformer (Roy et al., 2021). Formally, we define a set of B buckets, $\mathcal{B} = \{1, \ldots, B\}$, and learn functions $f_q, f_k : \mathbb{R}^d \to 2^{\mathcal{B}} \setminus \{\varnothing\}$, which assign a query or a key to one or more buckets. We will discuss in the sequel different design strategies for the functions f_q, f_k. Given these functions, the predicted graph is:

$$\hat{\mathcal{G}}_h = \{(\mathbf{q}_i, \mathbf{k}_j) \mid f_q(\mathbf{q}_i) \cap f_k(\mathbf{k}_j) \neq \varnothing\}, \tag{6}$$

that is, an edge is predicted between $\mathbf{q}_i$ and $\mathbf{k}_j$ iff they are together in some bucket.

We present three strategies, based on distance-based pairing (§4.3), quantization (§4.4) and clustering (§4.5). As a first step, all strategies require learning a metric that embeds the graph (projecting queries and keys) into a lower-dimensional space $\mathbb{R}^r$ with $r \ll d$, such that positive query-key pairs are close to each other, and negative pairs are far apart.

4.2 Learning projections

According to the α-entmax sparse-consistency property, in order to get a good approximation of $\mathcal{G}_h$, we would like that f_q and f_k produce a graph $\hat{\mathcal{G}}_h$ that maximizes recall, defined in Eq. 4. However, maximizing recall in this setting is difficult since we do not have ground-truth bucket assignments. Instead, we recur to a contrastive learning approach by learning projections via negative sampling, which is simpler and more scalable than constrained clustering approaches (Wagstaff et al., 2001; de Amorim, 2012).

For each head, we start by projecting the original query and key $\mathbf{q}, \mathbf{k} \in \mathbb{R}^d$ vectors into lower dimensional vectors $\mathbf{q}', \mathbf{k}' \in \mathbb{R}^r$ such that $r \ll d$. In practice, we use a simple head-wise linear projection for all queries and keys $g_\theta : \mathbb{R}^d \to \mathbb{R}^r$. To learn the parameters of the projection layer we minimize a hinge loss with margin ω for each head h:

$$\mathcal{L}_\theta(\mathcal{G}_h) = \left[\omega + \|\mathbf{q}' - \mathbf{k}'_{\mathrm{P}}\|_2^2 - \|\mathbf{q}' - \mathbf{k}'_{\mathrm{N}}\|_2^2\right]_+, \tag{7}$$

where $(\mathbf{q}', \mathbf{k}'_{\mathrm{P}}) \in \mathcal{G}_h$ is a positive pair and $(\mathbf{q}', \mathbf{k}'_{\mathrm{N}}) \notin \mathcal{G}_h$ is a negative pair sampled uniformly

[2] For the decoder self-attention the denominator in Eq. 5 becomes $n(n+1)/2$ due to "causal" masking.

at random. In words, we want the distance between a query vector to negative pairs to be larger than the distance to positive pairs by a margin ω. This approach can also be seen as a weakly-supervised learning problem, where the goal is to push dissimilar points away while keeping similar points close to each other (Xing et al., 2002; Weinberger and Saul, 2009; Bellet et al., 2015).

4.3 Distance-based pairing

To take advantage of the proximity of data points on the embedded space, we first propose a simple method to connect query and key pairs whose Euclidean distance is less than a threshold t, i.e. $\hat{\mathcal{G}}_h = \{(\mathbf{q}_i, \mathbf{k}_j) \mid \|\mathbf{q}'_i - \mathbf{k}'_j\|_2 \leq t\}$. Although this method also requires $O(n^2)$ computations, it is more efficient than a vanilla transformer since it reduces computations by a factor of d/r by using the learned projections. This method is also useful to probe the quality of the embedded space learned by the projections, since the recall of our other methods will be contingent on it.

4.4 Buckets through quantization

Our second strategy quantizes each dimension $1, \ldots, r$ of the lower-dimensional space into β bins, placing the queries and keys into the corresponding buckets ($B = r\beta$ buckets in total). This way, each $\mathbf{q}_i$ and $\mathbf{k}_j$ will be placed in exactly r buckets (one per dimension). If $\mathbf{q}_i$ and $\mathbf{k}_j$ are together in some bucket, Sparsefinder predicts that $(\mathbf{q}_i, \mathbf{k}_j) \in \hat{\mathcal{G}}_h$. Note that for this quantization strategy no learning is needed, only the hyperparameter β and the binning strategy need to be chosen. We propose a fixed-size binning strategy: divide each dimension into β bins such that all bins have exactly $\lceil n/\beta \rceil$ elements. In practice, we append padding symbols to the input to ensure that bins are balanced.

4.5 Buckets through clustering

The clustering strategy uses the low-dimensional projections and runs a clustering algorithm to assign $\mathbf{q}_i$ and $\mathbf{k}_j$ to one or more clusters. In this case, each cluster corresponds to a bucket. In our paper, we employed k-means to learn B centroids $\{\mathbf{c}_1, \ldots, \mathbf{c}_B\}$, where each $c_b \in \mathbb{R}^r$, over a small portion of the training set. This strategy is similar to the Routing Transformer's online k-means (Roy et al., 2021), but with two key differences: (a) our clustering step is applied offline; (b) we assign points to the top-k closest centroids rather than assigning the closest top-k closest points to each centroid, ensuring that all queries are assigned to a cluster.[3] At test time, we use the learned centroids to group queries and keys into k clusters each:

$$f_q(\mathbf{q}_i) = \underset{1 \leq b \leq B}{\arg \text{top-}k} -\|\mathbf{q}_i - \mathbf{c}_b\|_2^2, \tag{8}$$

$$f_k(\mathbf{k}_j) = \underset{1 \leq b \leq B}{\arg \text{top-}k} -\|\mathbf{k}_j - \mathbf{c}_b\|_2^2, \tag{9}$$

where the arg top-k operator returns the indices of the kth largest elements. As in the quantization-based approach, queries and keys will attend to each other, i.e., Sparsefinder predicts $(\mathbf{q}_i, \mathbf{k}_j) \in \hat{\mathcal{G}}_h$ if they share at least one cluster among the k closest ones. Smaller values of k will induce high sparsity graphs, whereas a larger k is likely to produce a denser graph but with a higher recall.

4.6 Computational cost

Let L be the maximum number of elements in a bucket. The time and memory cost of bucketed attention computed through quantization or clustering is $\mathcal{O}(BL^2)$. With balanced buckets, we get a complexity of $\mathcal{O}(n^{1.5})$ by setting $B = \sqrt{n}$. Although this cost is sub-quadratic, leveraging the sparse structure of $\hat{\mathcal{G}}_h$ in practice is challenging, since it might require specialized hardware or kernels. In general, we have $|\hat{\mathcal{G}}_h| = \sum_{b=1}^{B} n_b m_b \ll nm$, where n_b and m_b are the number of queries and keys in each bucket, since we have small complete bipartite graphs on each bucket. Instead of viewing quadratic methods only in light of their performance, we adopt an alternative view of assessing the tradeoff of these methods in terms of sparsity and recall of their approximation $\hat{\mathcal{G}}_h$. This offers a theoretical perspective to the potential performance of each approximation on downstream tasks, helping to find the best approximations for a desired level of sparsity.

4.7 Combining learned and fixed patterns

As pointed out in prior work (Voita et al., 2019), several attention heads rely strongly in local patterns or prefer to attend to a particular position, more promimently in initial layers. Therefore, we take inspiration from the Longformer (Beltagy et al., 2020) and BigBird (Zaheer et al., 2020) and combine learned sparse patterns with window and

[3]The difference relies on the dimension on which the top-k operation is applied. Routing Transformer applies top-k to the input dimension, possibly leaving some queries unattended, whereas Sparsefinder applies to the centroids dimension, avoiding this problem.

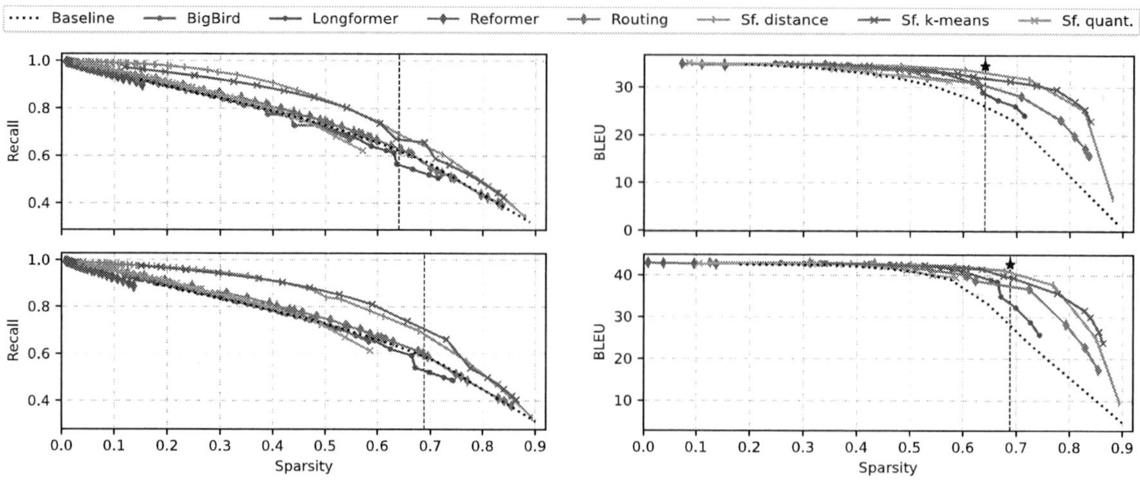

Figure 2: Sparsity-recall (left) and sparsity-BLEU (right) tradeoff averaged across all layers and heads on IWSLT EN→DE (top) and EN→FR (bottom). The vertical dashed line represents the gold sparsity obtained by the original α-entmax transformer (which requires quadratic computation), and the starred marks depict its BLEU score: 34.47 on EN→DE and 42.65 on EN→FR.

global patterns by adding connections in the predicted graph $\hat{\mathcal{G}}_h$ to improve the recall of all methods. Figure 1 illustrates how these patterns are combined in the last step.

5 Experiments: Machine Translation

Setup. We pretrain a *transformer-large* model (6 layers, 16 heads) on the Paracrawl dataset (Esplà et al., 2019). Next, we finetune it with α-entmax, fixing $\alpha = 1.5$ for all heads, on EN→DE and EN→FR language pairs from IWSLT17 (Cettolo et al., 2017). We use the 2011-2014 sets as validation data and the 2015 set as test data. We encode each word using byte pair encoding (BPE, Sennrich et al. 2016) with a joint segmentation of 32k merges. As Vaswani et al. (2017), we finetune our models using the Adam optimizer with an inverse square root learning rate scheduler, with an initial value of 5×10^{-4} and a linear warm-up in the first 4000 steps. We evaluate translation quality with sacreBLEU (Post, 2018). Training details, hyperparameters, and data statistics are described in §C.

Learning projections. To learn projections for queries and keys (§4.2), we randomly selected 10K long instances ($n > 20$ tokens) from the training set and extracted the α-entmax attention graphs $\mathcal{G}_h$ from the decoder self-attention for each head. This led to an average of 8M and 9M positive pairs $(\mathbf{q}_i, \mathbf{k}_j)$ per layer for EN→DE and EN→FR, respectively. In practice, due to the small number of parameters for each head (only 4,160), a single epoch with Adam was sufficient to optimize the loss in Eq. 7. The hyperparameters and the training details for learning projections can be found in §C.

Pareto-curves. Using the learned projections, we investigate the recall and the accuracy of all Sparsefinder variants by comparing them with Longformer, BigBird, Reformer, and Routing Transformer. To get a fair comparison, we analyze each method for different levels of sparsity by varying the following hyperparameters:

- **Distance-based methods**: the threshold t within $\{0.5, 1.0, 1.5, 2.0, 2.5, 3.0, 3.5, 4.0, 4.5, 5.0\}$.
- **Bucketing-based methods**: the number of buckets B within $\{2, 4, 6, 8, 10, 12, 16, 20\}$.
- **Fixed-pattern methods**: the number of random blocks of size 1 within $\{2, 4, 6, 8, 10, 12, 16, 20\}$ for BigBird; and the number of random global tokens within $\{2, 4, 6, 8, 10, 12, 16, 20\}$ for Longformer.

We also add global and local patterns to all methods, varying the window size within $\{0, 1, 3, 5, 7, 9, 11, 15, 19, 23, 27\}$ to get different levels of locality. We further compare all methods with a simple window baseline that only induces the window and global patterns. Since all methods exhibit a tradeoff between sparsity and recall/accuracy, we plot the scores obtained by varying the hyperparameters and draw their respective **Pareto frontier** to see the optimal Pareto-curve.

Methods whose points lie below this frontier are said to be **Pareto-dominated**, meaning that their recall/accuracy cannot be increased without sacrificing sparsity, or vice-versa. Concretely, each point on the curve is measured as a function of the approximation to the ground-truth α-entmax attention graph $\mathcal{G}_h$ by replacing it by $\hat{\mathcal{G}}_h$ at test time.

Sparsity-recall tradeoff. Pareto-curves for the sparsity-recall tradeoff are shown on the left of Figure 2 for both language pairs. Overall, both language pairs have similar trends for all methods. Sparsefinder's distance-based and clustering approaches Pareto-dominates the other methods, followed by Routing Transformer. Interestingly, Longformer, BigBird, Routing Transformer, and Sparsefinder's bucketing approach perform on par with the baseline, indicating that a simple local window is a hard baseline to beat. Since the LSH attention in Reformer shares queries and keys before hashing, the resultant buckets are also shared for queries and keys, explaining the high recall and the low sparsity of Reformer.

Sparsity-accuracy tradeoff. We show the tradeoff between sparsity and BLEU on the right of Figure 2. For lower levels of sparsity, all methods perform well, close to the full entmax transformer. But as sparsity increases, indicating that only a few computations are necessary, we see that the distance-based and k-means variants of Sparsefinder Pareto-dominate other methods, keeping a very high BLEU without abdicating sparsity. In particular, Sparsefinder's distance and clustering approaches perform on par with the full entmax transformer when the amount of sparsity is close to the original entmax transformer (around the vertical dashed line). Overall, these plots show that methods with a high recall for higher levels of sparsity also tend to have a higher BLEU score.

Learned patterns. We select some heads and show in Figure 3 examples of the pattern learned by our k-means variant on EN→FR. More examples can be found in §E. We note that the window pattern is useful to recover local connections. We can see that the k-means variant groups more query and key pairs than the actual number of ground-truth edges (left plots). However, due to the sparse-consistency property (right plots), most of these predictions receive zero probability by α-entmax, resulting in a very accurate approximation.

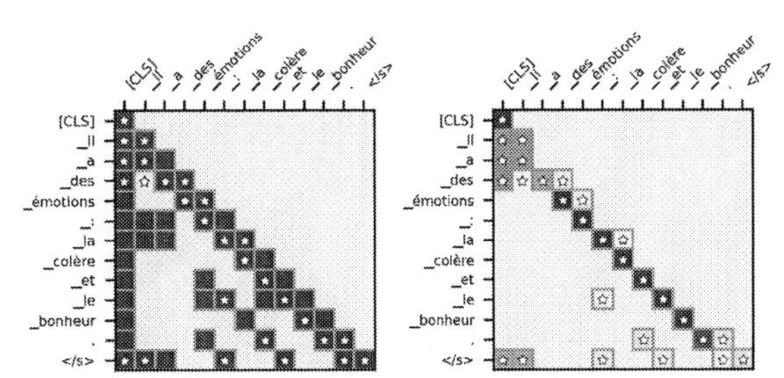

Figure 3: Learned patterns by Sparsefinder k-means (left) and the subsequent attention weights (right). Starred blocks represent ground-truth edges.

6 Experiments: Masked LM

Setup. Following Beltagy et al. (2020), we initialize our model from a pretrained RoBERTa checkpoint. We use the `roberta-base` model from Huggingface's transformers library, with 12 layers and 12 heads.[4] We finetune on WikiText-103 (Merity et al., 2017), replacing softmax by α-entmax with $\alpha = 1.5$ for all heads. Training details, model hyperparameters, and data statistics can be found in §D.

Learning projections. As done for MT experiments, we learn to project keys and queries from the original 64 dimensions into $r = 4$ dimensions. To this end, we use 1K random samples from the training set, each with length of 512, keeping half for validation. We extract the α-entmax attention graphs $\mathcal{G}_h$ but from the encoder self-attention of each head, leading to an average of 3M positive pairs per layer. Due to the small number of learnable parameters for each head (256), training was done with Adam for one epoch.

Results. Our full transformer trained with α-entmax achieved a perplexity score of 3.5004 with an overall sparsity of 0.9804 on WikiText-103. As in sentence-level MT experiments, we measure the sparsity-recall and the sparsity-perplexity tradeoff via the change of $\mathcal{G}_h$ with $\hat{\mathcal{G}}_h$ at test time. Moreover, since MLM has longer inputs, we increased the range of the window pattern to $\{31, 41, 51, 75, 101, 125, 151, 175, 201, 251\}$.

We show in Figure 4 the Pareto curves for the tradeoff between sparsity and recall (left), and the tradeoff between sparsity and perplexity (right). The curves for the sparsity-recall tradeoff are similar to the ones found in MT experiments, with the distance-based method outperforming all methods,

[4] `https://huggingface.co/roberta-base`

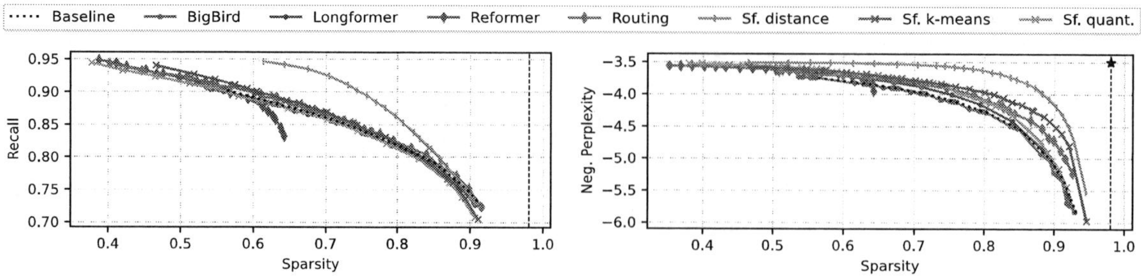

Figure 4: Sparsity-recall and sparsity-(neg-)perplexity tradeoff averaged across all layers and heads on WikiText-103. The vertical dashed line represents the gold sparsity obtained by the full α-entmax transformer.

followed by the k-means variant of Sparsefinder and Routing Transformer. In terms of perplexity, our distance-based approach also Pareto-dominates other methods, followed by our clustering variant and Routing Transformer. As in the MT experiments, the window baseline yields a similar sparsity-recall curve to other approaches, reinforcing the importance of local patterns. Although the distance-based method requires a quadratic number of computations, it reduces them by a factor of $d/r = 64/4 = 16$, as described in §4.3, and achieves better recall and perplexity than any other tested method. This finding indicates clear room for improvement in designing efficient attention methods that have a better tradeoff between efficiency and accuracy than existing approaches.

Learned patterns. In Figure 5 we show Sparsefinder k-means' predicted attention graphs for a specific attention head that originally learned to focus on coreference tokens. We can see that the pattern induced by Sparsefinder keeps the behavior of attending to coreferences. Concretely, our method achieves a high recall score ($\sim$ 80%) with a high sparsity rate ($\sim$ 75%) on this attention head.

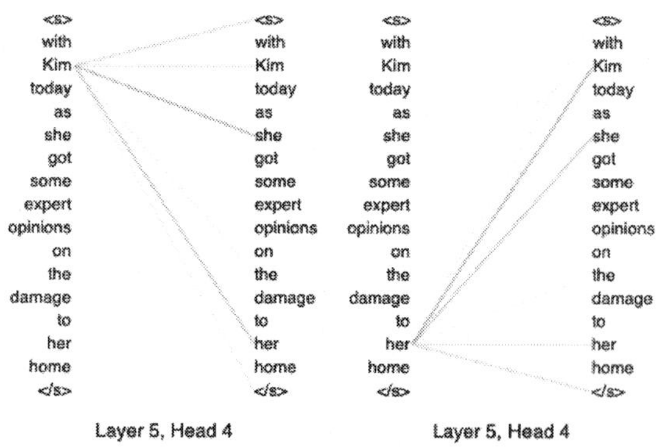

Figure 5: Attention pattern learned by Sparsefinder k-means that focus on coreference tokens.

Cluster analysis. To understand what is represented in each cluster learned by Sparsefinder k-means, we run the following experiment: we obtain POS tags using spaCy,[5] and calculate the distribution of each tag over clusters for all heads. We show an example in Figure 6, where Sparsefinder learned a cluster that makes verbs and nouns attend to themselves, and additionally to most auxiliary verbs.

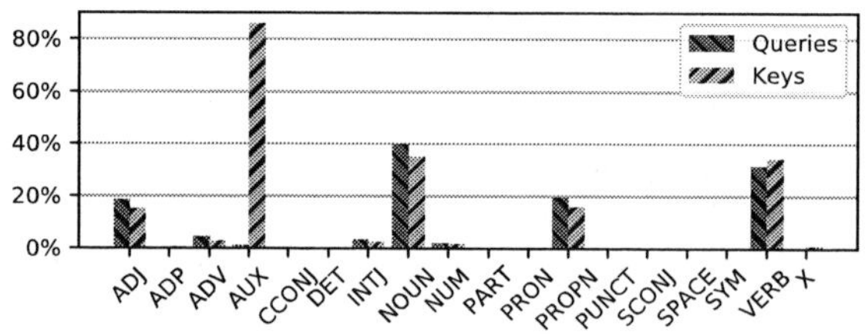

Figure 6: Percentage of POS tags assigned to a given cluster on the entire Wikitext 103 validation set.

7 Conclusions

We proposed Sparsefinder, a method to identify the sparsity pattern of entmax-based transformers while avoiding full computation of the score matrix. Our method learns a low-dimensional projection of queries and keys with a contrastive objective, and comes with three variants: distance, quantization, and clustering-based. We compared these variants against competing approaches on two tasks: machine translation and masked language modeling. We obtained favorable sparsity-recall and sparsity-accuracy tradeoff curves. Our theoretical sparsity provides a lower bound for how much computational sparsity can be achieved, and may guide future research on efficient transformers.

[5] https://spacy.io/

Acknowledgments

This work was supported by the European Research Council (ERC StG DeepSPIN 758969), by the P2020 project MAIA (LISBOA-01-0247- FEDER045909), and by the Fundação para a Ciência e Tecnologia through project PTDC/CCI-INF/4703/2021 (PRELUNA) and contract UIDB/50008/2020.

References

Aurélien Bellet, Amaury Habrard, and Marc Sebban. 2015. Metric learning. *Synthesis Lectures on Artificial Intelligence and Machine Learning*, 9(1):1–151.

Iz Beltagy, Matthew E. Peters, and Arman Cohan. 2020. Longformer: The long-document transformer. *arXiv:2004.05150*.

Tom B Brown, Benjamin Mann, Nick Ryder, Melanie Subbiah, Jared Kaplan, Prafulla Dhariwal, Arvind Neelakantan, Pranav Shyam, Girish Sastry, Amanda Askell, et al. 2020. Language models are few-shot learners. In *Advances in Neural Information Processing Systems (NeurIPS)*, volume 33, pages 1877–1901. Curran Associates, Inc.

Mauro Cettolo, Marcello Federico, Luisa Bentivogli, Niehues Jan, Stüker Sebastian, Sudoh Katsuitho, Yoshino Koichiro, and Federmann Christian. 2017. Overview of the iwslt 2017 evaluation campaign. In *Proceedings of the 14th International Workshop on Spoken Language Translation (IWSLT)*, pages 2–14.

Rewon Child, Scott Gray, Alec Radford, and Ilya Sutskever. 2019. Generating long sequences with sparse transformers. *arXiv preprint arXiv:1904.10509*.

Krzysztof Marcin Choromanski, Valerii Likhosherstov, David Dohan, Xingyou Song, Andreea Gane, Tamas Sarlos, Peter Hawkins, Jared Quincy Davis, Afroz Mohiuddin, Lukasz Kaiser, David Benjamin Belanger, Lucy J Colwell, and Adrian Weller. 2021. Rethinking attention with performers. In *International Conference on Learning Representations (ICLR)*.

Gonçalo M. Correia, Vlad Niculae, and André F. T. Martins. 2019. Adaptively sparse transformers. In *Proceedings of the 2019 Conference on Empirical Methods in Natural Language Processing and the 9th International Joint Conference on Natural Language Processing (EMNLP-IJCNLP)*, pages 2174–2184, Hong Kong, China. Association for Computational Linguistics.

Giannis Daras, Nikita Kitaev, Augustus Odena, and Alexandros G Dimakis. 2020. Smyrf - efficient attention using asymmetric clustering. In *Advances in Neural Information Processing Systems*, volume 33, pages 6476–6489. Curran Associates, Inc.

Renato Cordeiro de Amorim. 2012. Constrained clustering with minkowski weighted k-means. In *2012 IEEE 13th International Symposium on Computational Intelligence and Informatics (CINTI)*, pages 13–17. IEEE.

Jacob Devlin, Ming-Wei Chang, Kenton Lee, and Kristina Toutanova. 2019. BERT: Pre-training of deep bidirectional transformers for language understanding. In *Proceedings of the 2019 Conference of the North American Chapter of the Association for Computational Linguistics: Human Language Technologies, Volume 1 (Long and Short Papers)*, pages 4171–4186, Minneapolis, Minnesota. Association for Computational Linguistics.

Miquel Esplà, Mikel Forcada, Gema Ramírez-Sánchez, and Hieu Hoang. 2019. ParaCrawl: Web-scale parallel corpora for the languages of the EU. In *Proceedings of Machine Translation Summit XVII Volume 2: Translator, Project and User Tracks*, pages 118–119, Dublin, Ireland. European Association for Machine Translation.

Patrick Fernandes, Kayo Yin, Graham Neubig, and André F. T. Martins. 2021. Measuring and increasing context usage in context-aware machine translation. In *Joint Conference of the 59th Annual Meeting of the Association for Computational Linguistics and the 11th International Joint Conference on Natural Language Processing (ACL-IJCNLP)*, Virtual.

A. Katharopoulos, A. Vyas, N. Pappas, and F. Fleuret. 2020. Transformers are rnns: Fast autoregressive transformers with linear attention. In *Proceedings of the International Conference on Machine Learning (ICML)*.

Nikita Kitaev, Steven Cao, and Dan Klein. 2019. Multilingual constituency parsing with self-attention and pre-training. In *Proceedings of the 57th Annual Meeting of the Association for Computational Linguistics*, pages 3499–3505, Florence, Italy. Association for Computational Linguistics.

Nikita Kitaev, Lukasz Kaiser, and Anselm Levskaya. 2020. Reformer: The efficient transformer. In *International Conference on Learning Representations (ICLR)*.

Yinhan Liu, Myle Ott, Naman Goyal, Jingfei Du, Mandar Joshi, Danqi Chen, Omer Levy, Mike Lewis, Luke Zettlemoyer, and Veselin Stoyanov. 2019. Roberta: A robustly optimized bert pretraining approach. *arXiv preprint arXiv:1907.11692*.

Andre Martins and Ramon Astudillo. 2016. From softmax to sparsemax: A sparse model of attention and multi-label classification. In *International Conference on Machine Learning (ICML)*, volume 48 of *Proceedings of Machine Learning Research*, pages 1614–1623, New York, New York, USA. PMLR.

Stephen Merity, Caiming Xiong, James Bradbury, and Richard Socher. 2017. Pointer sentinel mixture models. In *5th International Conference on Learning Representations (ICLR)*.

F. Pedregosa, G. Varoquaux, A. Gramfort, V. Michel, B. Thirion, O. Grisel, M. Blondel, P. Prettenhofer, R. Weiss, V. Dubourg, J. Vanderplas, A. Passos, D. Cournapeau, M. Brucher, M. Perrot, and E. Duchesnay. 2011. Scikit-learn: Machine learning in Python. *Journal of Machine Learning Research (JMLR)*, 12:2825–2830.

Ben Peters, Vlad Niculae, and André F. T. Martins. 2019. Sparse sequence-to-sequence models. In *Proceedings of the 57th Annual Meeting of the Association for Computational Linguistics*, pages 1504–1519, Florence, Italy. Association for Computational Linguistics.

Matt Post. 2018. A call for clarity in reporting BLEU scores. In *Proceedings of the Third Conference on Machine Translation: Research Papers*, pages 186–191, Brussels, Belgium. Association for Computational Linguistics.

Alessandro Raganato, Yves Scherrer, and Jörg Tiedemann. 2020. Fixed encoder self-attention patterns in transformer-based machine translation. In *Findings of the Association for Computational Linguistics: EMNLP 2020*, pages 556–568, Online. Association for Computational Linguistics.

Alessandro Raganato and Jörg Tiedemann. 2018. An analysis of encoder representations in transformer-based machine translation. In *Proceedings of the 2018 EMNLP Workshop BlackboxNLP: Analyzing and Interpreting Neural Networks for NLP*, pages 287–297, Brussels, Belgium. Association for Computational Linguistics.

Aurko Roy, Mohammad Saffar, Ashish Vaswani, and David Grangier. 2021. Efficient content-based sparse attention with routing transformers. *Transactions of the Association for Computational Linguistics (TACL)*, 9:53–68.

Rico Sennrich, Barry Haddow, and Alexandra Birch. 2016. Neural machine translation of rare words with subword units. In *Proceedings of the 54th Annual Meeting of the Association for Computational Linguistics (Volume 1: Long Papers)*, pages 1715–1725, Berlin, Germany. Association for Computational Linguistics.

Simeng Sun, Kalpesh Krishna, Andrew Mattarella-Micke, and Mohit Iyyer. 2021. Do long-range language models actually use long-range context? In *Proceedings of the 2021 Conference on Empirical Methods in Natural Language Processing*, pages 807–822, Online and Punta Cana, Dominican Republic. Association for Computational Linguistics.

Yi Tay, Dara Bahri, Liu Yang, Donald Metzler, and Da-Cheng Juan. 2020. Sparse sinkhorn attention. In *International Conference on Machine Learning (ICML)*, pages 9438–9447. PMLR.

Constantino Tsallis. 1988. Possible generalization of boltzmann-gibbs statistics. *Journal of Statistical Physics*.

Ashish Vaswani, Noam Shazeer, Niki Parmar, Jakob Uszkoreit, Llion Jones, Aidan N Gomez, Ł ukasz Kaiser, and Illia Polosukhin. 2017. Attention is all you need. In *Advances in Neural Information Processing Systems (NeurIPS)*, volume 30, pages 5998–6008. Curran Associates, Inc.

Elena Voita, David Talbot, Fedor Moiseev, Rico Sennrich, and Ivan Titov. 2019. Analyzing multi-head self-attention: Specialized heads do the heavy lifting, the rest can be pruned. In *Proceedings of the 57th Annual Meeting of the Association for Computational Linguistics*, pages 5797–5808, Florence, Italy. Association for Computational Linguistics.

A. Vyas, A. Katharopoulos, and F. Fleuret. 2020. Fast transformers with clustered attention. In *Proceedings of the International Conference on Neural Information Processing Systems (NeurIPS)*.

Kiri Wagstaff, Claire Cardie, Seth Rogers, and Stefan Schrödl. 2001. Constrained k-means clustering with background knowledge. In *International Conference on Machine Learning (ICML)*, page 577–584.

Shuohang Wang, Luowei Zhou, Zhe Gan, Yen-Chun Chen, Yuwei Fang, Siqi Sun, Yu Cheng, and Jingjing Liu. 2021. Cluster-former: Clustering-based sparse transformer for question answering. In *Findings of the Association for Computational Linguistics: ACL-IJCNLP 2021*, pages 3958–3968, Online. Association for Computational Linguistics.

Sinong Wang, Belinda Li, Madian Khabsa, Han Fang, and Hao Ma. 2020. Linformer: Self-attention with linear complexity. *arXiv preprint arXiv:2006.04768*.

Kilian Q Weinberger and Lawrence K Saul. 2009. Distance metric learning for large margin nearest neighbor classification. *Journal of Machine Learning Research (JMLR)*, 10(2).

Eric P Xing, Andrew Y Ng, Michael I Jordan, and Stuart Russell. 2002. Distance metric learning with application to clustering with side-information. In *Advances in Neural Information Processing Systems (NeurIPS)*, volume 15, page 12.

Manzil Zaheer, Guru Guruganesh, Kumar Avinava Dubey, Joshua Ainslie, Chris Alberti, Santiago Ontanon, Philip Pham, Anirudh Ravula, Qifan Wang, Li Yang, et al. 2020. Big bird: Transformers for longer sequences. *Advances in Neural Information Processing Systems (NeurIPS)*, 33.

Biao Zhang, Ivan Titov, and Rico Sennrich. 2021. Sparse attention with linear units. *arXiv preprint arXiv:2104.07012*.

Guangxiang Zhao, Junyang Lin, Zhiyuan Zhang, Xuancheng Ren, Qi Su, and Xu Sun. 2019. Explicit sparse transformer: Concentrated attention through explicit selection. *arXiv preprint arXiv:1912.11637*.

A Sparse Attention

A natural way to get a sparse attention distribution is by using the **sparsemax transformation** (Martins and Astudillo, 2016), which computes an Euclidean projection of the score vector onto the probability simplex $\triangle^n := \{\mathbf{p} \in \mathbb{R}^n \mid \mathbf{p} \geq \mathbf{0},\ \mathbf{1}^\top \mathbf{p} = 1\}$, or, more generally, the **α-entmax transformation** (Peters et al., 2019):

$$\alpha\text{-entmax}(\mathbf{z}) := \underset{\mathbf{p}\in\triangle^n}{\arg\max}\ \mathbf{p}^\top \mathbf{z} + H_\alpha(\mathbf{p}), \tag{10}$$

where H_α is a generalization of the Shannon and Gini entropies proposed by Tsallis (1988), parametrized by a scalar $\alpha \geq 1$:

$$H_\alpha(\mathbf{p}) := \begin{cases} \frac{1}{\alpha(\alpha-1)} \sum_j (p_j - p_j^\alpha), & \alpha \neq 1 \\ -\sum_j p_j \log p_j, & \alpha = 1. \end{cases} \tag{11}$$

Setting $\alpha = 1$ recovers the softmax function, while for any value of $\alpha > 1$ this transformation can return a sparse probability vector. Letting $\alpha = 2$, we recover sparsemax. A popular choice is $\alpha = 1.5$, which has been successfully used in machine translation and morphological inflection applications (Peters et al., 2019; Correia et al., 2019).

Proof to Proposition 1.

Proof. From the definition of $\mathbf{z}|_\mathbf{m}$ and from Eq. 2, we have that

$$\begin{cases} z_j|_\mathbf{m} = z_j > \frac{\tau(\mathbf{z})}{\alpha-1} & \text{if } p_j^\star > 0 \\ z_j|_\mathbf{m} \leq z_j \leq \frac{\tau(\mathbf{z})}{\alpha-1} & \text{if } p_j^\star = 0. \end{cases} \tag{12}$$

We first prove that $\tau(\mathbf{z}|_\mathbf{m}) = \tau(\mathbf{z})$. From the definition of $\tau(\mathbf{z})$ we have that $\sum_j [(\alpha-1)z_j - \tau(\mathbf{z})]_+^{1/\alpha-1} = 1$. Plugging the (in)equalities from Eq. 12, we thus have

$$1 = \sum_j [(\alpha-1)z_j - \tau(\mathbf{z})]_+^{1/\alpha-1} = \sum_j [(\alpha-1)z_j|_\mathbf{m} - \tau(\mathbf{z})]_+^{1/\alpha-1}. \tag{13}$$

Since $\tau(\mathbf{z})$ satisfies the second equation – which is the condition that defines $\tau(\mathbf{z}|_\mathbf{m})$ – we thus conclude that $\tau(\mathbf{z}|_\mathbf{m}) = \tau(\mathbf{z})$. Combining the results in Eqs. 12–13, we see that the supports of α-entmax$(\mathbf{z})$ and α-entmax$(\mathbf{z}|_\mathbf{m})$ are the same and so are the thresholds τ, and therefore from Eq. 2 we conclude that α-entmax$(\mathbf{z}|_\mathbf{m}) = \alpha$-entmax$(\mathbf{z})$. □

B Computing infrastructure

Our infrastructure consists of 4 machines with the specifications shown in Table 1. The machines were used interchangeably, and all experiments were executed in a single GPU. Despite having machines with different specifications, we did not observe large differences in the execution time of our models across different machines.

#	GPU	CPU
1.	4 × Titan Xp - 12GB	16 × AMD Ryzen 1950X @ 3.40GHz - 128GB
2.	4 × GTX 1080 Ti - 12GB	8 × Intel i7-9800X @ 3.80GHz - 128GB
3.	3 × RTX 2080 Ti - 12GB	12 × AMD Ryzen 2920X @ 3.50GHz - 128GB
4.	3 × RTX 2080 Ti - 12GB	12 × AMD Ryzen 2920X @ 3.50GHz - 128GB

Table 1: Computing infrastructure.

C Machine Translation

C.1 Setup

Data. Statistics for all datasets used in MT experiments can be found below in Table 2.

DATASET	# TRAIN	# TEST	AVG. SENTENCE LENGTH
IWSLT17 (EN→DE)	206K	1080	20 ±14 / 19 ±13
IWSLT17 (EN→FR)	233K	1210	20 ±14 / 21 ±15

Table 2: Statistics for MT datasets.

Training and Model. We replicated the sentence-level model of Fernandes et al. (2021) with the exception that we used α-entmax with $\alpha = 1.5$ instead of softmax in all attention heads and layers. Table 3 shows some architecture (transformer large) and training hyperparameters used for MT experiments. We refer to the original work of Fernandes et al. (2021) for more training details.

HYPERPARAM.	VALUE
Hidden size	1024
Feedforward size	4096
Number of layers	6
Number of heads	16
Attention mapping π	1.5-entmax
Optimizer	Adam
Number of epochs	20
Early stopping patience	10
Learning rate	0.0005
Scheduling	Inverse square root
Linear warm-up steps	4000
Dropout	0.3
CoWord dropout	0.1
Beam size	5

Table 3: Hyperparmeters for neural machine translation models.

C.2 Projections setup

Data. Statistics for the subsets of IWSLT used in the projection analysis can be found below in Table 4.

	TRAIN			VALIDATION		
PAIR	# SENT.	# POS. PAIRS	AVG. SENT. LENGTH	# SENT.	# POS. PAIRS	AVG. SENT. LENGTH
EN→DE	9K	8M ±1M	35 ±16	1K	330K ±56K	36 ±17
EN→FR	9K	9M ±1M	37 ±17	1K	334K ±58K	37 ±16

Table 4: Statistics for subsets of IWSLT used for training and evaluating projections.

Training. After extracting the α-entmax graphs, we optimize the learnable parameters of Equation 7 with Adam over a single epoch. Moreover, we used the k-means implementation from scikit-learn (Pedregosa et al., 2011) for our clustering-based approach. The hyperparameters used both for training the projections and for clustering with k-means are shown in Table 5.

Projection analysis. We compare Sparsefinder, varying $B \in \{2, 4, 6, 8, 10, 12\}$ for bucket-based methods, and $t \in \{0.5, 1.0, 1.5, 2.0, 2.5\}$ for the distance-based variant, with the following methods:

- **Window baseline:** connect all query and key pairs within a sliding window of size $w \in \{0, 1, 3, 5, 7, 9, 11, 15, 19, 23, 27\}$.
- **Learnable patterns:** Reformer by varying the number of buckets within $\{2, 4, 6, 8, 10, 12\}$; Routing transformer by varying the number of clusters within $c \in \{2, 4, 6, 8, 10\}$ with top-k set to $\lceil n/c \rceil$ (i.e. balanced clusters).
- **Fixed patterns:** BigBird by varying the number of random blocks within $\{2, 4, 6, 8, 10\}$ with a block size of 1; Longformer by varying the number of random global tokens within $\{4, 8, 12, 16, 20\}$.

HYPERPARAM.	VALUE
Projection dim. r	4
Loss margin ω	1.0
Batch size	16
Optimizer	Adam
Number of epochs	1
Learning rate	0.01
ℓ_2 regularization	0
k-means init	k-means++
k-means max num. inits	10
k-means max iters	300

Table 5: Hyperparmeters for MT projections.

Sparsity-recall tradeoff per layer and head. Plots are shown in Figures 7 and 8 for EN→DE and EN→FR, respectively.

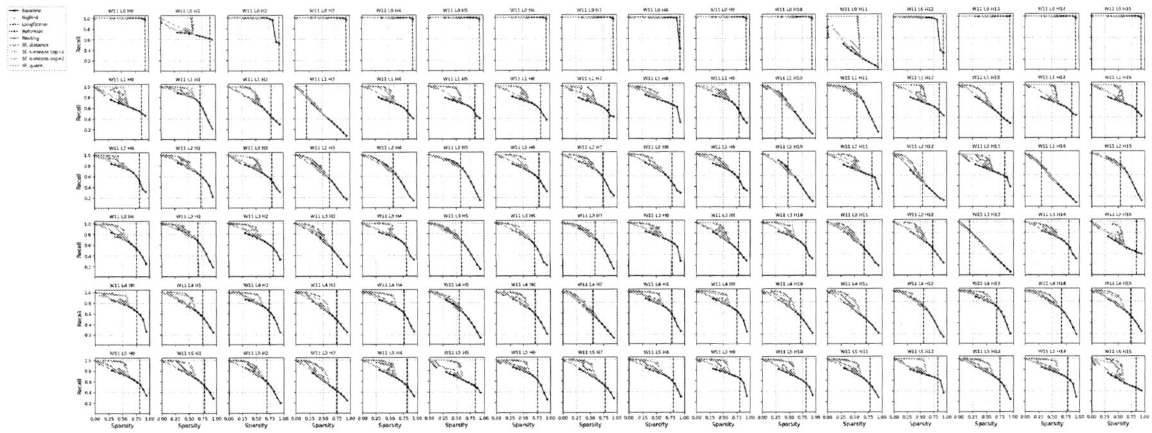

Figure 7: Sparsity-recall tradeoffs with a fixed window pattern of size 11 for EN→DE.

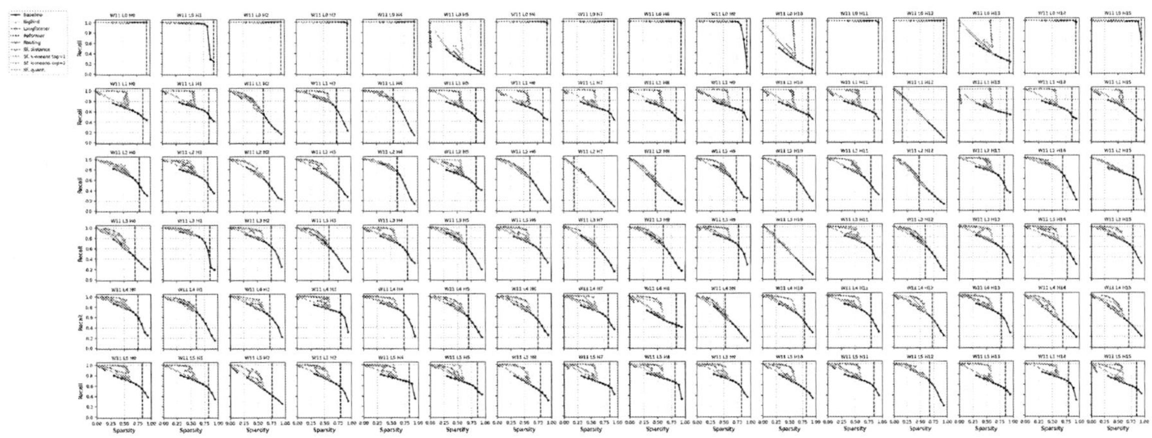

Figure 8: Sparsity-recall tradeoffs with a fixed window pattern of size 11 for EN→FR.

D Masked Language Modeling

D.1 Setup

Data and model. In order to have a transformer model trained with α-entmax, we finetuned RoBERTa-Base (Liu et al., 2019) on WikiText-103 (Merity et al., 2017) over 3000 steps with Adam (learning rate of

3×10^{-5}). To mimic the finetuning approach adopted by Longformer, we employed a batch size of 2 by accumulating gradients over 32 steps due to GPU memory constraints. Table 6 shows some architecture (transformer large) and training hyperparameters used for MT experiments. We refer to the original work of Liu et al. (2019) for more architecture details.

HYPERPARAM.	VALUE
Hidden size	64
Feedforward size	3072
Max input length	514
Number of layers	12
Number of heads	12
Attention mapping π	1.5-entmax
Optimizer	Adam
Number of steps	3000
Learning rate	0.00003

Table 6: Hyperparmeters for masked language modeling models.

D.2 Projections setup

Data and training. The subset used for Masked LM projections experiments contains 500 instances for training and 500 instances for validation. Moreover, all instances have a sentence length of 512 tokens. We got 3M (±1M) positive pairs for training and 2.5M (±1M) for validation. The hyperparameters for Masked LM are the same as the ones used in the MT experiments, shown in Table 5.

Projection analysis. We perform the same analysis as in MT, but now we vary the window size of the baseline within $\{0, 1, 3, 7, 11, 25, 31, 41, 51, 75, 101, 125, 151, 175, 201, 251, 301, 351, 401, 451, 501, 512\}$.

Sparsity-recall tradeoff per layer and head. Plots are shown next in Figure 9.

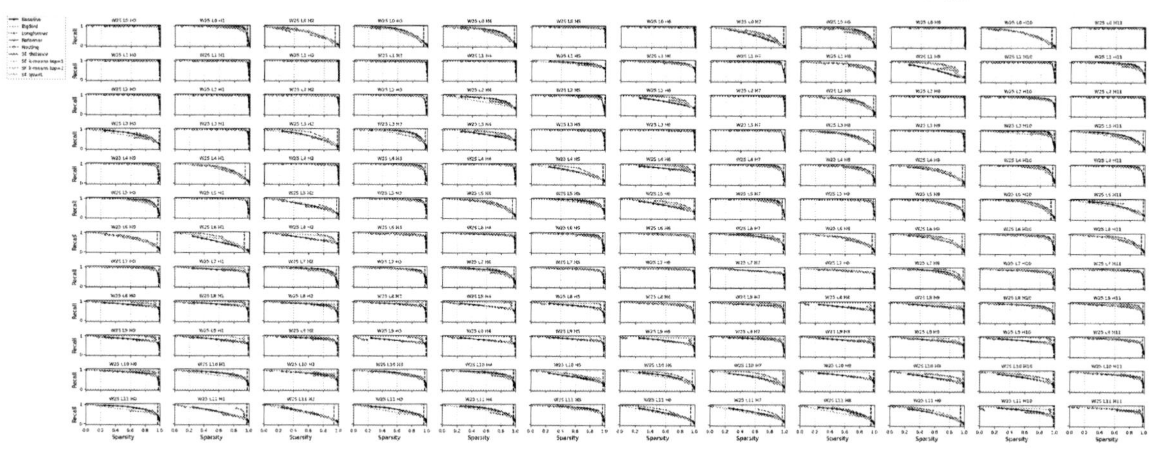

Figure 9: Sparsity-recall tradeoffs with a fixed window pattern of size 25 for MLM.

E Attention plots

Examples of attention maps can be seen in Figure 10 and 11.

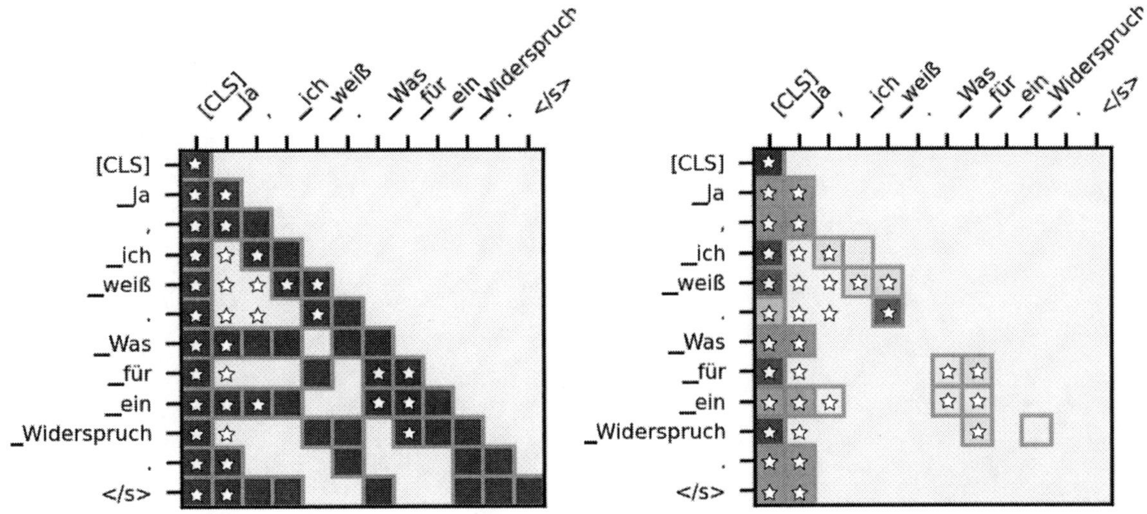

Figure 10: Learned patterns by Sparsefinder k-means (left) and the subsequent attention weights (right). Starred blocks represent ground-truth edges.

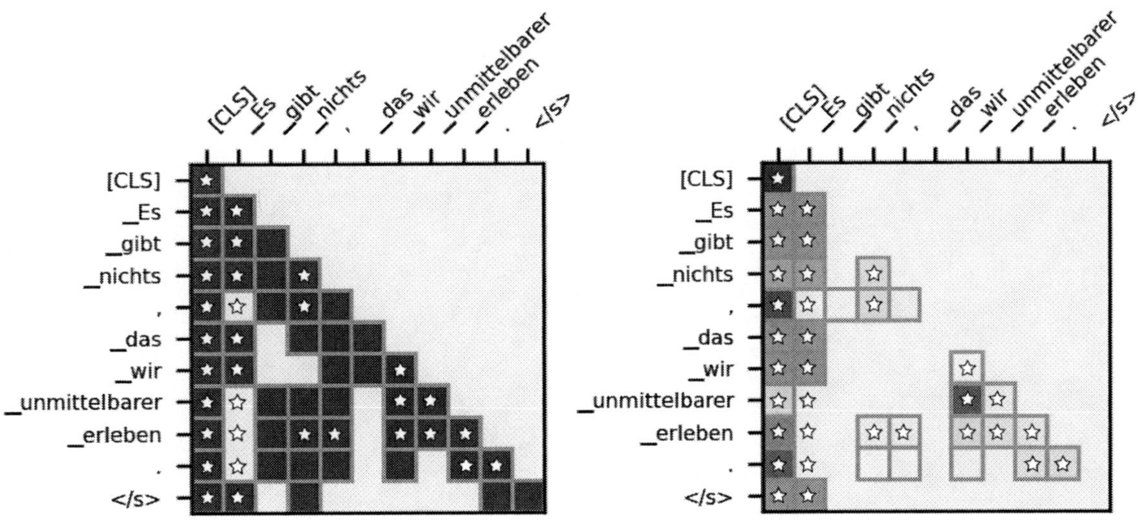

Figure 11: Learned patterns by Sparsefinder k-means (left) and the subsequent attention weights (right). Starred blocks represent ground-truth edges.

Author Index

Chiu, Jeffrey, 40
Cochez, Michael, 32

Daza, Daniel, 32
Ding, Zifeng, 22
Doshi-Velez, Finale, 40

Fernandes, Patrick, 67
Fonseca, Erick Rocha, 67
Fraser, Alexander, 52
Fu, Guirong, 22

Groth, Paul, 32
Góis, António, 67

Han, Zhen, 22
Hiraoka, Tatsuya, 11

Kando, Shunsuke, 1

Libovický, Jindřich, 52

Ma, Youmi, 11
Ma, Yunpu, 22
Martins, Andre, 67
Meng, Zhao, 22
Mittal, Rajat, 40
Miyao, Yusuke, 1

Noji, Hiroshi, 1

Okazaki, Naoaki, 11

Schubert, Matthias, 22
Sharma, Abhishek, 40

Tresp, Volker, 22
Treviso, Marcos Vinicius, 67
Tumma, Neehal, 40

Wattenhofer, Roger, 22

Association for Computational Linguistics
209 N. Eighth Street
Stroudsburg, Pennsylvania 18360

ISBN 978-1-7138-6753-1

9 781713 867531

CURRAN ASSOCIATES INC.
proceedings.com